THE SCHOOL CURRICULUM

The
School Curriculum

W. KENNETH RICHMOND

METHUEN & CO. LTD
11 NEW FETTER LANE · LONDON EC4

First published 1971 by Methuen & Co. Ltd
11 New Fetter Lane, London EC4
© 1971 by W. Kenneth Richmond
Printed in Great Britain by
Richard Clay (The Chaucer Press), Ltd
Bungay, Suffolk

SBN 416 14740 2
416 65760 5 paperback

This title is available in both hard and paperback editions. The paperback edition is sold subject to the condition that it shall not, by way of trade or otherwise, be lent, resold, hired out or otherwise circulated without the publisher's prior consent in any form of binding or cover other than that in which it is published and without a similar condition including this condition being imposed on the subsequent purchaser.

Distributed in the U.S.A.
by Barnes & Noble Inc.

WITHOUT COMMENT

I take it to be no small Error in the Affair of Education, to regard it as a Matter of mere SCIENCE or SPECULATION, rather than of PRACTICE; an ART or Method of furnishing the HEAD, rather than a DISCIPLINE of the HEART and LIFE.
David Fordyce *Dialogues Concerning Education*, XVII (1745–8)

Till within the last few years, the term used to define Education was INSTRUCTION. Give elementary and religious *instruction*, it was said and is still said, and this will be sufficient. Teach the poor to read the Bible, and forthwith you will make them good, holy and happy citizens – kind parents, obedient children – compassionate and honourable in their dealings; and crime will diminish. Hundreds of thousands of our population have received such an education. Are such the results?
David Stow *The Training System* (1836)

Contents

Acknowledgements *Page* viii

INTRODUCTION
1 New trends in curriculum planning 3
  Definitions of the curriculum 4
  The case for curriculum development 11
  Change, yes – but in what direction? 15
  Heritage and change 20
  Emergent guidelines for curriculum planning 28

PART I THE MANAGEMENT OF INNOVATION: PRACTICE
2 American education makes up for lost time 45
3 Response to change: the English experience 71
4 New directions for a new society: the French transformation 97
5 Authors, authorities and authoritarianism 112
  Proceed with caution: the Scottish situation 127

PART II THE MANAGEMENT OF INNOVATION: THEORY
6 Learning situations into life situations 149
7 Aims and/or objectives? Death is the only terminal behaviour 174
8 What knowledge is of any worth? 194
9 'Christ, what a way to grow up!': the drop-out generation 229

	Contents	vii
10	Stuff and nonsense in the curriculum	250
	The language of education	251
	Falling standards in the classroom	257
Index		275

ACKNOWLEDGEMENTS

The author and publishers wish to thank the following for permission to reproduce material from the publications listed below.

The Athlone Press of the University of London for *Educational Administration and the Social Sciences* edited by G. Baron and W. Taylor; Jonathan Cape Ltd and Alfred A. Knopf Inc. for *The Technological Society* by Jacques Ellul, translated by John Wilkinson; the Department of Audiovisual Instruction for *Trends in Programmed Instruction* edited by G. D. Ofiesh and W. C. Meierhenry; Faber and Faber Ltd and Harcourt, Brace and World Inc. for 'East Coker' by T. S. Eliot; Faber and Faber Ltd and Random House Inc. for '1st September 1939' by W. H. Auden; George G. Harrap and Company Ltd and UNESCO for *The Psychology of Audio-Visual Aids in Primary Education*; Harvard University Press for *The Process of Education* by J. S. Bruner, *General Education in a Free Society*, a Report of the Harvard Committee, *Dio Chrysostom: Thirteenth Discourse* translated by J. W. Cohoon, and *The Quality of Education in Developing Countries* by C. E. Beeby; Her Majesty's Stationery Office for *Report of the Working Party on the Schools Curriculum and Examinations (1964); McGill Journal of Education* for an article by W. J. Gushue in the Spring 1969 issue; the Organization for Economic Co-operation and Development for *Curriculum Improvement and Educational Development;* Scottish International Review Ltd for 'The Flowers of Scotland' by Edwin Morgan; *The Observer Ltd* for the 1 March 1970 issue; The University of Chicago Press for *The School and Society* by John Dewey; John Wiley and Sons Inc. for *Educational Anthropology* by George F. Kneller.

Introduction

CHAPTER ONE

New Trends in Curriculum Planning

What should children learn? What should the schools teach? To what ends – and how effectively? These are deceptively innocent questions, so much so that the layman may find it hard to understand why those in charge of the education system think it necessary to spend millions of pounds in trying to answer them. Policy-making, it seems, was much more clear-cut in Plato's day when the requirements of a small aristocratic ruling class could be satisfied by the simple formula, 'Music for the soul, Gymnastics for the body'.

Yet even within the gates of the Athenian city-state these issues were always contentious. Socrates' quarrel with the Sophists, his trial and self-inflicted execution bear witness to the seriousness with which they were taken. 'Opinion is divided about the subjects of education. All do not take the same view about what children should learn at school, either with a view to plain goodness, or with a view to the best life possible. Nor is the opinion clear whether education should be directed to the understanding, or mainly to the training of moral character.'[1] Aristotle's admission is a reminder that the problems facing curriculum planners, being central to the entire educational enterprise, are fraught with uncertainty and disagreement – a reminder, too, that both the uncertainty and the disagreement are likely to be permanent. Indeed, after reviewing the extensive literature which has grown up around these problems, and having taken stock of the numerous curriculum projects carried out in different countries, a cynic may well be left with the impression that the solutions now being propounded, if not altogether inconclusive, add little to the sum of conventional wisdom expressed in a short paragraph or two of Aristotle's *Politics*. Certainly they have brought home to us the truth of his saying that 'a great deal depends on the purpose for which actions are done or subjects are studied'.

DEFINITIONS OF THE CURRICULUM

The word 'curriculum' is decidedly blurred at the edges. When Bruner writes of the 'curriculum of a subject', what precisely does he mean? If certain of the school's activities are considered to be important, why are they referred to as 'extra-curricular' in England but usually in the U.S.A. as 'co-curricular'?

According to one view, 'the curriculum . . . is really the entire program of the school's work. It is the essential *means* of education. It is *everything* that the students and their teachers do. Thus it is twofold in nature, being made up of the activities, the things done, and of the materials with which they are done.'[2] According to another, there are three kinds of curriculum:

(1) *Subject curriculum*, which has the following distinguishing characteristics: (*a*) certain bodies of subject-matter are arranged in a logical order to facilitate exposition and are called subjects; (*b*) these subjects are determined in advance of the school lesson or pupils' learning experience; (*c*) teaching and learning are for the most part channelled into these already organized fields. This is the commonest form of curriculum. To arrange it, the teacher or administrator puts together a number of topics of suitable quality and difficulty dealing with a generally agreed upon field, and calls the result a subject—e.g. physics, French, etc. The curriculum then consists of a suitable collection of subjects which may be studied separately or in relation to each other.

(2) *Core curriculum* is not a group of subjects compulsory for all pupils. It is an arrangement of subject-matter according to the following principles: (*a*) the fundamental material to be studied consists of the rules, beliefs, facts and methods of thinking that are

shared by the society of which the school is part; (*b*) the study of this subject-matter is directed consciously towards the improvement of the society's beliefs, methods of thinking, etc.; (*c*) the subject-matter is arranged for study around current social problems or trends; (*d*) the main facts, values, skills and attitudes to be learnt are determined and arranged in advance by the teacher, but the actual problems studied and the manner of their study are decided by joint planning between teacher and pupils which takes careful account of the present needs and interests of the pupils. (3) *Activity curriculum* has no set subject-matter for study; it consists of things to be done, not things to be known – e.g. the pupil does not study the principles and history of telephonic communication, he makes and installs a telephone between two rooms and uses it; he does not study soil chemistry in the class room, he grows jonquils for competition in the local show. . . .'[3]

A rather different way of looking at the problem is summarized in the next extract:

Since only a fraction of the total accumulated experience of a culture can be included in a program of formal education, the curriculum worker is faced with the task of selecting content. How is the content to be selected? What kinds of experience should be provided? . . . In question form, the following five standards for subject-matter selection are presented:

1] Is the subject-matter significant to an organized field of knowledge?
2] Does the subject-matter stand the test of survival?
3] Is the subject-matter useful?
4] Is the subject matter interesting to the learner?
5] Does the subject matter contribute to the growth and development of a democratic society?[4]

A further move towards a more formal and rigorous definition of the curriculum is reflected in the discipline-centred approach typified by this oft-quoted passage from *The Process of Education*:

The curriculum of a subject should be determined by the most fundamental understanding that can be achieved of the underlying principles that give structure to that subject. Teaching specific topics or skills without making clear their context in the broader fundamental structure of a field of knowledge is uneconomical in several deep senses. In the first place, such teaching makes it exceedingly difficult for the student to generalize from what he has learned to what he will encounter later. In the second place, learning that has fallen short of a grasp of general principles has little reward in terms of intellectual excitement. The best way to create interest in a subject is to render it worth knowing, which means to make the knowledge gained usable in one's thinking beyond the situation in which the learning has occurred. Third, knowledge one has acquired without sufficient structure to tie it together is knowledge that is likely to be forgotten. An unconnected set of facts has a pitiably short half-life. Organizing facts in terms of principles and ideas from which they may be inferred is the only known way of reducing the quick rate of loss of human memory. Designing curricula in a way that reflects the basic structure of a field of knowledge requires the most fundamental understanding of that field. It is a task that cannot be carried out without the active participation of the ablest scholars and scientists. . . .

The 'spiral curriculum'. If one respects the ways of thought of the growing child, if one is courteous enough to translate material into his logical forms and challenging enough to tempt him to advance, then it is possible to introduce him at an early age to the ideas and styles that in later life make an educated man. We might ask, as a criterion for any subject taught in primary school, whether, when fully developed, it is worth an adult's knowing, and whether having known it as a child makes a person a better adult. If the answer to both questions is negative or ambiguous, then the material is cluttering the curriculum.

If the hypothesis with which this section was introduced is true – that any subject can be taught to any child in some honest form – then it should follow that a curriculum ought to be built around the great issues, principles, and values that society deems worthy of the continual concern of its members.[5]

Note the contrast between the relative looseness of Rugg's rationale in the first of these examples and the astringency of Bruner's in the last. It underlines the point made earlier that the curriculum is central to the entire educational enterprise. On the one hand, there are those who insist that the school's main duty is to foster moral training and the nurture of personal growth; on the other, those who would have it concentrate on the development of 'understanding' (as Aristotle called it). As Ben Morris says, 'We have to decide whether the school is primarily a place for instruction and intellectual development – as in fact it has been conceived in many countries – or whether the school is a place primarily for young persons to grow up in.'[6]

On this issue we are brought face to face with two rival claims of two schools of thought. While it is not really helpful to affix labels like 'traditional' and 'progressive', 'subject-centred' and 'child-centred', there are deep philosophical conflicts between them which give rise to distinct differences in theory and practice, and which help to explain why the curriculum means different things to different people. The origins of these two schools of thought can be traced back to Locke and Rousseau and beyond them to the writings of Comenius, at least so far as the modern period is concerned. The ideological disagreements between them were noted by John Dewey:

> Abandon the notion of subject-matter as something fixed and ready-made in itself, outside the child's experience; cease thinking of the child's experience as also something hard and fast; see it as something fluent, embryonic, vital, and we realize that the child and the curriculum are simply two limits which define a single process. Just as two points define a straight line, so the present standpoint of the child and the facts and truths of studies define instruction. It is continuous reconstruction, moving from the child's present experience out into that represented by the organized bodies of truth we call studies.
>
> On the face of it, the various studies, arithmetic, geography, language, botany, etc., are themselves experience – they are that of the race. They embody the cumulative outcome of the efforts, the strivings and the successes of the human race, generation after generation. They present this, not as a mere accumulation, not as a miscellaneous heap of separate heaps of experience, but in some organized and systematized way – that is, as reflectively formulated.
>
> Hence, the facts and truths that enter into the child's present experience, and those continued in the subject-matter of studies, are

the initial and final terms of one reality. To oppose one to the other is to oppose the infancy and the maturity of the same growing life; it is to set the moving tendency and the final result of the same process over against each other; it is to hold that the nature and the destiny of the child war with each other. . . .

The fundamental factors in the educative process are an immature, undeveloped being and certain social aims, meanings, values incarnate in the matured experience of the adult. The educative process is the due interaction between these forces. Such a conception of each in relation to the other as facilitates completest and freest interaction is the essence of educational theory.

But here comes the effort of thought. It is easier to see the conditions in their separateness, to insist upon one at the expense of the other, to make antagonists of them, than to discover a reality to which each belongs. The easy thing is to seize upon something in the nature of the child, or upon something in the developed consciousness of the adult, and insist upon *that* as the key to the problem. When this happens, a really serious practical problem – that of interaction – is transformed into an unreal and hence insoluble, theoretic problem. Instead of seeing the educative process steadily and as a whole, we see conflicting terms. We get the case of the child *v.* the curriculum; of the individual nature *v.* social culture. Below all other divisions in pedagogic opinion lies this opposition. . . .

From these elements of conflict grow up different educational sects. One school fixes its attention upon the importance of the subject-matter of the curriculum as compared with the contents of the child's own experience. It is as if they said: Is life petty, narrow and crude? Then studies reveal the great, wide universe with all its fulness and complexity of meaning. Is the life of the child egoistic, self-centred, impulsive? then in these studies is found an objective universe of truth, law and order. Is his experience confused, vague, uncertain, at the mercy of the moment's caprice and circumstance? Then studies introduce a world arranged on the basis of eternal and general truth; a world where all is measured and defined. Hence the moral: ignore and minimize the child's individual peculiarities, whims and experiences. They are what we need to get away from. They are to be obscured or eliminated. As educators our work is precisely to substitute for these superficial and casual affairs stable and well-ordered realities; and these are found in studies and lessons.

Subdivide each topic into studies; each study into lessons; each lesson into specific facts and formulae. Let the child proceed step by step to master each one of these separate parts, and at last he will have covered the entire ground. The road which looks so long when viewed in its entirety is easily travelled, considered as a series of particular steps. Thus emphasis is put upon the logical subdivisions and consecutions of the subject-matter. Problems of instruction are problems of procuring texts giving logical parts and sequences, and of presenting these portions in class in a similar definite and graded way. Subject-matter furnishes the end and it determines methods. The child is simply the immature being who is to be matured; he is the superficial being who is to be deepened; his is narrow experience which is to be widened. It is his to receive, to accept. His part is fulfilled when he is ductile and docile.

Not so, says the other sect. The child is the starting point, the centre, and the end. His development, his growth, is the ideal. It alone furnishes the standard. To the growth of the child all studies are subservient; they are instruments valued as they serve the needs of growth. Personality, character, is more than subject-matter. Not knowledge or information, but self-realization is the goal. To possess all the world of knowledge and lose one's own self is as awful a fate in education as in religion. Moreover, subject-matter never can be got into the child from without. Learning is active. It involves a reaching out of the mind. It involves organic assimilation starting from within. Literally, we must take our stand with the child and our departure from him. It is he and not the subject-matter which determines both the quality and quantity of learning. The only significant method is the method of the mind as it reaches out and assimilates. Subject-matter is but spiritual food, possible nutritive material. It cannot digest itself; it cannot of its own accord turn into bone and muscle and blood. The source of whatever is dead, mechanical and formal in schools is found precisely in the subordination of the life and experience of the child to the curriculum. It is because of this that 'study' has become a synonym for what is irksome, and a lesson identical with a task.[7]

The passage is worth reproducing at length for at least three good reasons: first, because it gives a balanced and humane concept of the curriculum which has yet to be bettered; second, because recent developments in the U.S.A. have seen 'discipline-centred' theories of the curriculum once more in the ascendant, with repercussions which have been felt in this country; third, because the sympathies of the ensuing argument are with Dewey – a Triton among the minnows of twentieth-century educational thought.

Before going on, it may be of interest to consider some definitions of the curriculum culled more or less at random from the *Journal of Curriculum Studies*. Between them, they are indicative of the contemporary movement of ideas in England:

1] All the learning which is planned or guided by the school, whether it is carried on in groups or individually, inside or outside the school.

(John F. Kerr)

2] That the curriculum consists of content, teaching methods and purpose may in its rough and ready way be a sufficient definition with which to start. These three dimensions interacting are the operational curriculum.

(Philip H. Taylor)

3] A programme of activities designed so that pupils will attain, as far as possible, certain educational ends or objectives.

(Paul Hirst)

4] The contrived activity and experience – organized, focused, systematic – that life, unaided, would not provide. . . . It is properly artificial, selecting, organizing, elaborating and speeding up the processes of real life.

(Frank Musgrove)

Wrenched from their contexts as they are, such definitions cannot fairly be taken as evidence of a return to 'subject'-centred theory and practice and the separation of learning from living of which Dewey complained. The English tradition has never been doctrinaire in these matters. On the other hand, it is perhaps not unfair to remark that its rationale, in so far as it can be said to have had one, has not been conspicuously child-centred. To this day, the common tendency is to equate the curriculum with the 'syllabus', a 'scheme of work', 'a course of study' or quite simply 'subjects' – something whose existence is taken for granted and which can be safely left to look after itself. If asked why they thought it necessary to teach this or that body of knowledge, the replies of nine out of ten teachers would probably be the same as Mallory's when pressed to give his reasons for wanting to climb Everest: 'Because it's there'.

Latterly, this easygoing frame of mind has had cause for serious second thoughts. In the mood of post-war reconstructionism there was no lack of talk concerning the need to get rid of lumber in the curriculum, but to begin with it was confined to relatively minor, piecemeal revisions of existing content and methods of teaching. Out of it grew the conviction that the dynamics of social and cultural innovation called for closer scrutiny than they had previously received, with the result that the early 1950s saw the concept of limited curriculum revision giving way to that of 'curriculum study' or (still more portentous) 'curriculum process'. If only at second hand, the impact of experimental projects – notably those mounted in the U.S.A. in the 'new' mathematics, physics, chemistry and biology – has been influential in popularizing an even more ambitious concept – 'curriculum development'.

THE CASE FOR CURRICULUM DEVELOPMENT

What *is* curriculum development? The question is worth asking, for it is only within the last ten years that the new term has crept into the language of educational discourse. Like other fashionable additions to our vocabulary, the term is liable to lead only to loose, pretentious talk unless it is adequately construed. It would be wrong to suppose that it is merely a fancy name for activities with which we are already familiar since it represents a bold advance beyond them. To the extent that curriculum development implies a fundamental recasting of the educational process as a whole, not just a spring cleaning of existing school syllabuses and a revamping of methods of teaching, it exemplifies a radical belief in the need for corporate planning. Hitherto it might be said that we have been too content to leave the curriculum to develop according to a process akin to natural selection, relying on the interplay between the forces of inertia in the education system and those energizing change in society. Broadly, the argument has been that the dead wood should be allowed to eliminate itself in its own good time to make room for new growths. Quite recently a very different persuasion has begun to gain ground, the conviction that unless positive, drastic, and immediate action is taken the dead wood will continue to pile up indefinitely and the non-stop accretions in an already overcrowded timetable will result in an impossibly chaotic situation. For the first time in history, educationists are being forced to the conclusion that innovation has to be *managed*.

Seeing that the quantitative aspects of educational expansion cannot be divorced from the qualitative, it is only natural that political and administrative decisions should be strongly influenced by the same conclusion. Policies of investment in human capital cannot expect that dividends will accrue automatically; the financial outlay in implementing them can only be justified if the courses provided are appropriate in terms of their objectives, content and methods of presentation. As the foreword to a recent O.E.C.D. report puts it,

> A new approach is urgently needed to curriculum construction and change, the main principles of which can be summed up as follows:
>
> (*a*) Curriculum development must be seen as an integral and continuing part of educational development policies and of educational planning.
>
> (*b*) A piecemeal approach to the several disciplines within the curriculum is no longer adequate, and an overall approach to the problem of curriculum development is now needed.

(c) In consequence, member countries should regard curriculum development as a continuing function which requires appropriate national permanent mechanisms to deal with it.[8]

A cursory inspection of the time allocations for the three main components of secondary school courses in O.E.C.D. countries – humanities (mother tongue, literature and languages), mathematics and science, and human sciences (i.e. social studies) – reveals some striking discrepancies. Some of these differences can be explained in the light of particular situations and conditions prevailing in the countries concerned, but in general it is apparent that the allocations are less a matter of rational planning than of tradition and social prestige. In fact, few countries have felt impelled to undertake an exhaustive examination of their education systems with a view to finding out whether the courses provided in schools are serving the national interest as well as they might. Nevertheless, 'It is one of the most striking characteristics of the recent educational history of the O.E.C.D. countries that the past few decades have witnessed a more thorough adaptation of the school curricula to contemporary needs than had been the case over the past few centuries.'[9]

The urgent need to find ways and means of ensuring continuous adaptation of the work of the schools in a rapidly changing world is now widely recognized. As we shall see, strategies of curriculum development vary from one national system to another, yet in all of them there is a discernible common pattern. There is, first, the recognition that the main sources of innovative power stem from outside the schools and that therefore they are not within the control of educationists alone. There is, second, the realization that the rates of change in the wider system are faster than those which take place in the educational sub-system, and that unless something is done to close the gap between the two rates of change the outcome will be a massive cultural lag – in other words, a further widening of the credibility gap which already exists between what is taught in the schools and what children learn from direct experience in the outside world. In a technological society in which, increasingly, the tendency is to say that if a

TABLE 1 Percentage of total time devoted to subjects in general secondary education (humanities and science sections)

Country	Section	Mother tongue	Classic languages	Modern languages	Total languages	Maths	Sciences	Total maths science	Human sciences	Arts (2)	Other subjects (3)
Austria	Class.	11·7	20·3	5·5	37·5	9·8	13·6	23·4	13·8	10·6	14·6
	Science	11·7	—	14·8	25·5	17·1	15·1	32·2	13·6	12·9	14·6
Belgium	Latin/Greek	14·4	22·1	15·3	51·8	11·1	7·1	18·2	9·6	6·8	13·5
	Mod/Maths	14·9	—	19·4	34·3	17·9	8·5	26·4	11·0	12·0	16·5
Denmark	Class.	13·0	18·2	19·3	50·6	10·2	6·8	17·0	12·5	6·8	13·0
	Scient.	13·0	0·0	19·3	32·4	16·4	17·0	33·5	13·0	7·9	13·0
France	Class. A.	13·9	21·0	11·5	46·4	9·7	8·2	17·9	19·5	8·0	8·3
	Mod/Maths	17·3	—	22·4	39·7	16·4	13·0	29·4	15·3	7·7	7·9
Fed. Germany	Class.	13·1	27·5	6·0	46·6	9·4	9·1	18·5	11·7	10·8	12·4
	Scient.	13·5	8·4	15·8	37·7	12·8	13·4	26·2	11·7	11·8	12·4
Greece	Class.	8·5	29·5	8·0	46·0	10·3	9·4	20·3	14·2	6·1	14·1
	Scient.	8·7	18·4	7·8	34·9	16·5	13·1	29·6	11·6	11·2	12·6
Iceland	Class.	13·4	7·1	29·1	49·6	11·8	19·2	31·0	9·9	9·2	9·5
	Maths/Sc.	13·5	1·6	23·6	38·7	15·9	19·2	35·1	9·6	9·2	9·6
Ireland	Class.	11·4	8·4	22·2	42·0	15·0	10·6	25·6	12·9	8·5	11·0
	Scient.	10·4	8·4	21·7	40·5	19·6	16·1	35·7	7·2	5·6	11·0
Italy	Class.	15·8	28·0	5·8	49·6	7·9	10·1	18·0	21·7	—	10·8
	Scient.	12·7	14·4	12·2	39·3	12·9	13·0	25·9	15·8	7·2	10·8
Luxembourg	Class.	18·2	29·9	9·8	57·9	9·8	7·0	16·8	9·4	4·2	11·6
	Modern	19·2	—	22·1	41·3	17·6	10·4	28·0	9·4	9·6	11·7
Netherlands	Lit.	9·1	33·3	18·2	60·6	8·6	6·5	15·1	14·1	2·5	7·6
	Science	10·9	—	23·7	34·6	17·5	18·2	35·7	15·2	6·6	7·9
Norway	Languages	13·9	—	35·6	49·5	10·6	8·3	18·9	11·7	7·2	12·7
	Science	13·9	—	23·4	37·3	16·7	13·9	30·6	12·2	7·2	12·7
Spain	Literature	10·6	17·6	9·7	37·9	6·9	12·1	19·0	16·2	4·2	28·7
	Science	10·0	4·2	10·0	24·5	13·9	18·6	32·5	16·2	4·2	28·7
Switzerland (Bern)	Class.	10·0	33·9	9·7	53·9	12·0	6·0	18·0	12·1	6·4	9·6
	Scient.	14·7	—	21·2	35·9	21·5	12·8	34·3	11·5	8·8	9·5
Turkey	Literature	15·7	—	12·5	28·2	13·0	17·8	30·8	19·8	9·5	12·0
	Science	13·5	—	11·5	25·0	16·7	21·3	38·0	15·6	9·5	12·0
United Kingdom	Literature	18·0	10·0	15·0	43·0	10·0	8·0	18·0	18·0	12·0	19·0
	Sciences	12·0	—	10·0	22·0	22·0	24·0	46·0	10·0	13·0	19·0
Yugoslavia	Lang/Soc. St.	12·9	3·2	12·9	29·0	8·9	18·5	27·4	20·2	4·9	19·5
	Sciences/Math.	10·5	3·2	8·9	22·6	13·7	31·5	45·2	12·1	2·4	17·7

1. Most data in the Report prepared by the Secretariat to the Fifth Conference of European Ministers of Education (Vienna, October 1965), Table 14.
2. Including 'practical arts' and 'aesthetic education'.
3. Including 'physical education', 'religious' and 'miscellaneous'.

Reproduced from O.E.C.D. Report, *Curriculum Improvement and Educational Development* (O.E.C.D., 1966).

thing works it is obsolete the danger is that both the subject-matter and its presentation will seem to be so outdated by events as to cause classroom instruction to lose any obvious relevance.

> Today in our cities
> most learning occurs outside the classroom.
> The sheer quantity of information conveyed by
> press-mags – film – TV – radio
> *far exceeds*
> the quantity of information conveyed by
> school instruction and texts.
> This challenge has destroyed
> the monopoly of the book as a teaching aid
> and cracked the very walls of the classroom
> so suddenly,
> we're confused, baffled.[10]

CHANGE, YES – BUT IN WHAT DIRECTION?

Acceptance of the need to come to terms with social, economic and technological change has been forced on educationists for a number of reasons which are now so familiar that it is scarcely necessary to list them. There would be no excuse for doing so were it not for the persistent conservative-mindedness which makes many people, parents as well as teachers, ambivalent in their attitudes, professing to welcome change with open arms while privately hoping and praying that things will remain as they are. These attitudes are proof against all the arguments and facts adduced against them, and it is as well to recognize that they are as widespread as they are deep-rooted in British culture. For all that, the facts speak for themselves.

1] The growth of population itself has made it imperative to cater for a much wider range of abilities and interests than ever before. If the answer to the question, 'What should children learn?' admitted of no straight answer in the Athenian city-state, when there was so much less to learn and only a handful of freeborn pupils to accommodate, it is infinitely more problematical in an industrial nation-state which is committed to the provision of equal opportunity for *all* pupils. As we shall argue in a subsequent chapter, one of the major headaches in the English system of education arises from the entrenched position of an academic curriculum originally designed for an able minority and geared to the occupational requirements of what used to be called the 'learned professions', and the difficulty of finding a non-academic equivalent for the majority of pupils who previously had had little or no chance of attending an extended secondary school course. New pupils – new in the sense that they were formerly left out of the reckoning – presuppose the need for new curricula. The alternative is to go on pouring old wine into new bottles.

2] In all the developed countries standards of living are steadily rising and so are levels of expectation and aspiration, with the result that the pressure of demand on the educational services is unprecedented and shows no signs of easing. Among other things, this means that the kind of treatment which was thought to be good enough for children, say, thirty years ago is not necessarily good enough for them today. More means different! This, in turn, implies that styles of teaching, quality of learning materials, and the organization of the school itself have to be continuously brought up to date and improved.

3] The explosion of information has affected every field of study, most spectacularly of course in the natural and applied sciences, but no less obviously elsewhere. As a consequence, the necessity of adopting criteria for selection has become more acute. The sheer impossibility of learning everything about something has also cast doubts on the possibility of learning something about everything. It is no longer so easy as it used to be to justify the retention of the traditional range of 'subjects' as well-organized bodies of knowledge, since for every one included there are others kept waiting outside with quite as good claims for admission. If physics and chemistry hold their places intact, what chance will there be for creative technology or (looking ahead to the space age) astronomy? If Latin and French occupy the No. 1 and No. 2 berths in the modern languages department, when (if ever) is Russian to get a look in and (again looking ahead), for that matter, Chinese? With so many options to think of, attention is inevitably being diverted from subject-matter (and the accumulation of facts and information to be committed to memory) to the search for organizing principles around which knowledge can be acquired. The habit of taking the various 'subjects' as they stand and deriving this or that alleged benefit from them is now held to be illicit, a case of putting the cart before the horse; instead, the curriculum planner now begins by asking what outcomes are desired and then proceeds to select the learning materials and experiences which are calculated to achieve his objectives.

> Far too often the element of purpose in learning is forgotten, and the subject itself is invested with a mystique and with powers that are totally unjustified. Usually this kind of claim rests upon ideas of faculty psychology and formal discipline, or misconceptions about the nature of transfer; as a result it is claimed that some subjects have greater power to train the mind than others. This leads to the idea that each of these subjects has its own logic, and that the study of the fact will not only reveal that logic, but somehow enable it to be assimilated and applied by the learner. In some mystical way the subject produces mental discipline, irrespective of the methods used in learning it; expose the learner to the facts and methods, and he will grasp the essentials and make use of them elsewhere.
>
> At its worst, this view can degenerate into advocacy of subject-matter mastery as the implied aim of education. Every time an educational crisis arises, there is a demand from laymen and specialists, sometimes even from teachers, for greater concentration on subject-matter. This ignores the part played by process, as well as a good deal of experimental evidence that mastery of subject-matter does not ensure effective application of learnings in relevant situations, that there is considerable difference between 'knowing that' and 'knowing how'. . . .
>
> The need for investigation of the problem of 'which subjects do what to the mind' is shown in a recent report on the curriculum of English schools preparing for sixth form work. From this, one

would be led to believe that almost any of some fifteen subjects is as effective as any other in achieving most of the general aims of education.[11]

4] The intricate division of labour in an advanced industrial society presupposes a wide range of occupational skills and a much larger proportion of highly skilled workers than was necessary during the nineteenth century or even during the first half of the twentieth century. The key positions in the middle and upper echelons of society are no longer occupied solely by members of the older learned professions for whom the cachet of a 'liberal' education was the passport to success. The demands of specialization being so heavy, a reinterpretation of the concept of 'liberal' education is clearly necessary. Can it be that England's misgivings about sixth formers taking three A-levels on one side or the other of the 'Great Divide' are misplaced after all? Is Sir Eric Ashby right in thinking that the way to culture in the modern world is through a man's specialism, not by by-passing it? The difficulty is to know how to strike a balance between the aims of general education (minimally defined as basic literacy and numeracy) and those of specialist training (which are more concerned with fitting pupils for their future occupational roles).

5] The universal trend is towards a longer school life. A combination of economic and social pressures serves to keep the young *in statu pupillari* until their middle or late 'teens, while for many the process of formal education carries on into adulthood. Because of the reduction in the number of unskilled and semi-skilled jobs – to mention only one reason – the effect is to confer a kind of indeterminate status on young people. Unless the curriculum for the ordinary run of fourteen- to sixteen-year-olds can hold their interest and attention, therefore, many will conclude that they are compelled to stay on at school for no better reason than the fact that there is nowhere else for them to go. Although the numbers staying on voluntarily for extended courses are increasing, so, too, are the numbers of drop-outs. The indications are, indeed, that many, many boys and girls feel that they have had more than enough of schooling by the time they reach the age of fourteen.

If so, this is another piece of evidence which suggests that all is not as well with the school set-up as the traditionalists are disposed to think.

6] At the same time we have to reckon with the secular trend towards earlier physical maturity. Throughout the Western world the onset of puberty has been taking place earlier in each successive generation for well over a hundred years, due, it is believed, to biological causes and not (as it is tempting to think) to environmental influences. Even so, this precocity is not entirely physical: it is accompanied by emotional, attitudinal and intellectual side-effects which proclaim themselves only too obviously in the home as well as in the classroom. School regulations, styles of instruction and methods of keeping discipline which have proved effective in the past are clearly not going to be anything like so acceptable in the future. Thanks to their greater self-assurance and sophistication, young people nowadays are much more inclined to be impatient of the restrictions imposed by school-bound learning and take less and less kindly to a regimen which confirms them in a submissive role. Still more important, their heightened and quickened emotional life has induced a craving for deeply-felt experiences which are more easily satisfied outside the school learning situation than in it. Moreover, the intellectual forwardness of the young must not be underestimated. In the past, the tendency has been to suppose that pupils who were not 'good at school subjects' could be more or less written off as failures, and, to the extent that the ability to pass examinations is still the main criterion of success, that tendency remains. While there is no evidence that low intelligence is compensated for by high creativity, it is now known that ability assumes a variety of forms. It is also known that many of these go undetected and unrewarded in the conventional classroom. Worse still, the suspicion is growing that the long-term effects of a teacher- and 'subject'-centred curriculum have been to discourage habits of independent inquiry, originality and self-expression. Can children learn French in the primary school? Can they learn French successfully in the secondary school after failing the 11-plus examination? Not so long ago the answers to both questions would (in England) have been an emphatic negative. If curriculum study has done nothing more at least it has alerted us to the need for revising our notions about what is and what is not possible in education. Instead of assuming that difficult accomplishments are beyond the reach of the average child, it would be nearer the truth to say that the latter's capabilities are pegged down by the average teacher's failure to exploit the resources at his disposal.

7] New media, new channels of communication, bring new methods and new approaches in their train. With vastly more work to be done and too few hands to do it, members of the teaching profession are under a moral obligation to play their part in an advancing educational technology. It is true that the latter has so far failed to alleviate the shortage of manpower in the schools, and that some of its techniques – programmed learning, for one – have made relatively little headway, but it has transformed the learning situation in a host of subtle ways and opened up dimensions of experience previously not dreamed of in the era of chalk-talk and books. More so, perhaps, than any other single factor it has produced a state of ferment in the hearts and minds of learners old and young, especially in the young. Technology is, by definition, implicated in the process of bringing about change and regulating it, and any educational policy which fails to understand this declares itself ostrichist.

HERITAGE AND CHANGE

On the face of it, the conviction that innovations in the schools can be managed has an air of resoluteness which commends it to forward-thinkers and to optimists. Just how feasible is a policy of curriculum development, however? With the possible exception of Sweden, no country has a fully implemented policy of this kind. Among the difficulties which are certain to be encountered there is, first, the difficulty of persuading individuals, institutions and agencies from different sectors of the education system to join forces and make common cause together; second, the difficulty of marshalling the necessary resources – research and development is a costly business, costlier still when it comes to the stage of full production and general usage; third, the difficulty of reconciling the need to work fast with the inevitably slow procedures in modernizing old-fashioned, established routines. How long would it take, for example, if a Stalinist Secretary of Education decreed that Russian and Chinese were to supplant French and German, and that astronomy and space technology were to replace physics and chemistry in our secondary schools, given that he had absolute powers to enforce a wholesale turnabout of this sort? The fact that such a hypothetical case is virtually unimaginable is itself an indication of the order of magnitude of the difficulties which stand in the way of any radical reform.

It may well be that the necessary conditions for corporate planning do not exist in some education systems. Where they do exist, and where affluence allows of adequate resources of money and know-how being made available, it may turn out that the time-lag problem is intractable. The secular trend to earlier physical maturity and the impact of the mass media are only two illustrations of the fact that the forces which determine social change – and hence our ideas about what constitutes useful knowledge – are not within the competence of the planners. Cultural anthropologists, on the whole, take a poor view of reform movements which set out with the intention of changing the face of society as if the tail could wag the dog: Kneller, for instance, is contemptuous of the 'progressive' education movement for this very reason.

In any case, there is a good deal of evidence to show that educationists are more often wrong than right when they seek to impose their own values. Professor Armytage points out that 'the illusion that historical education could effectively eradicate unpleasant principles was an old one. It animated the creation of the Regius chairs of History at Oxford and Cambridge in 1724 in the hope that 'Tory' principles would be eradicated, and it was certainly the hope of Dr Arnold at Rugby.'[12] What guarantee is there, then, that the claims now being made on behalf of curriculum development do not also rest on illusions? Plausible as they seem, can the claims be substantiated?

In the past it was generally understood that heritage and change went smoothly hand in hand. 'The old order changeth, yielding place to new' – a slow and natural process, no more to be questioned than the coming and going of the seasons or the waning of the moon. It is only during periods of social and cultural upheaval that the pace quickens and a sense of dislocation is aroused. The history of education provides many examples of these climacteric periods. Socrates, Plato and Aristotle lived through one of them, the early Christians through another, the Renaissance humanists through yet another, and so on down to the present day. All testify to the fact that long periods of stability are followed by relatively sudden and violent upsets which are in turn followed by a new order as resistant to change as the old one was. According to Max Weber, these alternations can be explained in terms of 'assertion' and 'domination'. Thus, to begin with, status group A and its ideas compete with other groups and their ideas, eventually gains the upper hand and the power to have its command obeyed, proceeds to institutionalize its ideas, leading to a period of domination during which the ideas of group A are held to be universally valid. But then a new contender, status group B, challenges the dominant group and gains sufficient organizing power to take over the leadership. Weber's model corresponds broadly to the interplay between government and opposition in British parliamentary politics, more accurately perhaps to the dynamics of a network of pressure groups.

Whether or not we accept this explanation, the process appears to be cyclical. Learning which is regarded as essential in one epoch is dismissed as trivial, irrelevant or positively harmful in another. Thus, the pride of place accorded to logic and dialectic as keystones of the *artes liberales* throughout the Middle Ages came to be held in disrepute by fifteenth- and sixteenth-century scholars and they were finally ridiculed as 'mere cobwebs of learning of no substance or profit' by Bacon. 'Grammar is the portal to all knowledge whatsoever', proclaimed Aeneas Sylvius – an enthusiasm shared by reformers like Erasmus, for whom 'knowledge of words' (i.e. literary studies as the royal road to the wisdom of the Ancients) was all important. In the same way, the gradual erosion of the monopoly of a liberal education based on the Classics and the ascendancy the natural sciences (embodying 'knowledge of things') can be traced during the second half of the nineteenth century. Spencer's essays, which put the cat among the pigeons of Victorian orthodoxy, and the confrontation between men of letters like Matthew Arnold and scientists like Thomas Huxley (anticipating the Snow-Leavis fracas) exemplify the stresses and strains involved in the constant tug-of-war between heritage ('domination') and change ('assertion').

On historical grounds it is evident that the intervals between these climacteric periods are getting progressively shorter. Once the reconciliation between Christian doctrine and Graeco-Roman learning had been effected by men like St Augustine and St Basil, the curriculum of the *artes liberales* remained more or less unchanged for nearly a thousand years. By comparison, Erasmus' revision of Lily's Latin primer held good for a mere two centuries. But if we compare the content of what is taught in schools today with what was taught fifty, or even ten, years ago we are immediately struck by obvious dissimilarities. Even the best textbooks, for example, suffer from the same built-in obsolescence which ensures that a 1970 car model is quickly outdated. Not only that, but the few elements which have kept their staying power and which serve to preserve some semblance of the *status quo* begin to look more like relicts rather than genuine survivals.

Yet in this state of flux there are two constants which are stubbornly resistant to change. One is the examination fetish. The other is the institutionalized power of a 'subject' centred curriculum. Between them they represent vested interests – academic, administrative, economic, social and political – which dominate the educational system to such an extent that the consensus of opinion is that any tinkering with them is inadvisable – and any move to get rid of them out of the question. Remove them and the education system would collapse – so runs the argument. Does not the organization of the secondary school – for that matter, the school building itself – depend upon an infra-structure of specialist teachers, just as the organization of a factory depends upon the division of labour among its workers? Team teaching, open plan, areas of inquiry and all the other latest fads may be all very fine in theory, but is it not significant that none of them has made much headway in practice and that as often as not those who tread the path of innovation end by reverting to type? What's in a name, anyway? 'Subject' barriers can be crossed easily enough: properly understood, they are no more than a means of ensuring that the content of courses is kept tidy and within reasonable limits. Without them, teaching and learning would sprawl all over the place and become an amorphous mess. Without examinations would there not be a serious loss of incentives? As for new-fangled methods like continuous assessment, is it any use pretending that they do the job anything like so well as an efficient examining board?

On the face of it, it appears that the odds against radical reform are too heavy. On the other hand, it is pertinent to remark that several of the stock 'subjects' in the timetables of our secondary schools are, relatively speaking, newcomers – English, for one; physics for another. Neither of these figured in the prospectus of the mid-nineteenth-century grammar school, and both had to undergo a hard struggle before gaining general acceptance and official recognition. Before 1867, the year which saw the establishment of the Cavendish Laboratory at Cambridge and the publication of Dean Farrar's *Essays on a Liberal Education*, the inclusion of physics had been as unthinkable as it was impracticable. As for the study of English literature, its arrival was delayed until long after the founding of the Oxford English School in 1894. The bitter controversies which attended the birth of physics and English and their early vicissitudes as secondary school studies are a reminder that 'subjects', as we have come to know them, are a fairly recent development; a reminder, also, that conflict is of the essence in the evolution of new curricula.

While it is easy to feel depressed by the apparent permanence of stereotypes in the schools which have outlived their usefulness, it is worth bearing in mind that their air of immutability is only apparent. To those engaged in it, the task of bringing about change may feel, most of the time, like a case of a not-so-irresistible force meeting an immovable object, yet a moment's reflection should tell them that their efforts are by no means as hopeless as they seem and that time is on their side. In education, as in art, there is a sense in which it can be said that *plus ça change plus c'est la même chose*, but the same is true of any organic process. Looking back, it is evident that many of our received opinions about what children should learn must be considered ephemeral in the eye of history. 'Subjects', now rated as essential, had no place in nineteenth-century schools and are certain to be replaced by others in the future. Reading and writing, presumably, will continue to be basic skills – but is it likely that they will be *the* basic skills in the world of the twenty-first century? To ask this is not to infer that they are necessarily on the way to being superseded, though so far as handwriting is concerned it is easy to see what is happening – and why. With numeracy vying for an equal place alongside literacy, with oracy in greater demand, and with pattern recognition threatening to oust learning by means of printed symbols, it is on the cards that several of the 'subjects' whose place in the scheme of things seems assured and inviolable will actually be superseded sooner rather than later.

Suppose, for the sake of argument, that geography were to disappear as a school 'subject'. Would it be missed? Would the mass of pupils be any the worse? Before the reader throws down the book in disgust let him ask himself how much of the geography he learned at school remains clearly identifiable in his mental make-up. How much of it is already within the experience of children who are daily surrounded by television, travel films, newspapers, advertisements and colour supplements?

It is at points like this that the polarization between traditional-minded and forward-thinking theory and practice is most clearly to be seen. It is that same polarization which Dewey noted between the formal intellectual concepts of adult knowledge and the informal vital experience of the immature child. Without the 'due interaction' between them, knowledge and experience are separated and a false dichotomy is set up between school-bound learning and the kind of learning which is as effortless and zestful as the process of growing up itself. The 'subject'-centred philosophy places its emphasis on the former. As Leff says,

> It is clearly untenable to regard mathematics, logic, language and various intellectual techniques as the purely transitory efflux of a particular historical and class (false) consciousness; by the very fact that they outlast any particular epoch they are of universal validity. They must, therefore, represent true knowledge quite independently of the uses to which they are put. . . . If we are to regard all those forms of consciousness as having been called forth from a certain economic structure for the purpose of sustaining the social order to which they belong, then the entire sphere of intellectual activity becomes incomprehensible.[13]

The trouble is that when it comes to asking wherein the universal validity of these central disciplines resides it is no longer possible to agree — at least it can no longer be taken for granted — that it is to be found in the intrinsic value of their content, in the mental training they provide, or in the transfer of training. *Pace* Bruner, Phenix and the rest, far from being able to predict which disciplines, which realms of meaning, which mental attributes will hold good a thousand years hence, we cannot even be sure whether or not the instruction given to five-year-olds will retain its relevance by the time they reach school-leaving age. What we can be sure of is that most learning occurs outside the classroom. Under the impact of modern media usage, the learning situation has been transformed, with implications which are as yet only vaguely appreciated and scarcely understood at all. Among other things, it has accentuated the discrepancy between the rates of social-cultural and educational change and helped to make the dislocation between schooling and living more painfully obvious than it has ever been.

New Trends in Curriculum Planning

In the contemporary situation, in short, there are grounds for thinking that the balance can best be redressed by a renewed assertion of the claims of child-centred theory and practice. Disparaged as they so often are, 'progressive' methods – as exemplified in the cult of 'activity and experience', 'self-expression', 'creativity', 'projects', 'guided discovery' and the 'integrated day' – are the outcome of a line of educational thought which is in many respects more convincing and more wholesome than the one which has come to dominate the education system. The mélange of romantic sentiment and divine discontent which inspired idle dreamers like Rousseau and dedicated idealists like Pestalozzi and Froebel was the source from which sprang empirical child-study and a systematic developmental psychology. It gave rise to an international reform movement and, so far as the primary school is concerned, it had a profound influence on policy-making in this country which can be traced in a succession of official reports from Hadow to Plowden. That it brought about a significant shift of ideas and a humanizing of case-hardened beliefs about what young children should learn and how they should be taught cannot be doubted. If the most troublesome problems in curriculum development today centre upon the secondary school, one very potent reason is that the secondary school was kept immune from this influence, apart from a short spell following the inception of the modern school which proved to be ill-fated.

Schemers who are impatient to initiate changes in the primary school – by introducing, say, the teaching of French or elements of the new mathematics tend to forget the long, slow struggle which followed the era of 'payment by results'. Whether they like it or not, and whether officialdom recognizes it or not, child-centredness has become the dominant ideology in the primary school, if nowhere else. The point, which hardly needs underlining, is that a new order cannot be accomplished overnight. Curriculum development may not be actually impossible, but it takes a great deal longer than some of its advocates would have us believe. Even when an assertive ideology succeeds in reaching a position of dominance it has still to provide convincing proof that the last state is better than the first, and proof is simply not procurable in the short term.

> Before it is fully accepted . . . any new curriculum should be carefully evaluated against the ultimate criterion – its long-range effect upon the children who study it. Such an evaluation takes time because it is not enough to know how the curriculum affects immediate test scores; we need to know how it influences the child's later success in college and in his career and also his adult life. The collection of test scores and other statistics is not evaluation but only the first step towards evaluation. Evaluation is not complete until someone has made the value judgements which are based upon empirical data but which interpret the evidence and draw conclusions from it in relation to a clearly stated philosophy of the proper goals of education.[14]

EMERGENT GUIDELINES FOR CURRICULUM PLANNING

Enough has been said to show that there is nothing new in the idea of curriculum renewal. The inevitability of change as a fact of life has always been conceded, however grudgingly. What *is* new is the determination to apply systematic techniques for controlling innovation, rather than leaving it to wayward trends and the whims of passing fashion. In the past, ways and means of doing this were within the competence of eminent scholars, working more or less single-handed, because the printed text was the main source of information, the touchstone for successful learning. Today, with a wider range of media opening up new possibilities and with the needs of pupils other than 'scholars' to be taken into account, the problem is immeasurably more complicated. If dispersal and duplication of effort, waste of resources, misunderstanding and muddle are to be avoided, a much closer get-together between the *disjecta membra* of the education system has to be contrived, otherwise the chances are that it will be a case of too many cooks spoiling the broth.

Unless we are content to go on believing that 'use and wont' provide their own rationale and that any changes taking place in schools owe more to *la puissance de l'accident* than to any other determinant, ways and means of understanding what is happening and what is likely to happen are demanded of us. Among the techniques of regulation and control, can systems analysis live up to the claims being made for it as a calculus of change? In assigning mathematic values to each variable, and by following a protocol which enables him to trace the lattices of transformation from one state to another, the systems analyst has achieved spectacular successes in mechanical engineering. Unlike the sceptics who say that problems in the field of human affairs are not amenable to such techniques, he is not deterred by the objection that he takes the term 'system' to mean anything he pleases; undeterred, also, by the size and complexity of the problems he undertakes to solve. One of the tenets of the systems analyst's creed is that it is unnecessary to know everything about a system in order to regulate it, just as it is unnecessary for the bridge builder to know about the sub-atomic dance of particles in the materials he uses. The larger the system, the greater the certainty that the sheer amount of information will be so overwhelming as to be unmanageable.

> When this occurs, what is he to do? The answer is clear: he must give up any ambition to know the *whole* system. His aim must be to achieve a partial knowledge that, though partial over the whole, is none the less complete in itself, and is sufficient for his ultimate practical purpose.[15]

In this sense, then, the analyst's system becomes 'not a thing but a list of variables' – i.e. a conceptual model (preferably computerized) which accurately represents the physical features of the actual system with which he is dealing. In the same way that a map reduces the landscape to manageable proportions by omitting inessential details for route-finding, so the analysis of, say, the education system makes it possible to tackle problems which would otherwise be regarded as intractable.

At the risk of over-simplification, the strategies of curriculum development adopted so far will be described in subsequent chapters as 'discipline-centred' in the U.S.A., 'teacher-centred' in

England and Wales, 'inspector-centred' in Scotland and 'systems-centred' in Sweden, but regardless of their country of origin all are agreed on the need for a conspiratorial attack on the forces of inertia – and all are converging in essentially the same direction. Although the tactics open to them depend upon the power structure and the climate of opinion in the country concerned, those who seek to bring about a managerial revolution in the conduct and affairs of the schools normally begin operations as a self-appointed élite whose avowed purpose is to take the citadel of the Establishment by stealth, not by storming it. If they are like-minded it is in agreeing that partial, discrete innovations – the kind that are left to voluntary free-enterprise – have little or no survival value, since experience shows that reversion to the *status quo* is almost invariably the rule. In their view, nothing less than an all-out effort is demanded, and this means pooling all the available resources of know-how, goodwill, materials and money.

Aware of the constraints placed upon them and the huge uncertainties which make theirs so dubious an enterprise, the planners nevertheless believe that there are certain conditions which provide an inescapable framework for curriculum development and certain guidelines which can be followed. Among the conditions which look like being irreversible, the following may be noted:

1] The declining demand for unskilled and semi-skilled labour.
2] The growing demand for occupational adaptability.
3] The exponential growth of knowledge (and its rapid obsolescence).
4] An increase in the amount of time available for leisure activities.
5] Greater expectation of life (both in terms of longevity and higher standards of living).
6] Earlier physical (and probably emotional and intellectual) maturity.
7] A marked decrease in the distinctions between the roles of the sexes.

8] An increase in the lateral transmission of knowledge and information (e.g. via the mass media) and a corresponding decrease in the vertical transmission (i.e. instruction of the young by parents and teachers).

Most of these have already been singled out for attention and call for no further comment. Each in its way is certain to be influential in revising existing notions about what the young should learn. Thus, the economic superfluity of middle and late adolescents practically guarantees that their school life will continue to grow longer, as it has been doing over the past century, which suggests that educationists will eventually have to face up to the truth of Rousseau's paradox: 'The great objective is not to save time but to waste it.' As things are, we know that many youngsters resent being forced to remain at school until the age of fifteen – let alone sixteen, seventeen or eighteen – that they are restive under the treatment they receive and find it stale, flat and unprofitable. Some of them are well aware of the fact that what they are doing in school is digging holes in order to fill them up again, thinks Musgrove: indeed, 'compulsory education over the past century has been essentially senseless'.[16]

Student power, as it is called, is only one manifestation of the refusal to stand for the kind of educational treatment which contrived to impose its own arbitrary values and pull the wool over the eyes of the young in the past – and it is only a matter of time before pupil power makes itself felt. The triangle of forces between the trend towards earlier maturity (and the demand for more active participation in decision-making which goes with it), the trend towards a more protracted school life (and the deferment of the recognition of young adults as fully-fledged citizens) and the pressure of demand for specialist training and paper qualifications creates so many tensions and is so snarled up with contradictions that the direction in which it is pointing, if there is one, is anybody's guess. If (and when) the age of automation arrives, will leisure pursuits provide the main aim and will the later adolescent years then be treated as a period of extended play, made bearable because general education will then be prized and enjoyed as a consumer good for its own sake? Not likely, thinks Musgrove, for the simple reason that 'a curriculum which is based largely on traditional upper-class leisure pursuits is not necessarily the most appropriate instrument for self-exploration for most of our children'.[17] Alternatively, what is to happen if, in a technological society, the contrast between the kinds of learning which are expected to take place in the school and those to which pupils are exposed willy-nilly in the outside world becomes even more pronounced than it is at present? It is not simply a contrast between formal and informal agencies, disciplined instruction and undisciplined experience, cognitive skills and affective motives: at the heart of it, it is between the educational process as it has been conceived so far and as it is going to be in the future. Accordingly, 'the business of the sociologist is to explore the systematic social relationships on which this artificial contrivance depends'.[18]

Sociological analysis, however, is only one component of the many-sided approach that is going to be needed if curriculum development is to be a manageable proposition. It may be that (like Newman's 'Idea' of a university as an assemblage of learned men brought together for the sake of intellectual peace to compose the differences between them) the attempt to find a common ground where educationists, sociologists, psychologists, economists, administrators and others can meet, on the understanding that no one among them can presume to have the casting vote, is doomed to failure.

The mixed bag of axioms which follows does not claim to be in any way original. It is offered in the full awareness that anyone who offers to lay down guidelines, however broad, runs the risk of being accused of trying to teach his grandmother to suck eggs. Each of these axioms has been derived from a comparative study of hard-won experiences in the field of curriculum development in other countries as well as in the United Kingdom. Each finds its support in a voluminous research literature. For the sake of brevity, the ten-point programme has been stated baldly, with a minimum of comment, and without making any attempt to quote chapter and verse, to summarize evidence, or to give a select bibliography.

Axiom 1: Management of conflict is a pre-condition for securing co-operation.

In any culture shades of opinion range from the ultra-conservative (those who would gladly leave things as they are) to extreme radicalism (those who urge the need for sweeping reforms). As a result, rival factions frequently find themselves at loggerheads. Free interchange of opinion is hindered by latent suspicion, misunderstanding, resentment, even open hostility. Fear of change, like the fear of the unknown, is the rule rather than the exception, and the strong prejudice against change, especially in the minds of the old, the middle-aged and those who are insecure, is not easily to be removed by rational argument. Learning to live with conflict is a necessary virtue in periods of cultural transition, such as the one we are passing through at the present time. Opposing viewpoints have to be listened to and accommodated, even if the outcome is only an agreement to differ. Conflict cannot be resolved dictatorially from above and may be destructive if attempts are made to stifle it. In the long run it can only be harmonized through the give and take of discussions involving all the interested parties – in which case it may become the basis for constructive co-operation.

Axiom 2: Since curriculum planning has to be related to the education system as a whole it is necessary to determine the state of the system.

Conflict itself is a sign that passive acceptance of the *status quo* is giving way to a dawning conviction of the need for change. Even in countries where established ways of doing things are largely unquestioned, school curricula rarely fail to arouse controversy. Does the content of courses need up-dating? Why are new methods being introduced and what is wrong with the old ones? To what ends, if not for the sake of gimmickry? Before attempting to answer such questions, it is vital to understand both the external and internal forces at work – in particular the ways in which the education system is likely to respond to these forces. Where the way of life and the general climate of opinion is conducive to change, as in the U.S.A., the chances of the education system being in a state of dynamic equilibrium are obviously greater, and the prospects for planning more favourable, than in cultures which are highly conservative. Sweden and Denmark and, to a lesser degree, England and Scotland provide interesting case studies of the ways in which styles of approach and strategies of innovation are affected by the wider system – i.e. the culture as a whole, including its history, national character, economy, ethos, etc. It does not always follow, however, that a country gets the kind of education system it deserves! The fact that curriculum planning has to be undertaken in the context of forces which are beyond its control makes it all the more necessary to investigate the patterns of power and the chain of command inside the education system. Goodlad[19] distinguishes between three levels of decision-making: (*a*) Societal (e.g. state agencies, local education authorities, mass media); (*b*) Institutional (e.g. universities, schools, professional associations); (*c*) Instructional (e.g. choice of methods of teaching in the classroom). This is one way of looking at the distribution of authority. With computable decision models in the offing, it becomes more than ever necessary to find out as much as possible about the structure of the education system and its modes of operation. Is the initiative shared among administrators, academics, teachers and others – or is the leadership in the hands of a few top people? Is there a clear differentiation of roles, so that each party knows what contribution is expected of it? Are there blockages in the system which prevent the pooling and cross-fertilization of ideas? Answers to questions of this sort may not satisfy the formal requirements of system analysis, but they do provide rough and ready indications of the state of affairs, and no viable strategy of planning can be considered until they are known.

Axiom 3: Curriculum planning needs to be carried out as a combined operation.

This is self-evident, or should be. It may be pertinent to add that the consortium of interests is not confined to representatives of the education system. Media men, publishers, manufacturers of school equipment, parents' associations, etc., also have a part to play. 'It is in the linkage between scholar and technician that the curriculum revision is most likely to fail.'[20]

Axiom 4: If it is to be effective, curriculum planning must be accompanied by appropriate learning materials.

Although shortage of cash is not the most serious impediment to innovation in the early stages, curriculum renewal costs a great deal of money in the long run. Although the production of packaged learning materials is not to be thought of as an end in itself, the fact is that none of the major projects carried out so far has made any impression without providing the necessary adjuncts – textbooks, audio-visual aids, apparatus. To date, most of the innovations in schools – e.g. the political decision to go comprehensive – have been imposed without providing adequate help for teachers implementing the new policies. Apart from isolated experiments in closed circuit television, film-making and programmed learning, relatively little has been done in the design, preparation, field-testing and development of high-quality learning materials. This is not because of any lack of resources but because the available resources are not being marshalled systematically and fully utilized. A great deal is said about the need for 'research', rather less about the advantages to be gained from an organized programme of research and development.

Without making extravagant claims on behalf of educational technology, curriculum planning needs to be informed by a thorough grasp of the principles behind the new media, techniques and instrumentation now at its disposal. If teachers and students are to be involved in the design and field-testing of learning materials, it seems that two of the best places for beginning curriculum renewal are to be found in courses of pre-service and in-service training. In addition, more practical demonstrations of new methods of presentation, and more opportunities for trying out unfamiliar equipment are required if the rank and file of teachers are to be convinced of their essential worthwhileness.

Axiom 5: In curriculum planning it has to be borne in mind that the emphasis is gradually shifting from the teacher as instructor to the teacher as manager of learning situations.

The role of the teacher as one-who-knows-telling-those-who-don't is clearly changing and may eventually become obsolete. The trend exemplified in programmed learning is symptomatic of a much wider trend which makes it impossible to envisage the emergence of the school as a resources-for-learning centre. The implications as regards school organization, methods of teaching and teacher-training are far reaching, not least in raising doubts about the existing compartmentation of the curriculum into 'subjects'. To say this is not to imply that 'lessons' are old-fashioned and that the time is at hand when pupils can safely be left to learn on a do-it-yourself basis. Neither does it ignore the fact that the me-and-my-children attitude of teachers is stoutly opposed to any move which looks like infringing or curtailing their authority. It does, however, reinforce the point of Axiom 4 – that the paramount need is for research and development.

Axiom 6: In curriculum planning selection of objectives comes before selection of content.

The easy-going philosophy which was content to equate the curriculum with 'the syllabus', 'subjects' or 'schemes of work' is no longer tenable. Content is important, certainly, but to derive purposes from a given body of knowledge, no matter how well organized, is to put the cart before the horse. In other words, the question, 'What outcomes are desired?', necessarily precedes the question, 'What are we going to teach?' While planning must disclaim any assumption that the shape of things to come can be pre-determined, it cannot fail to be strongly influenced by techniques of prediction, regulation and control. Common to all the strategies of the times – operations research, critical path analysis, systems engineering – is a preoccupation with knowable ends. As the cyberneticist insists, 'before any regulation can be undertaken or even discussed we must know what is important and what is wanted'.[21]

Praiseworthy as it seems, unfortunately, this determination to settle for visible, testable goals raises enormous difficulties for the educator. The distinction between *aims*, which too often are no better than vacuous hopes, and *objectives*, which make it plain what the learner is expected to do from the beginning of the course to its completion, is now widely appreciated. Just how agreed higher order objectives affecting the purposes of curriculum as a whole are to be stated is, to say the least of it, problematical. In theory it is easy enough to say that the desired outcomes ought to be decided first. In practice it is not easy to see how this axiom can be acted upon short of stopping the machine altogether and restarting from fresh premises. So long as the accent remains firmly on subject-matter, nevertheless, the readiness to accept because-it's-there arguments in favour of leaving things as they are will continue to go largely unquestioned.

Axiom 7: Continuous assessment and evaluation must be built into curriculum planning to ensure that it is self-correcting.

Testing as one goes is the watchword. Even the most carefully prepared plans will almost certainly need to be modified in the light of pupils' and teachers' reactions. At all stages, regular feedback of information, criticism and counter-suggestions from those trying out experimental courses to those responsible for initiating them is indispensable. At all costs the arrogance of supposing that any one party has the final solution has to be avoided. Only in this way can decision-making be effectively shared and off-course drift prevented.

This sounds like a truism, but arranging for self-correcting procedures is one of the most exacting tasks in mounting a curriculum project. Testing as one goes entails a great deal more than administering post-tests which give a measure of pupils' comprehension. No less important are the attitudinal and affective aspects of learning (and teaching). This kind of testing calls for sensitive, sophisticated skills, and it is as well to recognize that these skills are at present in short supply.

Axiom 8: In any education system the major forces for change stem from outside.

Tomorrow's five-year-old will go to school without ever seeing a farthing, a halfpenny or a half-crown, let alone the rod, pole or perch which hung on to their immemorial place in arithmetic books until quite recently. He will live in an environment in which steam locomotives are as romantic as stage coaches used to be during the first half of the twentieth century, in which propeller-driven aircraft are almost as antediluvian as hot air balloons, and the dirigible as far-away and fanciful as the dinosaur. These are only a few picturesque reminders of the fact that the prime movers of change in the schools are economic and technological ones. Among other forces which have to be reckoned with are: (*a*) the mass media; (*b*) the exploitations of pop culture; (*c*) commercial enterprise in the manufacture and sale of mechanical devices, aids to learning, school equipment of all kinds, etc. – one of the leading growth industries of our time; (*d*) a general speeding up of social mobility due to rapidly changing requirements in occupational skills and the ever-increasing speed of travel and other forms of communication.

Each of these affects the learning situation in some way or other. To deplore their effects is as idle as to wish that the H-bomb had never been invented: if they cannot always be approved of, they can never be ignored.

Axiom 9: The contemporary learning situation calls for a redefinition of the basic skills.

Throughout the nineteenth century *literacy* provided the main stock in trade of the schools. During the first half of the twentieth century the claims of science and mathematics have led to equal importance being attached to *numeracy*. Since 1950 more and more attention has been paid to the uses of the spoken word – '*oracy*'. More recently still, the Brynmor Jones Report has mentioned a fourth desideratum – 'picturacy'!

To what extent are new media and new systems of communication returning us to Quintilian's ideal of 'the good man skilled in speaking'? To what extent are reading habits being modified by constant viewing? What kinds of arithmetic are going to be needed in an age of decimalization and computers? Are the skills now being inculcated in the schools as fundamental as we like to think? In a permissive society is it any use looking for a code of fundamental values, or is it a case of anything goes, provided it can be justified on pragmatic, utilitarian grounds?

Axiom 10: Curriculum planning, like education itself, is a continuous process.

To say that adaptation to continuous change has become a condition of modern life is to state the blindingly obvious, and not very helpful. All Axiom 10 can do is to assert that, since the tempo of change is accelerating, some attempt has to be made to understand the dynamic interaction of the forces engaged, and to adjust the work of the schools so that what is taught (and how it is taught) does not fall so far behind the march of time as to seem prematurely archaic.

Whether, in the absence of a creditable curriculum theory, and without an all-out concerted effort, innovation can be regulated on the scale that is required remains questionable. The inertia of use and wont being so strong in the education system, the only sober appraisal of the situation facing up must be that 'the impossible takes a little longer'. The unresolved paradox is that, although the need to work fast is imperative, curriculum development is inevitably a slow business. To save time, and avoid duplication of effort and the waste of limited resources, nothing less than a confederate plan of campaign is required. The alternative is to fall back on a Micawberish approach which is as effete as it is ineffectual. Instead of bemusing ourselves by discussing the pros and cons of 'progressive' and 'traditional' methods, it would be more realistic to acknowledge that the opposite of progressive is unprogressive, the opposite of systematic is unsystematic, and that organisms which fail to adapt themselves to a changing environment doom themselves to extinction.

Broad as they are, then, the progressive stages by which a

corporate plan of curriculum development might conceivably be managed can be represented diagrammatically (the interconnecting feedback loops between the various stages have been omitted for the sake of simplicity):

| Preliminary study of the existing provision | → | Selection of desired outcomes (aims and objectives) | → | Preparation of pilot courses | → | Field-testing | → | In-service and pre-service training | → | Dissemination and use |

In reviewing the spate of recent and current curriculum projects in the U.S.A., France, Sweden,* England and Scotland in subsequent chapters, it is worth asking the following questions. Do they add up to a coherent national plan? How far do the strategies adopted answer to a common pattern? What value judgements are implicit in them? If significant improvements have been effected, how are they assessed? How are controversial issues dealt with? Where does the leadership come from? What procedures are followed for bringing about closer liaison and collaboration between teachers, administrators, research workers, etc?

For good measure, there is another axiom which is worth bearing in mind. *Axiom 11 states that: In most curriculum projects there is an inherent tendency to underestimate the learning capacities of the average child.* If there is one axiom that we are prepared to be dogmatic about, this is it. Its truth is confirmed by a substantial body of evidence which deserves to be made more widely known than it is, and acted upon accordingly. Granted, a fully prescriptive theory of instruction is still awaited, and a plausible curriculum theory nowhere in sight; but, with so many techniques and media asking to be exploited, there is no longer any excuse for the ungenerous habit of thinking that the 'lad o' pairts' is so rare a creature.

---

* The reader is referred to 'A systems approach to educational reform: the Swedish example', ch. 5 in W. Kenneth Richmond, *The Education Industry* (London, Methuen, 1969).

REFERENCES

1 Aristotle, *Politics*, viii, *passim*.
2 H. Rugg, *American Life and the School Curriculum* (Boston, Mass., Ginn, 1936), pp. 17–18.
3 W. F. Connell, 'A glossary of curriculum terms', *The Forum of Education*, XIV, 1 (July 1955).
4 B. O. Smith, W. O. Stanlet and J. H. Shores, *Fundamentals of Curriculum Development* (New York, Harcourt, Brace & World, 1957), p. 131.
5 J. S. Bruner, *The Process of Education* (Cambridge, Mass., Harvard University Press, 1960), pp. 31–2, 52–3.
6 Ben Morris, 'The school: how do we see it functioning (past, present and future)?', in The Schools Council, *The New Curriculum* (London, H.M.S.O., 1967), p. 4.
7 John Dewey, *The School and Society* (University of Chicago Press, 1910), pp. 11–12.
8 Organization for Economic Co-operation and Development, *Curriculum Improvement and Educational Development* (Paris, 1966), pp. 5–6.
9 ibid.
10 Marshall McLuhan, in G. E. Stearns (Ed.), *McLuhan Hot and Cool* (Harmondsworth, Penguin Books, 1968).
11 D. K. Wheeler, *Curriculum Process* (University of London Press, 1967), pp. 179–81. The report referred to by Wheeler was *The Curriculum of Secondary Schools Offering Advanced Studies* (University of London Press, 1962).
12 W. H. G. Armytage, *The German Influence on English Education* (London, Routledge & Kegan Paul, 1969).
13 G. Leff, 'The tyranny of concepts', *Heresy in the Later Middle Ages* (Manchester University Press, 1967), pp. 130–1.
14 Paul Woodring, 'Introduction', in R. W. Heath (Ed.), *New Curricula* (New York, Harper & Row, 1964), p. 4.
15 W. Ross Ashby, *Introduction to Cybernetics* (London, Methuen, University Paperbacks, 1964), p. 106.
16 Frank Musgrove, 'Curriculum objectives', *Journal of Curriculum Studies*, Vol. 1, No. 1 (November 1968).
17 ibid.

18 Frank Musgrove, 'The contribution of sociology to the study of the curriculum', in J. F. Kerr (Ed.), *Changing the Curriculum* (University of London Press, 1968), p. 101.
19 *Curriculum Innovation in Practice* (London, H.M.S.O., 1968).
20 J. R. Zacharias and S. White, 'The requirements for major curriculum revision', in R. W. Heath, op. cit., p. 74.
21 W. Ross Ashby, op. cit., p. 219.

Part I

THE MANAGEMENT OF INNOVATION

Practice

CHAPTER TWO

American Education Makes up for Lost Time

Education, like trade, has its booms and recessions. In affluent societies, moreover, it does not follow that economic prosperity and cultural advancement occur simultaneously. The low ebb to which the schools of the U.S.A. had slumped in the years following the end of World War II may perhaps be illustrated by recounting an incident which took place in the long hot summer of 1953. In a classroom somewhere in Kansas a group of fourth graders were holding a kind of birthday party, talking among themselves, passing around jars of cookies, sucking iced lollies, sprawled in their chairs or recumbent on the floor. Outside, the shade temperature was topping the 100° F mark; inside, the atmosphere was stifling, which was some excuse for the general torpor. Relaxed at her desk, the teacher (a young miss straight from college), eyed the goings-on around her with sleepy indifference. After twenty minutes of perspiring embarrassment, the visitor who had strayed into this seven sleepers' den felt impelled to ask what it was all in aid of and received an illuminating reply. Laying aside her handbag (she was busy fixing her eye-shadow when the question was popped), she drawled, 'Well, ah figure we kinda sit around and wait for experiences.'

To such base uses the theory and practice of 'progressive' education were reduced during the years following the death of John Dewey. This was the era of the Macarthyite political witch hunts, the heyday of a nation-wide cult of so-called Life

Adjustment Education which pandered to two of the less reputable features in American life, its anti-intellectualism and its practicalism. In retrospect, it is easy to conclude that an all-time low in standards of teaching and scholastic attainment had been reached, and that the nadir can be dated somewhere between 1950 and 1955.

Before jumping to this conclusion, however, it is necessary to know something about the genesis of the American high school, which grew naturally as an upward extension of the local community's elementary school and enjoyed the same freedom from state control and from university entrance requirements. Like the elementary school in Britain, the American 'grade' school had a curriculum based on the Three Rs, but over and above this it was committed to a very different ideology, as the authors of *Who Shall be Educated?* made clear:

> In the common elementary school American boys and girls should assimilate the literature, history and biography that will bind them together with a common background of tradition and emotional experience. The democratic values should be experienced and related to the affairs of everyday life. Holidays should be celebrated – both national holidays such as Washington's Birthday and Thanksgiving, and societal holidays such as Christmas and Easter. Thus the common loyalties of Americans should be inculcated along with the common skills of communication which are always taught in the elementary school.
>
> The American school system does all these things fairly well. Present practice in these matters is, on the whole, good practice. Occasionally, however, an effort to improve the teaching of the fundamental skills conflicts with the teaching of fundamental loyalties and values. Tendencies towards segregation of pupils for more efficient teaching of the fundamental skills should be examined carefully to see that they do not threaten the teaching of the common loyalties.[1]

The presuppositions here may seem to an outsider to be more patriotic and quasi-religious than rational, but they have always been at the heart of New World ways of life and thought; and even today, when they are being seriously questioned, they impose the sternest of all requirements – that whatever else it succeeds in doing the school must not fail in its duty of turning out good Americans.

As an outgrowth of the common elementary school, the success story of the American high school is best explained as a triumph of Jacksonian democracy and egalitarianism over Jeffersonian democracy and élitism – though only at the cost of drastic oversimplification. As late as 1893, the Committee on Correlation of Studies was advocating the teaching of Latin to eight-year-olds, and the main course offered in most high schools was a college preparatory one, essentially similar in its components to that of the English grammar school. How abrupt was the revulsion against an academic approach can be gathered from the fact that by 1918 the Commission on the Reorganization of Secondary Education contented itself with a statement of seven cardinal principles, in which the 'liberal arts' received neither mention nor recognition: health, command of the fundamental processes, worthy home membership, vocation, civic education, worthy use of leisure, ethical character. In the interregnum the high school had been swamped by a tidal wave of enrolments for which it was totally unprepared. Instead of having to cater for a relatively small fraction of the nation's youth, it was now called upon to cope with a heterogeneous mass of children. From 357,000 in 1890, the high school population rocketed to 7,113,000 in 1940. Housing the hordes was no problem, finding a pabulum to suit all tastes certainly was. The solution, never more than a makeshift and the only one possible in the circumstances, was to replace the traditional academic studies by a simple 'core curriculum' and to lay on as wide a variety as possible of optional courses to accommodate different levels of intelligence and interest. A mechanical unit-and-credit plan was adopted by which pupils ('students') could tot up the necessary points on an *à la carte* basis, a credit in Latin counting the same as one obtained in laundry. Inevitably, this led to a wholesale proliferation of Mickey Mouse courses – glee club, radio speaking, cosmetology, consumer buying, home mechanics – some of which owed their popularity, if not their *raison d'être*, to the spirit of fun and games. The mindless togetherness induced by this 'rope of sand' curriculum presents the seamy side of the formative period of the high school, one which many educated Americans would gladly forget. Even at the time its excesses exposed it to bitter ridicule and its woeful inadequacy made it the butt of savage criticism.

An over-statement? Francis Keppel, former Dean of the Harvard Graduate School of Education and U.S. Commissioner of Education, disagrees:

> But the majority trend of thinking both by the public and the educators seemed to favour a variety of programs within the same high school, with a good deal of common experience for all students. This became the comprehensive high school, the twentieth-century version of the old idea of the common school. Here the pupils could, if they wished and if they improved their ability to learn, move from one kind of program to another. Such a pattern of flexibility took care of two objections which were made to the idea of curricula linked directly to individual differences: the objection that no test of native ability was really accurate since many tests fail to allow for cultural differences, and therefore that fixed assignments to particular curricula might penalize children who might improve as they grew older. The system of flexibility gave room for the powers of moral courage to come to play. It allowed the effects of sheer hard work and persistence to be felt. In short, it made it more nearly possible for citizen and educator alike to say that each child while in school had equal opportunity – which is to say that the school was carrying out its part of the bargain with the idea of perfectibility and the idea of education for all. And the onus of decision was left, at least in theory, to the individual, not to society operating through the teacher.[2]

For all that, credit must be given to the Jacksonians for their insistence on keeping education close to the people. It has become a cliché to speak of the 'power at the grass roots', but how is it possible to explain the sheer dynamism of the American education system, the most highly decentralized in the world, without resorting to clichés? With all its faults, despicable as they often were, the high school offered something for everybody; and if it showed scant regard for scholastic prowess it was because it owed its main allegiance to the broad mass of children, not to a chosen few. If the shared experience championed by Dewey was misinterpreted, and 'progressive' methods so travestied as to become a mockery in the back-slapping ballyhoo and the mumbo-jumbo which heralded the advent of Life Adjustment Education, it nevertheless provided the essential springboard for future reforms. Whether we trace it back to conditions of life at the frontier, or to the political ideals of the Founding Fathers, the Declaration of Independence and all that, togetherness is part and parcel of the American mentality. With it goes the belief that everyone has a part to play, that practical abilities deserve just as much consideration as any other kind of ability, and that provided all are given the chance to find their own level of accomplishment there is really nothing wrong with a system which allows them to learn in their own good time. Even so captious a critic as Dr Conant, therefore, is prepared to defend the high school:

> If one can speak of a typical American arrangement where such wide variety exists, it would be fair to say that in the United States we attempt little differentiation in our public schools until age fifteen. As a consequence, the American student enrolled in a public school studies few of the academic subjects believed essential for University work in Great Britain or Australia. Furthermore he rarely studies them as intensely as the corresponding boy or girl in the other English-speaking countries. We can correct this situation somewhat and to good advantage within the framework of a comprehensive school. But we cannot correct the situation to the degree that those accustomed to the British or Continental tradition would think wise. For these foreign observers have not thought through the contrast between a selective system of education starting at eleven or twelve and a system of general education. There are advantages in the British system in terms of mastery of intellectual skills but they are far outweighed, to my mind, by the negative factor.[3]

That the situation needed correcting after 1950 was apparent from some of the crazier pronouncements of the devotees of Life

Adjustment. One of them quoted statistics showing that the percentage of pupils studying foreign languages had fallen from 38·7 in 1890 to 17·6 in 1930, arguing that this represented 'one of the great triumphs of American democracy'. Another professed to being scandalized on finding that there were five times as many failures in mathematics as there were in home economics, and asserted roundly that 'there is no justification for this prevailing condition'. Harold Spears, author of *The High School for Today*, asked his readers in all seriousness which was more important:

> To find out what's under the cover of Scott's *Ivanhoe*, or to find out what's under the cover of Ford's Mercury?
> To repair the weak construction of a complex sentence, or to repair the weak construction of a complex relationship in one's home?
> To be able to date the Battle of Hastings, or to be able to date the captain of the football team?
> To recognize a split infinitive, or to recognize a split personality?
> To be able to recite the pronouns that rightly govern the accusative in German, or to be able to recite the forces that falsely accuse Congress in Washington?
> To understand Ohm's law, or to understand the law of supply and demand?[4]

— the inference being, of course, that in each case the second alternative was the only possible one.

The counter attack was not long delayed. Public opinion, already shaken by the disclosure that the number of pupils completing twelfth grade had actually fallen in 1945, became increasingly perturbed by a series of reports showing that standards of attainment were dangerously low. In New York State a Board of Regents inquiry reported that 'every third pupil is not adequately prepared for the duties of citizenship'. In Chicago, according to Dr R. Hutchins's estimate, 50 per cent of the male population were functionally illiterate. Back in 1941, in an examination for entrance to the Naval Reserve Officers' Training Corps given to college freshmen, 68 per cent had failed to pass the Arithmetical Reasoning Test. Three years later a fact-finding survey carried out by the *New York Times* in thirty-six liberal arts colleges found evidence of so much ignorance and misinformation that it concluded that history was evidently not being taught at all in most high schools. Yet another independent survey, reported in *What the High Schools Ought to Teach*, offered the opinion that 'a great many pupils in these schools have reading abilities of the fifth or even of the fourth grade level'.

It was in this context and in this chastened mood that the work of curriculum development began in earnest. The cheap witticism which says that public interest in reform (not to mention governmental support) was launched by Sputnik I contains more than a grain of truth, for unquestionably the Russian success in getting the first satellite in orbit came as a mighty jolt to national pride. Incredible that any other nation could beat America to the punch! If proof were needed for the axiom which holds that the major forces for change stem from outside the education system, here it was. To say that for the next ten years the high school was running scared under the impact of this demonstration of technological know-how by a foreign power may be an inelegant, but not altogether inaccurate way of describing what happened.

Disaffection inside the education system had been stirring for more than a decade, however, and the preliminary moves in at least one of the major curriculum projects had been made long before 1957. Still, the fact remains that none of them got off the ground until after 1957. When they did, they gathered momentum with extraordinary rapidity and left no one in any doubt about their ability to get things done in the grand manner.

The speed and efficiency with which the Physical Science Study Committee set about the task confronting them may be taken as typical. The project was sparked off by Professor Zacharias of the Massachusetts Institute of Technology in a memorandum dated March 1956:

> In an effort to improve the teaching of high school physics I want to propose an experiment involving the preparation of a large number of moving picture shorts . . . complete with text books, problem books, question cards and answer cards . . . but before taking up the

detailed mechanism it is necessary first to look at the subject-matter. Success or failure depends to a large extent on having the entire apparatus of the experiment really right. Like a high fidelity phonograph, one must have besides the machine a good piece by a good composer played by an artist. The room must be good, not too noisy, and the people have to want to listen, but that all depends upon the piece.

... The tidy notions of classical mechanics still predominate in the way we try to introduce the subject of physics and it usually happens that these notions are dull as presented because it is so difficult to present arresting experiments to liven them up. Because one needs to understand many of the basic ideas and mathematical methods before gaining a profound comprehension, it always seems logical to begin with the basic ideas of vectors, velocities, statics, hydrostatics, force, mass, etc. Now I think that physics can be divided up into the following parts: (1) the particles and the bodies, (2) between these bodies we have laws of force, (3) under the action of these forces the things move with the laws of motion. . . .[5]

This proposal was shrewdly timed. The Physical Science Study Committee was formed, recruited from top-flight scientists, technologists, industrial and educational experts who forthwith got down to discussing the broad outlines of the course and the detailed arrangements for bringing it into being. It was agreed (1) that the course must be intellectually challenging, (2) that it must reflect the structure and 'feel' of advanced, contemporary thinking and investigation in physics, (3) that it should engage the learner in active exploration, inquiry and discovery, (4) that it should be accompanied by a varied array of packaged learning materials, in particular a first-rate textbook. Drafts of the latter were prepared and ready for try-outs in selected schools during the summer of 1957, and in 1958–9 a film studio went into production, summer institutes were organized to familiarize teachers with the new course and its collateral learning materials. The revised version of the textbook was published in the autumn of 1960 and had involved the participation of some eight hundred schools and nearly a thousand teachers. Within the space of a twelvemonth period half a million copies had been distributed, at which point the project ceased to be experimental and developments in the schools were left to gather their own momentum.

From the start, the P.S.S.C. project had received generous backing from the National Science Foundation and other funding agencies. To handle the business side of its work, which very quickly assumed proportions too vast and too onerous for a team of academics to manage, an administrative machinery was created in 1958 in the form of a non-profit corporation linked with the federal government under the title of Educational Services Incorporated (E.S.I.). 1958, incidentally, was the year of the National Defense Education Act which facilitated the giving of federal aid (hitherto one of the toughest bones of contention in the U.S.A.), and which was itself strongly influenced by the shock waves from Sputnik I. Thereafter, the Office of Education was in a position to play a more active role, always bearing in mind the need to respect the autonomy of the several States as defined in the Tenth Amendment of the Constitution.

While it would be wrong to think that the trail-blazing of the P.S.S.C. project paved the way for what has come to be called 'alphabet soup' curriculum development in the U.S.A., its success certainly boosted morale and served as a stimulus for other ventures which sought to emulate it. Of these, the biggest and best known was the School Mathematics Study Group (S.M.S.G.), formed in 1958. Here again the initiative came from professional mathematicians and research workers in the field of higher education. Their motives for wishing to see an improvement in the content and methods of teaching in schools can be summarized as follows:

1] Mathematics is a key discipline in the modern world. More people need to possess a basic understanding of mathematical concepts and procedures than ever before – and the need is certain to become even greater in the future.
2] Without an adequate supply of highly trained mathematicians manpower requirements in science and technology are seriously jeopardized.

3] As normally taught in schools, mathematics tends to be uninteresting and difficult, with the result that many pupils are left with a positive distaste for it.

4] Professional mathematicians are chiefly concerned with branches of their study which have grown up fairly recently, but because they have refrained from finding out what goes on in the schools these new and significant aspects of mathematics have not found their way into the curriculum.

5] Conventional methods of teaching mathematics rely too heavily on rule-of-thumb computation and the mechanical manipulation of number symbols. Heuristic learning is blighted by the importance attached to rote-learned rules.

6] The field of mathematics has become so diverse that its complexities can only be resolved by experts who have the perspectives and the insights which are needed in the elucidation of its essential structure and underlying principles.

The emphasis on abstraction in the new approach to mathematics was poles apart from the approach favoured in most high schools during the early 1950s when a lunatic fringe came near to dismissing it as an un-American activity. Now at last academic opinion made itself heard. If it did not always speak with one voice, its arguments were both forceful and consistent:

> When we stop to compare the mathematics of today with mathematics as it was at the close of the nineteenth century, we may well be amazed to note how rapidly our mathematical knowledge has grown in quantity and complexity, but we should also not fail to observe how closely this development has been involved with an emphasis on abstraction and an increasing concern with the perception and analysis of broad mathematical patterns. Indeed, upon closer examination we see that this new orientation, made possible only by the divorce of mathematics from its applications, has been the true source of its tremendous growth during the present century.[6]

A few years earlier such an argument would have been hooted out of court, but in a climate of opinion in which anxiety verged on or near hysteria, induced by the Soviet threat to American supremacy, it was listened to with deference. That it made sense to the politicians may be gauged by the fact that during the first two and a half years of its existence the S.M.S.G. project was able to spend five million dollars. Like other projects which were under way by this time, its first priority was the production of a textbook incorporating the ideas of some hundred university teachers and an equal number of high school teachers who shared the work of writing the various drafts. Within a year the first texts and teachers' manuals were ready for use. They were tried out by four hundred teachers in forty-five states during the 1959–60 school year and the results analysed and evaluated so that the revision teams could get busy with the job of editing a final version for publication and distribution.

Leaving aside for the moment the charge that the whole drift of S.M.S.G.'s thinking was in favour of return to college preparatory courses and that it was too demanding for the ordinary boy and girl – a charge which is not altogether ill-founded – it is impossible not to be impressed by the clockwork efficiency of this high-powered operation, the way it adhered to a tight schedule, the scrupulous care in meeting its deadlines, its dovetailing of the handiwork of hundreds of contributors, all like-minded in working to a common brief. As a case study of the philosophy of shared experience, S.M.S.G. would be hard to beat.

Next to get into the act were the biologists who had long been aware of serious deficiencies in the teaching of life sciences at both school and college levels. Their reasons for thinking that an all-round reform was overdue were similar to those of their colleagues in physics and mathematics:

1] Biological knowledge is practically doubling itself in each succeeding decade, so that unless frequent reappraisals of the content of courses are made what is taught is bound to be hopelessly in arrears.
2] In any case, the practice of teaching biology as a body of established information is too static and quite out of keeping with the spirit of experimental science; it places too heavy a premium on memorization, inhibits inquiry, prevents the

honest weighing of evidence, and turns the laboratory into a museum where demonstrations are occasionally carried out by the teachers, not a workshop where pupils are regularly engaged in first-hand investigations.

3] The life sciences are now so diversified and embrace so many different aspects (and methods of inquiry) that unless some principle of unity-in-diversity can be found courses will suffer from lack of coherence. It is an illusion to suppose that a single approach or a fixed sequence capable of satisfying all pupils can be found; the best way of organizing secondary school courses is, therefore, itself a problem for investigation.

4] Whatever approach is attempted, certain basic themes– biochemical, physiological, genetic, evolutionary, ecological – should provide the conceptual framework.

5] An understanding of biological principles is a *sine qua non* for any educated person in the modern world. Accordingly, the foundations for a study of the life sciences should be laid in the early years of the secondary school, and should not be postponed because of the prior claims of physics and chemistry with the result that many pupils leave without any clear understanding of biological principles.

Sponsored by the American Institute of Biological Sciences, and with substantial financial support from the National Science Foundation, the Biological Sciences Curriculum Study (B.S.C.S.) was launched in 1959. Having run out of superlatives in the case of S.M.S.G., it seems that there is nothing for it but to relapse into the language of the Hollywood film advertiser ('Gigantic', 'Spectacular', 'Stupendous' 'Colossal' . . .) in describing the ways in which the B.S.C.S. team tackled the job of bringing about a renaissance in the life sciences. Having cleared the ground in advance by defining its broad objectives and deciding its strategy, it went to work with a will. A task force of college and high school teachers, administrators, illustrators and clerical staff was assembled from all over the U.S.A. at Boulder, Colorado, during the summer of 1960. For eight weeks they lived together, ate together, thought and worked together. University and college biologists were paired with high school teachers, each pair being assigned to a section of the textbook which it was asked to write – an arrangement which was intended to ensure that accuracy and up-to-dateness of content was taken care of by the academic expert and appropriate style of presentation by the practising teacher. Once a section had been drafted, it was circulated for comment and criticism. Inter-group discussions of work in progress, many of them heated, were the order of the day. The outcome of it all was that after seven weeks of hard communal slog the texts were ready to go to press. Since the team had been unable to agree about the precise sequence which the course ought to follow, there were, in fact, three different texts.

The *Blue Version* ('Molecules to Man') starts off at the molecular biochemical level and retraces the story of evolution under the headings of: (1) Biology as the interaction of facts and ideas, science as inquiry, etc.; (2) The Living Cell; (3) The Evolving Organism; (4) Multicellular Organisms – reproduction and development; (5) Multicellular Organisms – energy utilization; (6) Multicellular Organisms – integration systems and behaviour; (7) Higher levels of organization – populations, societies, and communities. The *Yellow Version* ('Biological Science: An Inquiry into Life') began with an examination of cell structure and incorporates a number of basic conceptual themes: (1) Cells, (2) Micro-organisms, (3) Plants, (4) Animals, (5) Genetics, (6) Evolution, (7) Ecology. The *Green Version* ('High School Biology') reversed the order and preferred to approach the study of biology from the behavioural and ecological aspects. On the whole, its treatment was broader and rather less analytical than either of the other versions as a summary of its sections indicates: (1) The Biosphere Dissected – the living world, individuals, populations and communities; (2) Patterns in the Biosphere – life on land, life on inland waters, life in the seas, the history of life, the geography of life; (3) The Individual Dissected – the cell, the functioning plant, the functioning animal, reproduction development and heredity; (4) Evolution, Behaviour and Man – mechanisms of evolution, behaviour, the human animal, man and the biosphere.

Approximately two-thirds of the information was the same in all three versions. All were addressed to the junior high school level and were intended to meet the needs of pupils who did not go on to four-year college studies as well as those who did.

Even by American standards of mass production, the B.S.C.S. achievement in getting its printed materials ready for printing, distribution and preliminary trials in a matter of months must be accounted a notable feat. As early as November 1959 they were being used in schools throughout the U.S.A. and an elaborate testing and evaluation service had been organized with fifteen testing centres staffed by teachers and college consultants.

But all this represented only one side of the B.S.C.S. joint endeavour. While the task force appointed by the Committee on Course Content had been busy, the Committee for Innovation in Laboratory Instruction had simultaneously been devising a programme of controlled experiments and work assignments which were designed to capture the interest and imagination of pupils and place them in a learning situation akin to that of the trained biologist himself. In addition, the Committee on Gifted Children had been sounding out professional opinion in colleges and universities and had drawn up a list of one hundred research topics, many of them still unsolved, which it was thought might be suitable for assignment to extremely able pupils.

The immediate response to these prodigious efforts was encouraging. The laboratory package-deal, in particular, was well received, many teachers saying that it had come as a godsend to them and a revelation to their pupils. On the other hand, none of the three textbooks came through their trials unscathed. This, it was agreed, was because the exposition had not succeeded in bringing out the major conceptual themes which the authors had had in mind: despite all the precautions that had been taken, the texts were still over-cluttered with factual detail, and they were too difficult to hold the attention of the average pupil.

Back to the drawing board, then. In the summer of 1961 there was a reunion at Boulder and the work of collaboration, discussion and revision began all over again. The *Blue Version*, for example, was pared to the bone to highlight a conceptual structure comprising two major themes: the origins of life and its evolution, and the nature of scientific inquiry. The number of testing centres was increased to thirty-five and before the end of the year more than 50,000 pupils in high schools ranging from Vermont to Hawaii were using B.S.C.S. texts and equipment. The new course entered its final phase of general adoption and use in 1963, by which time its reputation had attracted the attention of educationists in several countries, including Britain.

How to sum up the significance of the B.S.C.S. new deal?

One might say two principal things in reply. For the first time in the history of American education we now see a large number of research scientists, from the colleges and universities, taking part in a cooperative effort with high-school teachers of science and science supervisors to replace an antiquated body of knowledge and outlook with subject matter and perspective that are truly current. The Physical Science Study Committee and the School Mathematics Study Group, the two curriculum studies begun earlier, moved in this direction. But I believe that only in the Biological Sciences Curriculum Study has this fruitful collaboration been fully realized. The result is as astounding to the research biologist as to the high school teacher. How nearly fatal that until so recently no one seemed to realize that this must be the way – the only way, in an ever-accelerating pace of scientific advance – to provide the well-orientated education in the sciences that modern man must have.

That is one answer to the question. The other is this. For the first time, I think education in the natural sciences, at least at the secondary level, has assigned the acquisition of scientific information and concepts a place of lesser importance than the understanding of the very nature of scientific enquiry and of the scientific enterprise in which modern man is embarked.[7]

As to that, the Foreword in each of the B.S.C.S. laboratory manuals speaks for itself:

No matter now much you learn about the facts of science, you will never understand what makes science the force it is in human history, or the scientists the sorts of people they are, until you have shared with them such an experience. The laboratory and field are the scientists' workshops. Much reading and discussion are essential in scientific work, but it is in the laboratory and field that hypotheses are tested.

Of the other large-scale projects which followed in the wake of the first three – CHEMStudy (1960–3), the Chemical Bond Approach (C.B.A.), Project English and the rest – little needs to be said. Reviewing the series as a whole the only possible verdict must be: so far so good. The only question is, 'Did they go far enough?'

Despite all disclaimers to the contrary, there can be little doubt that thoughts of national security were uppermost in the minds of the instigators of these projects: after all, the fact that science and mathematics were the first to receive attention can hardly have been accidental. The 'Return to Learning', as it has been called, would not have been expedited with anything like the same urgency if it had been left to professors of history, English and foreign languages to make the first move, and might never have occurred at all; yet, as we have seen, history, English and foreign languages were in bad shape in American high schools at the time. That the lead given by eminent academics helped to bring about an enhanced respect for scholarship that was sorely needed is obvious enough. Their willingness to lend a helping hand, often at great personal sacrifice, their zeal for promoting their particular field of study, their immense energy and the enthusiasm they displayed in bringing together people from different walks of life – all these were invaluable. Their acumen in seeing textbooks and packaged learning materials as the most effective means of bringing about the improvements they wanted to see (including a closer articulation between high school and college) is not to be faulted, either, for one of the weak links in the American education systems has always been the low level of professional competence of its teaching body. A sound textbook is not everything, but it is a good deal better than nothing in classrooms where most of the instruction given centres upon it.

In Woodring's view, then,

The curricular revisions of the present day represent, to some extent, a return to the older tradition that dominated the secondary schools before the progressive revolution. It is true that the content is new but once again the emphasis is on subject matter organized within the separate academic disciplines. Once again university scholars and scientists are playing a large part in deciding what is to be taught in the secondary schools and the part played by those professional educators, whose graduate degrees are in education rather than in an academic discipline, has been correspondingly reduced in importance. It is true that most of the new curriculum committees include secondary school teachers but, in most cases, these have been carefully selected on the basis of a firm grounding in an academic discipline and demonstrated success as teachers rather than for their professional training.

'Curriculum revision' seems to mean the preparation of new and improved educational materials: textbooks, supplementary readings, visual aids, laboratory equipment, and examinations for use in the classroom. This concept of the curriculum represents a departure from the approach most popular during the twenties, thirties, and forties, when the view was widely accepted that a curriculum was the total experience of the child and that what took place outside the formal school setting was no less important than what took place in the classroom.[8]

Before going on to look at some of the deficiencies of this 'discipline-centred' strategy it is only fair to summarize its positive achievements. First, and best, it shifted the onus of learning firmly on to the side of the pupil by placing him in situations and providing him with materials which helped him to draw conclusions, appraise evidence and test hypotheses for himself. Second, in insisting that the learning process should be intellectually demanding, it appealed to the sense of wonder (Whitehead's 'Stage of Romance'). Third, it sought to minimize the load of information which the learner had to carry by breaking down the field of study into its essentials. Finally, it injected into the melting pot of the high school curriculum a solid dose of quality, both in its thinking and in the goods it delivered, which evoked a healthy response from the schools and a determination on the part of federal, state and teachers' professional organizations to carry on the good work.

Yet in acknowledging that the project-by-project approach did far more than dent a few surfaces, it suffered from one serious disability – that of moving one piece on the board at a time without reference to what was happening to the others. By way of extenuation it may be argued that it is never possible to do more than one thing at a time, and that in view of their impressive record of achievement there is no excuse for looking on these projects as a succession of crash programmes which failed to add up to a coherent plan for modernizing the curriculum as a whole. At least they demonstrated that American working parties really *worked* and did not degenerate into mere talking shops (as happens all too often in Britain); better still, they demonstrated the kinds of organization, techniques and scale of operation that were needed.

In a sense, however, the lead given by the academic community laid itself open to the accusation that it had taken the law into its own hands. In side-tracking the schools boards and state administrations on the one hand, and in cold-shouldering the university schools of education and the teachers' colleges on the other, the scholars may have been astute; astute, certainly, in seeing textbooks and packaged learning materials as the key to the problem. But, as the quotation from *Who Shall Be Educated?* makes plain, the tension between Jacksonian and Jeffersonian principles in American education is permanent, which means that any move which seeks to improve the quality of education has to be watched very carefully in case it interferes with equality of opportunity. While there is no excuse for thinking that what the academics wanted was to put back the clock to 1890 (when the Committee of Ten had sought to restrict the high school to a college preparatory course), it seems clear that their sympathies were mainly on the side of the abler pupils. If they earned credit for showing that the capacities of the average learner had been grievously underestimated, that was incidental; they also invited the reproach that their strategy overlooked the most important factor of all in the management of innovation in the schools – the inability of the average practitioner to cope with the new materials and to adapt his styles of teaching to the new techniques. Like Comenius centuries before them, the academics had fallen into the error of supposing that the production of a good textbook was the answer to their problems. As the B.S.C.S. teams soon discovered, however, the new materials were most successful in the hands of competent specialist teachers, decidedly less successful when left to those with indifferent scientific and professional backgrounds; this, despite a lavish provision of teachers' guides, bulletins and supportive literature.

After 1965, then, the tactics changed. Many lessons had been learned, not least the realization that so far as curriculum development was concerned a policy of more haste, less speed had much to commend it. However reluctantly, the official view now was that 'the time-lag between a researchable idea and its final dissemination as a usable tool throughout the schools approaches forty years in the field of education' – another way of saying that even in the U.S.A. innovation cannot be hurried. If anything, this admission that the impossible *does* take a good deal longer than the optimists like to think led to a redoubling of the efforts that had already been made.

Some inkling of the determination to harness all available resources for a more concerted logistic support programme than had been possible before 1963 can be gained from the President's 'Message on Education' addressed to the first session of the 88th Congress:

> The Federal Government – despite increasing recognition of education as a nationwide challenge, and despite the increased financial difficulties encountered by the states, communities and private institutions in carrying this burden – has clearly not met its responsibilities in education. . . . I do not say that the Federal Government should take over responsibility for education. That is neither desirable nor feasible. Instead its participation should be selective, stimulative, and where possible, transitional. . . . The proper Federal role

is to identify national educational goals and to help local, State and private authorities build the necessary roads to reach those goals. Federal aid will enable our schools, colleges and universities to be more stable and therefore more independent.

These goals include the following:

First, we must improve the *quality* of instruction provided in all of our schools and colleges. We must stimulate interest in learning in order to reduce the alarming number of students who now drop out of school or who do not continue into higher levels of education. This requires more and better teachers – teachers who can be attracted to and retained in schools and colleges only if pay levels reflect more adequately the value of the services they render. It also requires that our teachers and instructors be equipped with the best possible teaching materials and curriculums. They must have at their command methods of instruction proven by scientific research into the learning process and by careful experimentation.

Second, our educational system faces a major problem of *quantity* – of coping with the needs of our expanding population and of the rising educational expectations of our children which all of us share as parents. . . .

Third, we must give special attention to increasing the *opportunities* and *incentives* for all Americans to develop their talents to the utmost – to complete their education and to continue their self-development throughout life. . . .

To enable the full range of educational needs to be considered as a whole, I am transmitting to the Congress with this message a single, comprehensive education bill – the National Education Improvement Act of 1963. For education cannot easily or wisely be divided into separate parts. Each part is linked to the other. The colleges depend on the work of the schools; the schools depend on the colleges for teachers; vocational and technical education is not separate from general education. This bill recalls the posture of Jefferson: 'Nobody can doubt my zeal for the general instruction of the people. I never have proposed a sacrifice of the primary to the ultimate grade of instruction. Let us keep our eye steadily on the whole system.'

The growing interest and the more active role assumed by the Federal Government during the Kennedy and Johnson administrations are graphically illustrated in Fig. 1. By 1966, the Office of Education's annual budget was of the order of $100 million, a hundred times larger than it had been ten years earlier.

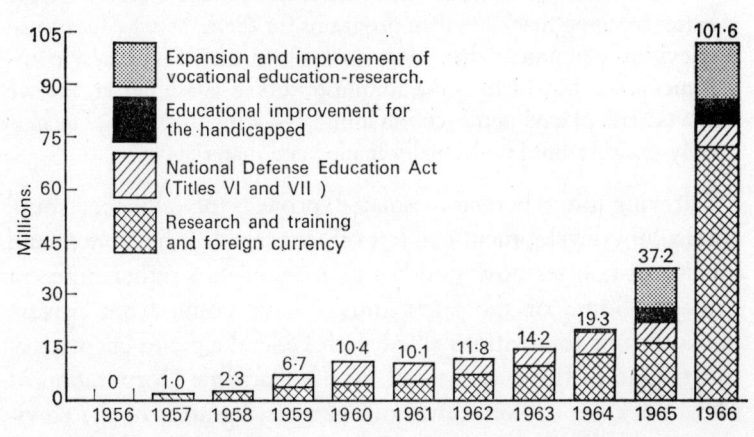

[Bar chart showing Office of Education financial assistance (in Millions) from 1956 to 1966:
- 1956: 0
- 1957: 1·0
- 1958: 2·3
- 1959: 6·7
- 1960: 10·4
- 1961: 10·1
- 1962: 11·8
- 1963: 14·2
- 1964: 19·3
- 1965: 37·2
- 1966: 101·6

Legend:
- Expansion and improvement of vocational education-research.
- Educational improvement for the handicapped
- National Defense Education Act (Titles VI and VII)
- Research and training and foreign currency]

SOURCE: Office of Education of the U.S. Department of Health, Education, and Welfare.

FIG 1   Office of Education financial assistance for educational research

Undoubtedly, all this was due to the recognition that a systems approach designed to promote an all-round raising of standards, and capable of linking the efforts of some 30,000 schools boards, fifty states and nearly 3,000 institutions of higher learning, was beyond the management of any but the central government. As it was, giant corporations such as IBM, Xerox and Time were forging ahead in the field of educational technology and the mounting pressure of salesmanship for their wares might well be seen as a potential take-over bid from Big Business which needed to be matched by equally powerful organizations inside the education system. As one observer noted,

> These parent companies are buying smaller firms in the various aspects of the education industry and will present in due time a co-ordinated line of teaching materials and equipment to the schools.
>
> The potential virtue of this co-ordination is great. Books and films and teaching machines and the rest can be related as never before and can provide for teachers a lift comparable to the introduction of

free textbooks in the 1890s. The potential dangers are no less obvious. As with federal dollars coming before ideas for their use, in the education industry we have technical devices of great sophistication before we have clear ends, much less materials, for them. We have better teaching machines than programs for them, better educational television equipment than ideas on how to use it. The new companies are as impatient as the administrators in Washington, and we run the risk of having the schools inundated with quantities of technically exciting but intellectually inadequate materials.[9]

Carrying on where the isolated projects of 'alphabet soup' curriculum development had left off, concern for the content and quality of courses now finds its expression in a rather different strategy. Some of the latest moves have come from private philanthropic foundations allied with Federal aid and encouragement. One of these, sponsored by the Carnegie Corporation of New York has explored methods of assessing areas of the curriculum which are *not* controversial – e.g. how soon and how well children learn to read, how far they understand fundamental scientific principles, how far they are able to grasp ideas embodied in the Constitution, etc. – with a view to establishing norms of scholastic achievement. Financed by the U.S. Office of Education, four regional Educational Laboratories, based on universities, began operations in 1965. The intention is to cover the country with a network of these, which are in effect curriculum development centres. Like their forerunners, they rely of co-operative effort and the active participation of all concerned, on linking all forms of research – psychological and sociological as well as 'discipline'-centred – above all, on keeping channels of communication between institutions and individuals in the education system open. In short, the kind of working party dominated by distinguished academics is being replaced by a more varied and representative team of all the talents. In so far as this signifies a new departure it is because experience has shown that

> Equality of educational opportunity did not square with type or program or quality of offering. New curricula would have to be brought in line with social goals and educational realities as well as

with advances in knowledge and psychological theories of learning. It was not only that new approaches in particular subjects – mathematics or history or physics – were needed: such approaches had to be related in new ways to one another and to the values of the society in which the learners lived. Simply to reform a particular course might not have a lasting effect. What was needed was the larger view of the curriculum as a whole, of the forest rather than only the trees.[10]

In reviewing the train of events since 1957 it may seem odd to characterize the United States as a developing country. Yet if there is one feature in a society or a culture which, more than any other, accounts for its willingness to countenance the need for rational and continuous changes in its education system, it is its awareness of its own immaturity. Countries with long histories tend, on the whole, to be more traditional-minded and the essence of traditional-mindedness is in thinking of itself as mature. The model proposed by W. W. Rostow in *The Stages of Economic Growth*, in which tradition-bound societies are led step by step to take off en route to the stage of mass consumption, has been adapted by educationists like C. E. Beeby who sees the drive towards quality in education taking place in four progressive phases. (cf. Fig. 4, p 223). At the 'Dame School' stage teachers are neither educated nor trained. At the stage of 'Formalism' teachers are trained but poorly educated. At the stage of 'Transition' teachers are trained and better educated but still lack full professional competence. At the stage of 'Meaning' teachers are well educated and well trained.

Beeby's thesis is that none of these stages can be skipped. If he is right – and the experience gained from a succession of projects in the U.S.A. suggests very strongly that low-level competence on the part of the rank and file of teachers was the Achilles heel in curriculum development – then the only strategy open to the planners must be a long-range one.

If it be true that there are recognizable stages in the development of school systems, the social and professional resistances to change will obviously affect the speed at which any system will pass through the stages, but without closer analysis, this pattern of resistances is not sufficient in itself to explain the existence of the stages. What is at issue here is not the *attitude* toward change of either parents or teachers but the actual *ability* of the teachers to bring about the changes necessary to raise a school system to a higher stage.

And again:

For the teacher, as for the clergyman, what he achieves is in large measure a function of what he believes, and most administrators will admit that they have changed very little in the work of the classroom merely by issuing instructions to teachers. Understanding, of course, must accompany acceptance; the travesty that can result from the misinterpretation of a reform by a proportion of the teachers can do more to discredit it than does straight opposition. A teacher using a technique that he has accepted but not understood can, by some strange inverted alchemy, turn the most shining idea to lead. No technique seems proof against this. . . . This is not to suggest that teaching methods are irrelevant, but only that good results can be achieved by enthusiastic and able teachers using very different methods, and that the best of methods will fail in the hands of uncomprehending and uninspiring practitioners. The significance of this for educational reform is capital.[11]

Even if it has the backing of scientific research and exhaustive field-testing, innovation in the classroom may fail to catch on for any one of several reasons:

1] Because teachers do not know about it.
2] Because the new materials and equipment are too costly or simply not available.
3] Because pupils do not respond to the new methods.
4] Because the new methods call for knowledge, understanding and other abilities that the majority of teachers do not possess.
5] Because teachers and administrators are conservative and suspicious of new techniques.

With the exception of the first, we know little enough about any of these reasons (says Beeby), but it is the fourth that is most commonly overlooked. We are inclined to assume that, if a pilot project shows that selected teachers can use the technique successfully with sample cases in any area, one can safely plan for making the practice universal. Any opposition can then be attributed to the fifth of the reasons, sheer conservatism. Yet every administrator knows that it is just at this point, where practice has to be spread from the few to the many, that his real problems usually begin. Children are much more adaptable than those who teach them. J. S. Bruner has taken as a working hypothesis 'that any subject can be taught effectively in some intellectually honest form to any child'. There is now some basis for this hypothesis, but, administratively speaking, the vital question is, 'Can it be taught by any teacher?'[12]

So long as the range of professional competence among teachers remains wide, any advance on a broad front will be held up, and regardless of the resources which may be made available for it, curriculum development will be largely a matter of throwing good money after bad. So long as the educational services themselves exhibit a wide range of standards this state of affairs is likely to continue, since teachers are the products of the education system: a system which tolerates good, bad and indifferent schools must expect to breed good, bad and indifferent teachers. Isolation, lack of clearly stated objectives and inadequate equipment are three of the factors which inhibit the onset of the stage of 'Meaning' – and which can be mitigated – but in the last resort the process of development can only be consummated by raising standards of teacher education. The Americans have learned the hard way that no other strategy will suffice. It speaks well for their philosophy, which has always been 'What's past is prologue', that at least it has preserved them from the foolishness of pretending that their education system has got beyond the stage of 'Transition'.

REFERENCES

1 W. L. Warner, R. J. Havighurst *et al.*, *Who Shall Be Educated?* (London, Routledge & Kegan Paul, 1946), p. 155.
2 Francis Keppel, *The Necessary Revolution in American Education* (New York, Harper & Row, 1966), p. 106.

3 J. B. Conant, *Education and Liberty* (Cambridge, Mass., Harvard University Press, 1953), pp. 66–7.
4 Harold Spears, *The High School for Today* (New York, American Book Co., 1950), pp. 57–8.
5 James R. Killian, 'The return to learning', in R. W. Heath (Ed.), *New Curricula* (New York, Harper & Row, 1964), pp. 253–4.
6 Marshall H. Stone, quoted by B. Demott, 'The math wars', in R. W. Heath, op. cit., p. 61.
7 Bentley Glass, 'Renascent biology: a report on the A.I.B.S. Biological Sciences Curriculum Study', in R. W. Heath, op. cit., pp. 116–17.
8 Paul Woodring, 'Introduction', in R. W. Heath, op. cit., p. 4.
9 Dean Theodore Sizer, quoted by Francis Keppel, op. cit., p. 120.
10 Francis Keppel, op. cit., p. 117.
11 C. E. Beeby, *The Quality of Education in Developing Countries* (Cambridge, Mass., Harvard University Press, 1966), p. 37.
12 ibid., pp. 27–8.

CHAPTER THREE

Response to Change
THE ENGLISH EXPERIENCE

'Minister knows nowt about curriculum'.

Twenty-odd years on, George Tomlinson's priceless utterance has a strange ring, rather as if the managing director of some vast consortium had placed it on record that he had not the faintest idea what the companies under his charge were up to, and that he was quite happy to remain ignorant about them. This seemingly ingenuous remark, so redolent of *laissez-faire* policy-making, sought to make a virtue out of necessity by acknowledging that prior to 1944 the administrative arrangements in England and Wales had allowed the schools considerable freedom in framing their own courses. It was, no doubt, a way of reassuring a mistrustful public opinion that despite the powers of direction and control newly vested in him, the Minister intended to abide by the non-interference precedents set by a long line of nonentity presidents of the defunct Board of Education; a way, too, of paying tribute to the traditional English habit of rationalizing muddle by calling it diversity.

In fact, there were two traditions, one ancient and bourgeois, the other bred of nineteenth-century utilitarianism and proletarianism. The problem of fusing these sub-cultures and of bringing together the institutions in which they are embodied on a common ground has been, and remains, beset with immense difficulties. Throughout its long history, the grammar school had not been subjected to governmental control. It was firmly established centuries before the setting up of the Board of

Education in 1899 and of the local education authorities in 1902. It had its own curriculum, based originally on the medieval trivium and quadrivium, later on the classics, a curriculum which grew like Topsy during the second half of the nineteenth century when modern languages, the natural sciences, physical education and games were added to its central core of literary studies. Being geared to the ambitions of the professional classes, and having links with the universities, the grammar school enjoyed both prestige and a measure of independence comparable with that of the public school, at any rate up to the time of the Taunton Commission, and to a lesser extent right up to 1944.

The origins of the elementary school were altogether humbler and its curriculum more Spartan. Where the grammar school taught Latin, French, English literature and mathematics, the elementary school taught reading, writing and arithmetic. Indeed, as the Cockerton Judgment of 1899 indicated, any attempt on the part of the elementary school to rise above this modest level of attainment was held to be illegal. True, after 1906 the regulations of the Revised Code were relaxed, and as the *Handbook of Suggestions* was pleased to put it,

> The only uniformity that the Board of Education desire to see in the teaching of public elementary schools is that each teacher should think for himself, and work out for himself such methods of teaching as may use his powers to the best advantage and be best suited to the particular needs and conditions of the school. . . . It is not possible to lay down any rule as to the exact number of the subjects which should be taken in any individual school.

But this velvet glove language concealed the iron fist which had stamped its bleak philosophy on the elementary school before, during and after the era of Payment by Results. It had always been understood that the Three Rs and precious little else provided its stock in trade. Despite the polite fiction of giving its teachers *carte blanche*, the elementary school had been bound hand and foot by economic, social and political constraints from the beginning.

Until the depression years of the 1920s and early 1930s its staff was exclusively non-graduate, two-year college-trained men and women with more than a fair sprinkling of uncertificated personnel, which ruled out any pretence of academic studies. This in itself implied that a 'subject' listed in the timetable of an elementary school was quite different in content, method, aim and general ethos from the same 'subject' as listed in the grammar school course. Thus, nature study, which became increasingly popular after 1900, was introduced mainly because it was cheap, the kind of 'subject' which required no elaborate equipment and which could be dealt with as a variant of reading. Obviously, it bore little or no relation to the more systematic teaching of biology, still less to that of physics and chemistry as pursued in the grammar school. Geography, history and other 'subjects' likewise tended to be watered down versions of fields of study which only assumed a systematic form in the longer, academic-type course leading to university entrance. Latin and French – two 'subjects' which class-conscious parents regarded as a *sine qua non* in any genuinely secondary course – were, needless to say, ruled out from the start. The solitary exception to this poverty-stricken state of affairs was the break-through in child art, an exception which proves the rule – that innovation in the curriculum is held in check by the requirements of external examinations.

Apart from the 11-plus examination, the elementary school had no incentives – it was a terminal course which led straight to the world of work. As the Hadow Committee noted, many of its senior pupils were marking time, a finding which, more than any other, clinched the decision that the time had come to remove the vertical distinction between the elementary and grammar school systems and replace it with a horizontal division (the 'clean break' at 11-plus) under which primary and secondary education would be conceived of as stages, not as separate *kinds* of school. Throughout their report, *The Education of the Adolescent*, it is only too clear that the writers were themselves horribly unsure whether the newly styled secondary modern school was to be 'secondary' or merely 'post-primary'.

We are not authorized by our reference, nor do we desire, to explore the form of environment which goes by the name of the secondary school (they averred). We are concerned with the growth – which has already begun, and which we desire greatly to accelerate – of selective and non-selective central schools and of senior departments in elementary schools. This growth, in our view, will run side by side with, but in no sense counter to, the growth of secondary schools; and while *it will be different in kind*, it will not be inferior in its promise or quality. The central schools and senior departments, like the secondary schools, will give a humane and general education. It will be shorter in duration; it will terminate at the end of three or four years; but it will be directed as long as it lasts to the general fostering of mental power. Two methods, which will differentiate them to some extent from secondary schools, will generally be followed in central schools and senior departments. One will be the method of practical instruction and manual work, on which we set high hopes, believing that there are many children who think as it were with their hands and will profit greatly by a method of instruction which follows the natural bent of their capacity. Another will be the method of giving a trend and a bias, which for want of a better word we may call by the name of 'realistic', to the general course of studies.[1]

So, by resorting to all manner of terminological inexactitudes (as the Committee said, 'There is magic in words'), the illusion of parity of esteem was born. The secondary modern school was to be left to find its own *modus vivendi* and (despite Hadow's recommendations) freed from any commitments in the shape of a leaving certificate. Although no clear directives had been given, it was generally understood that 'activities', 'projects' and 'centres of interest' were to be encouraged, history and geography were to be regrouped under the heading of social studies – and there was endless talk in favour of integrating and co-ordinating other 'subjects'. Some of this influence spilled over from the primary school and was partly motivated by child-centred theory and practice and the progressive education movement, partly by the belief that almost anything would be better than the *status quo*.

Although the Spens Report went out of its way to defend it, the organization of the curriculum on a 'subject' basis came in for increasing criticism in the late 1930s and early 1940s. These criticisms have been aired so frequently that it is scarcely necessary to recapitulate them. There is first the objection that any curriculum organized around 'subjects' lacks unity, consisting as it does of an assembly of largely unrelated studies which are taugh in airtight compartments. There is next the objection that, so far as the majority of children are concerned, a 'subject' approach is too formal. A third objection is that 'subject'-centred teaching puts far too heavy a premium on content and so encourages fact-grubbing, memorization and the inculcation of inert ideas. A fourth is that once a 'subject' finds its way into the timetable it is almost impossible to get rid of it. A fifth is that aesthetic, practical, moral and religious experience tends to wither once it is brought under the aegis of a 'subject', which explains why the more readily examinable studies get the lion's share of time and attention.

The most telling criticism of all, however, is one made by the Council for Curriculum Reform in 1945:

> We are prepared to accept without argument in this place the individual and social qualities summarized in such terms as scientist, mathematician, historian, linguist, and that these people as experts in their subjects are of value to the community. What we do not accept is that these same values and qualities can be achieved for the child of sixteen by simply snipping off a certain length of the 'subject' as defined above, like a piece of tape. The 'subject' in this reduced sense, as it appears in school courses up to sixteen, is an entirely different proposition and it is unsound to justify it by smuggling in values to be obtained only by much more prolonged study. For those children who are going on to such higher study we agree that the study of subjects as such would emerge from the general studies of the school at a particular point. . . . But the implication that the general body of secondary students can become in any real sense scientists, historians, or linguists seems to us fantastic. The crucial question is the test by results. 'What attitudes, skills, knowledge, will remain with these pupils at the end of their course?' We must plan our courses for objectives which can be achieved and

pointed to in this way. Otherwise we risk falling into the ancient teacher's trap of assuming mental discipline but not ensuring it.[2]

How far, if at all, this view of a 'subject' as a truncated 'discipline' has been modified in the light of experience gained in curriculum development projects launched since 1960 is an interesting question, and one which is better left open for the moment. In the event, for all the hard things said about them, 'subjects' are still the main building-blocks for the curriculum-maker. In England, as in the U.S.A., the search for a viable alternative, for non-academic equivalents, and for a common core, has so far proved abortive. As the interim report of the Council for Curriculum Reform predicted, 'The apple turns out to be an orange, segments but no core.' As late as 1952 the authors of the N.U.T. Report on The Curriculum of the Secondary School still clung to the hope that some unifying principle might be found.

> The conception of the curriculum as the sum of many isolated parts is an unfortunate development, especially when it leads a teacher to limit his teaching to a narrow 'subject' field. The curriculum should move away from restricted subject treatment and towards integration. It should be 'of a piece', its parts related, its whole having pattern, meaning, and purpose. It is for this reason that we prefer to consider the content of the curriculum in terms of areas of activity rather than in terms of separate subjects. Though we believe that a curriculum may be weakened by overcrowding or by the construction of artificial subject barriers, we desire that, within a simplified organization of the curriculum, a pupil may sample as wide a range of different forms of activity as possible. In a new activity, he may find an interest, a talent, an unsuspected opportunity for self-fulfilment and success, an enthusiasm which may lead him into new fields of worthwhile endeavour.[3]

These worthy sentiments, which find their answering echoes in many a curriculum working paper today, cut no ice in most secondary modern schools for a number of reasons. One was that the average teacher, like the young man who said 'Damn!', actually preferred to run on tram-lines rather than use his freedom and embark on adventure courses ('You know where you are so long as you stick to "subjects". Better still, you can see the results', etc., etc.). This 'me-and-my-subject' attitude is itself the outcome of physical immurement within a classroom and a school building whose design favours the continuance of chalk-and-talk methods. A more potent reason has been the demand from parents, employers and pupils for some kind of paper qualification, and the widespread dissatisfaction with a terminal course which was a cul-de-sac. In their eyes, no amount of 'activity and experience' could compensate for the fact that the secondary modern school was all dressed up and had nowhere to go.

If, then, the two traditions represented by the academic grammar school and the non-academic ex-elementary school have showed signs of drawing closer together in recent years, it has been under the pressure of examination requirements – a pressure which in turn can only be accounted for in terms of a growing demand for vocational skills and qualifications. The path to general education was paved with good intentions which led the modern school to fall in behind the grammar school and set its sights on the O-level General Certificate Examination.

To be fair, however, between 1944 and 1963 (the year of the Beloe Report) the relative freedom enjoyed by the secondary modern schools resulted in some healthy experimental developments. In Professor Dent's estimation,

> The twenty years following 1944 saw in the Secondary Modern school a process of evolution unmatched for speed and significance in the history of English education.... The courses covered: Art and Crafts; Catering; Homecraft; Needlework and Design; Automobile Engineering; Mechanical Trades; House Maintenance and Furnishing; Practical Crafts; Craftsmanship; Rural Science; Farming and Gardening; Music; Seamanship; General Science; Electrical Science; Commercial Subjects; Nursing; Academic subjects for G.C.E. The last was the largest group of all.[4]

Even more gratifying was the increasing numbers staying on beyond the compulsory school age, and (though by no means everyone found it a cause for satisfaction) the tenfold increase in the number of modern schools presented for G.C.E. and other public examination between 1953 and 1963, the year which saw the introduction of the Certificate of Secondary Education. Designed to overlap with O-levels at one end and to provide the mass of average ability pupils with an opportunity of gaining some tangible token of success at the end of five years of secondary education, the new certificate was awarded on a subject basis and could be taken in a variety of modes. While it supplied an incentive which had previously been lacking and undoubtedly acted as a spur to flagging morale among teachers and pupils alike, there were many who regarded it as a retrograde step, a sop to ill-advised professional opinion. As an editorial in *New Education* observed at the time:

> It marks a radical departure by teachers themselves from the spirit of the 1944 Education Act, which sought to abolish examinations for at least all those who were not concerned with a university career, as well as Sir David Eccles's strongly worded Circular 289 eleven years later, in which the Minister said emphatically: 'all examinations restrict to some extent the teacher's freedom'.
>
> The justifications for this highly expensive operation (with teachers to-ing and fro-ing all over the country on subject panel groups) are flimsy. It is claimed that employers are demanding a national measure of competence. Yet there is no evidence that in the C.S.E. their demands are being met. Quite the contrary. The regional boards are spending a good deal of time 'selling' the C.S.E. to employers, and explaining its intricacies to them.
>
> It is also claimed that parental pressure demanded some piece of paper for their children to wave upon leaving school. This sort of presssure, if it existed, ought to have been resisted if it could not be justified on educational grounds – and there are ample reasons for believing that, on those grounds, the C.S.E. will prove a dangerous innovation. By being based on subject examinations (some schools are offering as little as one subject on the Certificate), it introduces specialization into schools which until now have been free from these false pressures. By once again sub-dividing education in this way, it virtually ensures that all-round education will be discarded in favour of individual grades. Worst of all, it sets up yet another artificial barrier in the education system. By 1970, between

four and five million children will be involved to some degree in the C.S.E. Above them will be the G.C.E. O-level students. Above these the G.C.E. A-level scholars, and beyond these the undergraduates. At the bottom of this pyramid there will emerge a large body of children who, already labelled 11-plus failures, can now also assume the tag of 'unexaminables'.

As the elaborate juggernaut of the C.S.E. begins to bundle forward this month, it may seem too late to protest at its creation. The fact remains that it represents a false god. Another hurdle has been created in an education system that already resembles a Grand National course. And unlike horses, who may be shot if severely injured, children carry the scars of combat all their lives.[5]

Whether or not this bitter indictment was deserved, it can hardly be doubted that the demand for a second-best certificate examination stemmed mainly from the schools themselves. In so far as it was prompted by the recognition that social and economic circumstances were vastly more powerful in shaping the curriculum than any educational theory, however enlightened, this demand may be thought to have been realistic. In a meritocracy scholastic prowess is essential. Experience had shown that the promise of 'separate but equal' status could not be honoured: there was only one way for the secondary school to earn esteem and that was by vying with the grammar school, even if vying meant aping. The 1950s had seen a hardening of opinion against progressive methods, and the provision of extended courses had been made possible by the presence in the schools of a substantial minority of pupils who had been borderline cases at the 11-plus stage.

The year 1963 marks a turning point. Overshadowing the Beloe recommendations were those of the Newsom Report, which stressed the need for increasing the proportion of trained and technical manpower in the working population, and pointed to the untapped reservoirs of talent in the broad mass of average and below-average ability pupils.

Will a substantial investment in their education produce people capable of fulfilling the industrial roles indicated above? (it asked)

If we look at what has happened when popular education has been extended in the past, the answer is an optimistic 'Yes'. New provision has always elicited new responses. Intellectual talent is not a fixed quantity with which we have to work but a variable that can be modified by social policy and educational approaches. The crude and simple answer was given by Macaulay 139 years ago: 'Genius is subject to the same laws which regulate the production of cotton and molasses. The supply adjusts itself to the demand. The quantity may be diminished by restrictions and multiplied by bounties.'

A more subtle investigation into what constitutes the 'restrictions' and the 'bounties' in our society is of far more recent growth. The results of such investigation indicate that the kind of intelligence which is measured by the tests so far applied is largely an acquired characteristic. This is not to deny the existence of a basic genetic endowment; but whereas the endowment, so far, has proved impossible to isolate, other factors can be identified. Particularly significant among them are the influences of social and physical environment; and since these are susceptible to modification they may well prove educationally more important.[6]

1963 also saw the publication of Professor William Taylor's book, *The Secondary Modern School*, which gave a sober and critical appraisal of its work from a sociological point of view. It showed that the changes which had taken place in the curriculum over the years were mostly peripheral, and that the distribution of subjects and the lay-out of the timetable remained much the same as they had been in the senior departments and higher grade elementary schools at the turn of the century. Normal practice was to allow five periods per week for English and arithmetic, two periods for history and geography (sometimes combined as social studies), religious instruction, music, art and science, two or three periods for physical education and games, plus a morning or afternoon devoted to woodwork, metalwork, domestic science, gardening and other practical activities.

> One interesting feature of this basic curriculum is the extent to which it has withstood the onslaughts of educational ideas which at one time might have seemed likely to alter substantially the 'subject-centred' timetable in favour of projects, centres of interest, individual

assignments and subject groups. Schools in which the work is based on such approaches are objects of comment and clearly exceptional in the general run of Modern schools.[7]

The general run, in other words, had entered for the G.C.E. stakes, undeterred by the heavy handicaps which made high failure rates inevitable. Although the steady rise in the numbers of candidates presented by the Modern schools may have boosted morale, there was no getting away from the fact that less than 10 per cent of them succeeded in gaining five or more O-level passes and that nearly half of them gained only a single pass. Disquieting, too, was Professor Vernon's disclosure that of 800 boys tested at the age of eleven, and again at fifteen, those who attended grammar schools gained an average of seven points of I.Q. over those who went to non-selective schools. So much for 'the placing of youth, in the hour of its growth, "as it were in the fair meadow" of a congenial and inspiring environment', which the Hadow Committee had talked of so airily a quarter of a century earlier. In Professor Taylor's judgement,

> the scholastic atmosphere of the Modern school, its position in the educational and social structure, may tend to depress performance and aspirations, and its examination streams and advanced work may not be fully effective in countering this effect. Social and economic pressures combine to demand higher standards, more systematic teaching, a secondary education that is both deeper and broader than that provided in the past for the mass of the population.... Secondary education in a mass society must be thought of in total terms, rather than with reference to the education of the 'average' and the élite. The attempt to fit such a total concept of education within a tripartite structure in the years after 1944 failed, first, because the terms in which this concept was thought out were socially and educationally unrealistic, and, secondly, because the strength of the traditional elements in this structure were underestimated.[8]

But if the logic of events was pointing to the adoption of the comprehensive school principle, it was also pointing to the need for a more systematic approach to the problems of curriculum design. The first moves in this direction had scarcely been propitious and had led to a false start. In a debate in the House of Commons on the Crowther Committee's Report (21 March 1960), Sir David Eccles had let it be known that the central authority was seriously considering the advisability of venturing into 'the secret garden of the curriculum'. Two years later, without prior consultation with the local authorities and the teachers' professional associations, came the announcement of the formation of a Curriculum Study Group consisting of H.M.I.s, administrators and co-opted 'experts'. It was envisaged as a 'small commando-like unit' (the Minister's own description) which would function more or less on the lines of the Development Group in the Ministry's Architects and Building Branch. The latter had already proved its worth in improving the design and cutting down the costs of school buildings and equipment, and the official view was that a closely knit team might effect similar improvements by making raids into the curriculum. In a letter addressed to the educational associations, the Permanent Secretary outlined the rationale for such a departure.

> At a time characterized above all by the speed of change, we believe that the Ministry and Inspectors have a useful contribution to make to thinking about the educational process, arising partly from the knowledge we obtain from the view we have of the whole educational field, partly from our contacts, through central government, with some of the mainsprings of change, and partly from our opportunity (which we share with some large local education authorities) to form interdisciplinary teams capable of bringing to bear on current and future problems a considerable concentration of skill and experience. And it seems to us peculiarly important that we should make this contribution where it is a matter – as it so often is today – of foreseeing changes before they become apparent on the ground, and of placing before our partners in the educational service a range of possible solutions to future problems.

Neither the Association of Education Committees nor the National Union of Teachers approved of this line of argument, which smacked too strongly of unilateral intervention and which, in their view, threatened a shift in the balance of power. Both urged the Ministry to think again and demanded a more broadly based planning authority.

Of all the moves made in 1963, none was more significant than the convening of a representative meeting by Sir Edward Boyle to examine the lines on which action might be taken and to conconsider a proposal to establish a Schools Council for the Curriculum and Examinations. The Minister had prepared the ground by setting up a Curriculum Study Group to supplement the work carried out by the existing Secondary School Examinations Council and, without saying that the outcome of their deliberations was a foregone conclusion, the working party under the chairmanship of Sir John Lockwood lost no time in reaching unanimous agreement. The case for devising co-operative machinery to stimulate, organize and co-ordinate fundamental curriculum changes' was, in their view, proved. In drawing the outline of a constitution for a Schools Council for the Curriculum and Examinations, and defining its functions, the working party's report was suitably diplomatic.

> We noted that it has long been accepted in England and Wales that the schools should have the fullest possible measure of responsibility for their own work, including responsibility for their own curricula and teaching methods, which should be evolved by their own staff to meet the needs of their own pupils. We re-affirm the importance of this principle, and believe that positive action is needed to uphold it.
>
> The responsibility of the individual schools for their own work is not, however, an exclusive responsibility. It has inevitably to be exercised within a wider framework which takes account of the general interest of the community, both local and national, in the educational process. Within this general framework, individual schools have to take a wide range of particular decisions on educational content and methods.
>
> The work of the schools also has to be related to the requirements of the many and varied establishments of higher and further education to which many of the pupils will go on leaving school, and to the

training arrangements and entry requirements of a wide range of professional bodies and of employers generally. There is thus a complicated, and constantly changing, relationship between the work of the schools and many particular outside interests.

The responsibility of the schools is a heavy one. If it is to be successfully carried, the teachers must have adequate time and opportunity for regular re-appraisal of the contents and methods of their work in the light of new knowledge, and of the changing needs of the pupils and of society. A sustained and planned programme of work is required, going well beyond what can be achieved by occasional conferences and courses, or by the thinking and writing of busy teachers in their spare time.

We concluded therefore that there was no need to define a new principle in relation to the schools' curricula and examinations. Our task was rather to examine how far the existing principle is being realized in practice, and whether new arrangements are needed to uphold it and interpret it.[9]

Having paid their respects to the sacrosanct legend of free enterprise in English education, the working party reinforced their argument by noting that there were forces at work over which the schools had no control – forces which could in time seriously diminish their responsibility and lead to excessive standardization. The only way of avoiding this was by bringing all the agencies concerned in the educational enterprise into closer association.

In short, our conclusions on the nature of the problem are as follows:

(1) The present arrangements for determining the curriculum in schools and the related examinations are not working well: in particular, teachers have insufficient scope for making or recommending modifications in the curriculum and examinations.

(2) Different arrangements are needed to achieve the balanced co-operation of the teachers, the Local Education Authorities, the Ministry of Education, the establishments of higher and further education, and others, in a continuing process of modifying the curriculum and examinations.

(3) More resources and more effort should be devoted to co-operative study research and development in this field.[10]

The working party's report was dated 5 March 1964 – and the Schools Council started work on 1 October 1964. Financed jointly by the Ministry and the local education authorities, the new body was to be fully independent, with its own staff, free to decide its own priorities within the general terms of reference laid down for it by the Lockwood working party.

The job entrusted to the Schools Council in 1964 was, basically, to find ways and organize means of reviewing – and reforming – the school curriculum of England and Wales. That it was a necessary job was generally accepted. Some valuable work was already being done. The Council had to bring together those whose activities were independent yet complementary – a job of co-ordination. It had, also, to extend what had been begun elsewhere to a wider range of pupils, and it is here that progress is most conspicuous, particularly in mathematics, science and modern languages, in which the Council is co-operating with the Nuffield Foundation.

But this is only one aspect of the job. The greater part of the Council's energy so far has been absorbed in initiating curriculum development in new fields. This has meant deciding priorities, estimating costs and finding funds, identifying the resources and people from whom it can commission new work, ensuring that what is commissioned matches the priorities. Each of these requirements has had to be met with very little previous national experience on which to draw. Each has exposed the Council to some hard questioning.[11]

The whole prehistory and evolution of the Schools Council can be seen as being in keeping with the English tradition in education, a case of state-wide organization taking over from dispersed voluntary effort. Just as 1870 marked the end of *laissez-faire* in the provision and maintenance of schools, so 1964 spelt its end in the curriculum. In its initial stages the only viable strategy had, of necessity, to be in the nature of a compromise. Unlike the Swedish Board of Education, which decided that large-scale innovations could only be managed effectively through its central planning bureaux, the Council has had to tread warily for fear of alienating a highly sensitive professional opinion. Any strong lead would have been resented. Any suggestion of figuring in other than an advisory and supportive role had to be avoided. To date, the Council has done so through an array of interlocking committees which ensures that decision-making represents all shades of interest and opinion, and by disseminating information about its varied activities in the form of working papers, bulletins and regular news reviews. The Council assumed responsibility for the work previously carried out by the Secondary Schools Examinations Council and by the Curriculum Study Group, and during its early years has co-operated in jointly sponsored projects with the Nuffield Foundation, 'broadly on the basis that the Nuffield teams are wholly responsible for the development of teaching materials while the Council provides field services . . . and evaluation'.[12]

With an annual budget of nearly £1½ million at its disposal, the Council is an extremely powerful body. It is as yet far too early to look for tangible returns from this, on the face of it, lavish expenditure; and it may well prove that considerably greater resources will be needed as the work of curriculum development gathers momentum. Influential as they have been, major projects of the Nuffield type might be compared with skin grafts rather than heart transplants, in the sense that they have not affected the system as a whole – this despite the very substantial sums spent upon them. Moreover, some of these grafts have not 'taken', and there have been innumerable local and regional pilot schemes which have begun life promisingly only to peter out ineffectually after a year or two. The scale of operations needed to bring about fundamental, nation-wide changes in the educational services, and to keep them abreast of social, economic and technological developments, is so immense that it can hardly be exaggerated.

Regardless of what its critics may think, therefore, the Schools Council is committed by its own terms of reference to the cause of innovation, 'to organize a more rapid, and more effective, response to change'. A gentle giant, it prefers to offer a helping hand where it is asked for rather than seem to impose its own authoritative ideas. In the first six years of its existence it has performed a number of useful tasks quietly and unobtrusively. One of the first, a left-over from the Beloe Report, was to issue a stream of Examination Bulletins outlining the basic techniques for teachers in their new role as assessors, and reporting work in progress on the devisal of more efficient measuring instruments of attainment. Next, as an essential prerequisite for more active teacher participation, the Council got busy organizing teachers' centres in collaboration with local education authorities (which contribute roughly 60 per cent of its funds). Again, by commissioning investigations only when it foresees a visible return in terms of help for teachers, it has helped to popularize the case for research-and-development – 'action research' as it is sometimes called. Research-and-development differs from research *per se* in so far as it is geared to immediate practical problems and is undertaken on the understanding that its findings will be used. This is not to belittle the importance of 'pure' research, nor to suggest that there is any difference between the two methods of investigation. The great failure of educational research in the past, however, has always been that it was so detached as to seem merely esoteric.

The Council has also initiated its own series of experimental projects covering a wide gamut of problems in primary and secondary schools. Through its Resources for Learning Project it has kept in close touch with the latest developments in teaching aids, new media and learning systems – a link nicely illustrated by the fact that it shares the same premises as the National Council for Educational Technology.

Each of these projects is carefully phased, beginning with a survey of existing practice and the clarification of objectives, followed by the preparation of trial materials, field-testing (involving large numbers of schools during the life of the project), distribution and, where possible, some final evaluation of the changes effected. As might have been expected, there has been overt and covert resistance to any moves on the part of the Council which looked like 'selling' packaged learning kits to the schools. It seems that the leaders of more than one of these projects have been forced to think more than twice about the feasibility – not to mention the desirability – of aiming at an end-product which left itself open to the criticism that it was 'teacher-proof'. No doubt the lessons learned from 'alphabet soup' curriculum projects in the U.S.A. were partly responsible for this, but in the conditions prevailing in English schools it is hard to see how any strategy other than a teacher-centred one could have been adopted.

Be this as it may, in their diplomatic and circumspect way, these projects have undoubtedly served to stimulate widespread and serious rethinking about the aims of courses, about content and methods, and about problems of assessment. In particular, the conventional division of the school timetable into discrete 'subjects' has come under closer scrutiny than it had previously received: better still, practical proposals for alternative approaches have been put forward. As regards the teaching of science to average and below-average ability pupils, the Council's Working Paper No. 1 recommended the organization of courses around a number of broad major themes. Working Paper No. 2 took a new look at the humanities and suggested that courses should be built round a set of topics or social issues.

> The problem is to give every man some access to a complex cultural inheritance, some hold on his personal life and on his relationships with the various communities to which he belongs, some extension of his understanding of, and sensitivity towards, other human beings. The aim is to forward understanding, discrimination and judgement in the human field – it will involve reliable factual knowledge, where this is appropriate, direct experience, imaginative experience, some appreciation of the dilemmas of the human condition, of the rough hewn nature of many of our institutions, and some rational thought about them.[13]

Pursuing the same line of development, Working Paper No. 11 (*Society and the Young School Leaver*) advocated a course based on 'areas of inquiry'. Of those listed – 'Epidemics', 'Public Utilities', 'The Organization of Labour', 'Clothes', 'Churches', 'Religions of the World', 'Law and Order', 'The Population Explosion', etc. – some are not readily distinguishable from the projects and centres of interest of yesteryear, not that this is to be held against them. As an attempt to move away from the arid formalism of 'subjects' and to bring greater relevance, immediacy and realism into school-learning for teenagers, the organization of courses on theme-and-topic lines clearly represents a return to the child-centred practice which had been tried and found wanting during the years of the locust between Hadow and Beloe. The difference is that, whereas projects and centres of interest formerly tended to be haphazard affairs carried out in hit-or-miss fashion, the rationale for the new courses is more deeply pondered and the assistance and advice given to teachers much greater. Working Paper 11, for example, is full of illustrations drawn from imaginative work in schools which have succeeded in breaking down 'subject' barriers and using intelligent opportunism in devising an integrated course. In singling out examples of forward-thinking practice for approbation, the hope is that other schools will be encouraged to follow suit. Increasingly, the view taken is that a break from normal 'lesson' routines at the end of the third year of the secondary school course is desirable and beneficial for many youngsters, especially those whose interests are swayed by outside influences.

Following on from these working papers, the Humanities Curriculum Project has explored the possibilities of synthesizing the social sciences, the arts, religion and ethics through discussion of controversial issues. Its aim is 'to develop understanding of the nature and structure of certain complex value issues of universal human concern'. These are: War, Education, The Family, Relations between the Sexes, People and Work, Poverty, Living in Cities, Law and Order, and Race Relations. The assumption is that the very fact of their being controversial – issues for which no universally accepted solution has been found – warrants their being aired in the classroom, to which end the strategy is 'to attempt to devise a method of teaching which should within itself guarantee that the teacher is doing all he can to protect pupils from his own bias, while advancing their understanding'. In short, the emphasis is upon procedures which will enable the teacher to retain his position as *primus inter pares*, while observing strict neutrality as leader of the discussion group. This, it is thought, might become the basis for a new professional ethic. For each of the nine issues the project team has assembled a collection of illustrative reading and study materials – poems, extracts from novels and plays, letters, memoirs, newspapers, advertisements, statistical tables, graphs, maps, plans, cartoons, still photographs, slides of paintings and audio-tapes. These are in every sense raw materials, to be drawn on as and when the need arises: they are not arranged in any predetermined sequence. The pattern of teaching envisaged would be in accordance with the following characteristics:

1] The fundamental educational values of rationality, imagination, sensitivity, readiness to listen to the views of others, and so forth, must be built into the principles of procedure in the classroom.
2] The pattern of teaching must renounce the authority of the teacher as an 'expert' capable of solving value issues since this authority cannot be justified either epistemologically or politically. In short, the teacher must aspire to be neutral.
3] The teaching strategy must maintain the procedural authority of the teacher in the classroom, but contain it within rules which can be justified in terms of the need for discipline and rigour in attaining understanding.
4] The strategy must be such as to satisfy parents and pupils that every possible effort is being made to avoid the use of the teacher's authority position to indoctrinate his own views.
5] The procedure must enable pupils to understand divergence and hence must depend upon a group working together through discussion and shared activities. In such a group opinions should be respected, and minority opinions should be protected from ridicule or from social pressure.
6] In sensitive issues, thought must be given to preserving privacy and protecting students, e.g. illegitimate children, children from broken homes, children of prostitutes, should be borne in mind when discussing the family or relations between the sexes.
7] Above all, the aim should be understanding. This implies that one should not force pupils towards opinions or premature commitments which harden into prejudice. Nor should one see particular virtue in a change of view. The object is that the pupil should

come to understand the nature and implications of his point of view, and grow to adult responsibility by adopting it in his own person and assuming accountability for it. Whether or not the pupil changes his point of view is not significant for the attainment of understanding.[14]

It would be hard to think of a better way of explaining the changeover from the lackadaisical pre-war approach to a curriculum in terms of 'activity and experience' and the contemporary drive for improved styles of teaching than by contrasting the stringency of the requirements listed above with the happy-go-lucky ways in which most classroom projects used to be undertaken. Often a project engaged the interest and enthusiasm of pupils temporarily, but normally it was self-contained and came to a full stop, with the result that the course built around it lacked continuity and coherence. Worse of all, since it did not fit in with the requirements of external examinations, pupils formed the impression that it was largely a waste of time – and relatively few teachers felt able to avail themselves of the opportunities afforded for internal assessment within the C.S.E. framework.

The fact of the matter is that, although no one had ever dared to say so openly, the obstinate fiction that 'each teacher should think for himself, and work out for himself such methods of teaching as may use his powers to the best advantage' had long acted as a brake on progress. In the great majority of cases, the professional training of the teacher was inadequate and the conditions in which he worked inhibiting. Although it was no longer fashionable to declare themselves in favour of a return to 'progressive' methods, the authors of Working Paper No. 11 noted that:

> A frequent cause of failure seems to be that the course is often based on the traditional belief that there is a body of content for each separate subject which every young school-leaver should know. In the least successful courses this body of knowledge is written into the curriculum without any real consideration of the needs of the boys and girls and without any question of its relevance. Of course there are many schools where a gifted teacher is able to keep the

pupils interested, but sometimes this depends upon a special talent rather than a well thought out course. The schools that appear to be making most progress are moving in a different way. It is not the content of the course which gets first attention but the needs and interests of the youngsters.[15]

In all the developments now going forward under the aegis of the Schools Council the accent is upon teamwork. Closer collaboration – between schools, local education authorities, university departments, colleges of education, research institutes and other agencies, between project teams and local development groups, between head-teachers and their staffs, between teachers from different schools, between teachers and pupils, and (not least important) between pupils themselves – is becoming the order of the day.

How far the lump of conventional practice can be leavened by the more dynamic approaches at present being tried out up and down the country remains to be seen. Whether the demands made upon teachers by a curriculum conceived in terms of 'areas of inquiry' can be met is an open question. Whether such a curriculum is capable of extension to all pupils irrespective of age and ability is even more doubtful. It may be true that, 'If the entering points or centres of interest can be identified, it is possible to teach not less but more of the individual disciplines because they are learnt, not for their own sake, but to make clear the answer to part of a larger problem' – but so long as the academic streams remain examination-controlled any prospect of achieving a fully integrated common course must be considered distant. The spectre of the 'Two Nations' still casts its shadow over much of the School Council's literature, with its frequent references to the Newsom children on the one hand and to sixth-formers on the other. The latter are, indeed, 'a sub-group which often constitutes a society in its own right', as Working Paper No. 5 freely acknowledged.[16] Can the conflict between egalitarian and élitist motives in English education be reconciled, or is it going to be a case of oil and water? Can such a reconciliation be effected by teachers whose cultural background and training are themselves conditioned by a tacit acceptance of the propriety of differential treatment – 'discipline-centred' courses for the few, 'child-centred' ones for the many? Can the ideals of 'equality' and 'excellence' be married?

While it may be true that there is sufficient unity of ideas and methods to make clear the sort of curriculum reforms which the Schools Council is endeavouring to set in motion, the tentative moves made so far are best described as exploratory. No matter how smoothly the machinery for all-round co-operation runs, it is going to be a long haul converting the patchwork quilt of English education, with all its divisive influences and sectional interests, into the seamless web of a national system. In the long run, the reliance on a teacher-centred strategy may prove to be the wisest, quite apart from the fact that practical politics conspire to make it the only viable one. The motive power is to come primarily from local development groups, in which teachers will have regular opportunities to meet together, work out new methods of teaching and assessment through joint discussions with researchers and academics from the universities and colleges, local authority advisers, H.M.I.s and others.

The big question, yet to be decided, is whether the rank and file can raise their sights to meet this challenging demand, or whether their outlook will continue to have closer affinities with a trade union rather than of a genuinely professional body. In an imperfect world there is no point in looking for perfect teachers. It has to be remembered, however, that the perfectibility of mechanical aids to teaching and packaged learning materials proceeds apace – much faster, certainly, than improvements in the training of teachers (pre-service as well as in-service). Courses planned around areas of inquiry and themes of universal concern call for greater skills, greater devotion to duty and greater readiness to take calculated risks than those which follow the line of least resistance in sticking to the habitual 'subjects'. Continuous assessment, properly done, is more time-consuming than marking an end-of-term test or a batch of examination scripts – and teachers who have yet to learn the new procedures of assessment complain that 'marking' is a big enough burden as it is.

The irony of the situation is that whereas Scotland has a General Teaching Council, charged with the duty of safeguarding standards of entry and professional qualification, but no agency for managing research and development, England now has a Schools Council but no agency capable of sinking the differences between graduate schoolmasters and non-graduate teachers. Neither country has the built-in machinery which is provided in France by the *conseil de classe*, the *cahier de classe* and other devices to ensure that the prognosis of individual differences is carried out in an informed, systematic fashion during the early years of the secondary school course. It may be that the political decision to introduce this machinery, which has already gone far to democratize French education and force the *professeur* and the *instituteur* to work alongside each other on a common ground, was expedited by the explosive events of May 1968. It may be that England's native conservatism needs a similar jolt, and that nothing short of legal compulsion will transform the freedom which teachers theoretically enjoy into a practical reality.

Meantime, the gentle giant is left to do what it can. Compulsion is not its way: it prefers a supportive role, working within the schools and sharing their problems in the belief that in the course of time good practice will drive out the bad. The English experience has always been such as to confirm the view that the quality of an education system is neither better nor worse than the quality of its teachers, a view to which American pragmatism and go-getting have been driven by a rather more roundabout route. This view, needless to say, is popular because it seems to be so flatteringly axiomatic, but it may be that time is not on its side and that developments in the field of educational technology will cause it to be revised sooner rather than later. It *could* be that a strategy which chooses to be teacher-centred is backing a loser.

In suspending judgement, therefore, it is as well to keep one's fingers crossed. Ronald Manzer's verdict, based on a political analysis of the in-fighting that has been going on between the various pressure groups in the English system of education since 1944, is as well-informed as it is noncommittal:

Whether the Schools Council does provide leadership in curriculum development, or not, the argument surrounding it is not ended. Advance and adaptation with the agreement of all important interests concerned is comfortable, but it is also notoriously slow. In a time demanding fairly quick responses to changing situations, where policy decisions must be renewed much more rapidly than previously, it is likely to be highly frustrating and costly as well. The criticism of the Schools Council reflects both the frustration of those wanting more rapid change and the discontent of those concerned to protect traditional values and prerogatives. That criticism is certain to continue so long as pressure for curricular change continues. But whatever the differences between teachers and administrators, they have been limited to the education sub-government. Common agreement that the broad interests of society need to be better represented and inserted more positively into the process of curriculum formation has not resulted in any effort to improve the representative function of the sub-government by going outside it, for example, to Members of Parliament. As a result the Schools Council may be regarded as an assertion of orthodoxy and, quite possibly, an opportunity lost.[17]

REFERENCES

1 *The Education of the Adolescent*, Report of the Consultative Committee of the Board of Education (London, H.M.S.O., 1926).
2 *The Content of Education*, Interim Report of the Council for Curriculum Reform (University of London Press, 1945), p. 44.
3 *The Curriculum of the Secondary School*, Report of the Consultative Committee appointed by the Executive of the National Union of Teachers (London, Evans Brothers, 1952), pp. 24–5.
4 H. C. Dent, *The Educational System of England and Wales* (University of London Press, 1969), pp. 118–19.
5 *New Education* (December 1963).
6 *Half Our Future*, Report of the Central Advisory Council (England) (London, H.M.S.O., 1963), paras. 15–16.
7 W. Taylor, *The Secondary Modern School* (London, Faber & Faber, 1963), p. 84.
8 ibid., pp. 162–3.

9 Report of the Working Party on the Schools' Curriculum and Examinations (London, H.M.S.O., 1964), paras. 6–10.
10 ibid., para. 15.
11 The Schools Council, *The First Three Years 1964–7* (London, H.M.S.O., 1968).
12 The Schools Council, *Change and Response: The First Year's Work* (London, H.M.S.O., 1965).
13 The Schools Council, *Raising the School Leaving Age*, Working Paper No. 2 (London, H.M.S.O., 1965), para. 60.
14 Lawrence Stenhouse, *The Discussion of Controversial Value Issues in the Classroom* (unpublished paper).
15 The Schools Council, *Society and the Young School Leaver*, Working Paper No. 11 (London, H.M.S.O., 1967), paras. 16–17.
16 The Schools Council, *Sixth Form Curriculum and Examinations*, Working Paper No. 5 (London, H.M.S.O., 1966).
17 Ronald A. Manzer, Teachers and Politics: *The Role of the National Union of Teachers in the Making of National Educational Policy in England and Wales since 1944* (Manchester University Press, 1970), p. 97.

CHAPTER FOUR

New Directions for a New Society:

THE FRENCH TRANSFORMATION

Management of innovation is a good deal easier in a monolithic state than it is in a democracy. In the eastern European countries decisions taken at the highest level can be implemented with a minimum of delay and with little or no dissent, a case of when-Father-turns-we-all-turn. Because policy-making can afford to be uncompromising, changes in school organization, in the content of courses and in methods of teaching, can be brought about almost overnight. Khruschev's 'Life and Work' reforms in Soviet secondary schools typify the sudden switches which are possible in a totalitarian régime. As the Preamble to the 1961 Education Act of the Hungarian People's Republic explains:

1] The development of the education system must be determined by the needs of a socialist society.
2] The system must be uniform both in its organization and its aims.
3] The responsibility for providing and maintaining the educational services belongs exclusively to the state.

The overriding principle insists that the aims of education must be prescribed by, and consonant with, those of a planned economy, and closely related to them at all points and at all stages of the learner's life. To this end, the Preamble continues:

> The building of socialism calls for men and women who possess general culture, but in addition tomorrow's citizens are entitled to

expect a school education which enables them to participate in creative work according to their aptitudes and abilities.... Our schools must be linked more closely with life and practical training and production. All schools, regardless of the types to which they belong, must prepare their pupils for active, productive work. Standards of instruction in general and vocational studies based on the natural sciences must be raised. In deciding the content of curricula due care must be paid to the stages of maturation to avoid overburdening the pupils.

Disrespectful as it may seem to say so, the transformation which has taken place in French education in recent years – a transformation which is still far from being complete – invites comparison with similar developments in Eastern Europe. This is not to infer that the ideology behind the transformation and the methods used are the same, only that the long-term objectives and the broad pattern of change are alike in many ways.

The land of Louis XIV, of Napoleon and General de Gaulle is also the land of Descartes, of Condillac and Condorcet, a land where political dictatorship and rational planning have a way of going hand in hand. From the Revolution down to the present day the French education system has always been highly centralized. Historically, this concentration of power and authority in the hands of a Paris-based officialdom can be accounted for in a variety of ways – by the predominant position of the capital in what until fairly recent times was a rural, peasant economy, by the need for strong government in the event of military invasion (*sécurité d'abord*) and by the fear of internal disruption in the regions, several of which still cling to their distinctive way of life, their own language or patois ('*la France une et indivisible*').

Before 1945 French education was decidedly two-track, more so, if anything, than was the case in England. For a select minority of children, mainly those from a comfortable middle-class background, the *lycée* offered a rigorous, classical course leading to the baccalauréat examination, success in which gave candidates the chance to go on to the university or, better still if they were exceptionally able, to try their luck in the vastly stiffer competitive examinations (*concours*) in the hope of gaining a place in one or other of the Grandes Ecoles. The latter were, and remain, the training ground from which the upper echelons of the civil service were recruited. Even among this gifted minority failure rates were extraordinarily high, and the educational scene was littered with countless *déclassés* – the unfortunate ones who had not quite made the grade. For the great majority, the elementary school offered a utility-type terminal course which catered for children destined for artisan and agricultural occupations, and which scarcely ranked even as a second best. In short, the class distinctions which have bedevilled English education were more accentuated in France. From its Napoleonic origins, the *lycée* had always been a more prestigious institution than the grammar school ever was, and the social distance which separated the *professeur agrégé* from the humble *instituteur* was considerably greater than that which existed in England between the graduate schoolmaster and the two-year college-trained teacher.

Dissatisfaction with this state of affairs had been steadily mounting between 1918 and 1939 during which period sundry pressure groups, notably Les Compagnons de l'Université Nouvelle and teachers' professional associations, urged the need for wholesale reforms. Their arguments were as consistent as they were cogent: the system was undemocratic, a flagrant denial of equality of opportunity, over-rigid, out of date, not in keeping with the national interest, wasteful of human resources, a bar to economic growth. None of them made much impression. It was as though France needed to lose a war and suffer the humiliations of the Occupation before reconstruction could be begun in earnest and fresh foundations laid.

What has been accomplished since 1945 may well be accounted an educational miracle on a par with the much-publicized economic miracle in West Germany. In outlining France's national goals and ideals, W. D. Halls quotes Michelet:

> God must indeed illuminate it more than any other nation, since in the depths of night it sees what others can see no longer; in the frightful darkness that often descended in the Middle Ages, and later,

none could discern the heavens. France alone saw. . . . That is what France is. With her nothing is finished; everything has to be begun again.[1]

In the context of 1945 the quotation is certainly apt.

Immediately following the Liberation the first tentative moves were made with the introduction of the 'Classes Nouvelles'. These were authorized by the Ministry in a number of selected pilot schools which were given a more or less free hand in experimenting with child-centred approaches and activity methods in the first year ('sixième') classes in secondary schools. Teacher:pupil ratios were generous so as to allow for aesthetic, creative, practical and social activities, the emphasis on theoretical studies was relaxed, examination requirements were waived, environmental studies and extra-curricular activities were encouraged and more attention was paid to individual differences and interests. Eventually the 'Classes Nouvelles' were followed through to the school-leaving stage, whereupon the experiment was called off, but not before its results had been carefully evaluated and assimilated by the system as a whole.

The French genius for 'planification', forced underground or driven into exile during the war years, emerged afresh once hostilities had ended. Under the inspired leadership of politicians like Jean Monnet and Maurice Schumann, groups of civil servants, industrialists and businessmen immediately entered into joint discussions with a view to setting the ravaged economy on its feet again. 1946 saw the establishment of a national planning agency, the Commissariat Général au Plan, and the initiation of the first of a series of economic plans. The first of these, covering the years 1946–53, was designed to clear up the mess left over from the war years and to prepare the ground for a concerted drive for increased industrial output. Its first priorities were to estimate manpower needs, restore essential services, allocate materials which were in short supply and retool and re-equip factories; to begin with any thoughts of educational reform had to wait upon these. The Le Gorgeu Commission, appointed in 1951, was given the task of surveying such things as school buildings, estimating the number of places required, reviewing the position as regards the supply, recruitment and training of teachers, and only gradually moved on to considerations of policy-making affecting the curriculum itself as the economic situation improved. The second plan ran from 1954-7, the third from 1958-61, the fourth from 1962-5, the fifth from 1966-9 and the sixth, now under way, will be completed in 1973. Any attempt to understand the striking transformation which has taken place in French education, a transformation no less remarkable than the one which has seen France restored to a position of power and influence in the European Economic Community (entered into in 1958, the year which ushered in the Fifth Republic), has to be related to the cumulative effects of these national economic plans.

Unlike the early Stalinist five-year plans, 'planification' as the French understand it is not in the least totalitarian: its purpose is not 'dirigiste' but 'indicatif', that is to say, it is content to set objectives and to state general principles for their achievement, and otherwise to rely on the force of persuasion to bring about the necessary consensus. Where this fails, political controls may be resorted to, for example by manipulating the stock exchange, but for the most part the plans are formulated on a take-it-or-leave-it basis.

Again, 1946 saw the publication of the Langevin-Wallon Plan, an ambitious blueprint if ever there was one, which envisaged free education for all between the ages of three and eighteen, and which laid down lines of development that have in effect been followed, although the proposals failed to win the approval of the National Assembly and were never formally adopted. The plan was nothing if not bold in its conception: it sought to remove the vertical class distinction between the *lycée* and the elementary school, which had operated within separate and self-contained sub-systems hitherto, and replace it by a unified system in which all pupils would follow a common course with little or no differentiation before the age of fifteen. Instead of the education system being divided into different types of school, the plan advocated its division into 'cycles', more or less on the lines of three progressive stages of the 1944 Education Act in England and Wales, but with one very important difference. At age eleven, selection was to be scrapped and the first two years of secondary schooling were to be devoted to 'observation', to be followed by a further two-year period of guidance ('orientation') to allow for adequate opportunities for continuous assessment of each child's aptitudes and abilities. Between the ages of thirteen and fifteen the range of options would be widened and a certain amount of streaming might be allowed, but any commitment to a specialized type of course or to study in depth was to be deferred until after fifteen, when the 'cycle de détermination' began.

Quite apart from its being impracticable on economic grounds, the Langevin Plan stood little chance of getting official backing in the confused political set-up of the immediate post-war era in which coalition governments came and went with monotonous regularity. In any case, it encountered stiff resistance from the traditionalists who feared – and still fear – that any attempt to implement it would lead to a 'baisse de niveau culturel' (the French equivalent of the more-means-worse criticism which is frequently voiced in Britain). If anything, this resistance is stronger than it is in this country and the strategies and tactics adopted by the planners in order to overcome it provide an interesting case-study for the comparative educationist. In our own case, the extent to which the 'septic debris of past social history' (to borrow a phrase from Sir Fred Clark) still distorts policy-making is only now becoming clear, and it is fair to say that if anything is more intransigent than the British prejudice in favour of liberal studies and the disparagement of vocational-technical ones it is the Gallic belief in the efficacy of *culture générale*.

> The idea itself is bivalent (says Halls). On the one hand, it was conceived of as a corpus of knowledge that embraced philosophy, literature, science, history and the arts. Yet it also implied a mode of intellectual discipline, a means of training the mind, in which the chief instruments would be the classics and mathematics. This instrumental aspect is possibly the more important. Through familiarity with the

great works of Antiquity, of which French classical literature was the true continuation, the student would come to the concept of excellence. Minute, detailed study was necessary. No matter that such study was sometimes dull and dreary: interest would arise as appreciation deepened, and in any case the striving after understanding represented a good mental training. Similarly, mathematics yielded up *l'esprit de géométrie* – a Pascalian quality of logical thinking. Reason becomes the dominant characteristic of such an education, a residue that remains when knowledge has been lost. Edouard Herriot has said of *culture générale* that it is 'what remains when all else has been forgotten'.[2]

This firm adherence to a theory and practice predicated on mental training is reminiscent of Seneca's apologia: 'Why do we teach the liberal arts? Not because they give virtue but because they prepare the mind to receive virtue. Our duty is not to study them but to *have* studied them' – a view which had survived intact since Roman times and one which most educated Frenchmen have never been disposed to challenge. At its best, as exemplified in Montaigne's preference for 'la tête bien faite' rather than 'la tête bien pleine', it produced the kind of analytical, incisive mind which the French have always prized above all others; at its worst it was excessively intellectual, disinterested to the point where it became meaningless, and so élitist as to rule out any hope of success for the mass of average-ability pupils. As a basis for the training of a small professional class, *culture générale* had served France well enough, but in its pre-war forms it was totally unsuited to the requirements of an advanced industrial state. That it should have been enlarged in order to grant parity of esteem to technology is perhaps not altogether surprising: what *is* surprising is that the modernization of the French education system has been engineered so smoothly and gone so far as it has in so short a time.

It has been said that the purpose of French-style planning is to indicate the broad lines of advance, not to compel people to follow them. However, a centralized education system has no compunction about telling its teachers what to do and how to do it. France has no body on a par with the Schools Council in England and Wales. Since 1956 its National Institutes of Pedagogy at Sèvres and St Cloud have carried out various curriculum projects assigned to them by the Minister, to whom any findings or recommendations have to be submitted for approval. Teachers may undertake research investigations on their own account provided they obtain the necessary authorization from Paris, but the fact is that only investigations carried out by the National Institutes in specially selected pilot schools stand any real chance of being acted upon and must receive official blessing before that happens. Once he is satisfied that a change is justified, the Minister can bring it about on a nation-wide basis by law, by decree or more simply (if the change is a relatively minor one) by issuing a circular. The latter may not necessarily be mandatory, but when occasion demands its wording leaves no doubt that the instructions are to be followed closely. In addition, all schools receive a weekly *Official Bulletin*, the contents of which have to be made known to all members of staff and discussed by them with the head teacher.

Many of the day-to-day innovations in organization of schools and in methods of teaching are effected through this regular information service. For example, the *Official Bulletin* of 1 December 1950 set out in great detail the new methodology and curriculum for modern languages. Not only did it state such general principles as the need for giving instruction throughout in the foreign language concerned and the advisability of avoiding translation into the vernacular except where it was absolutely necessary, but it specified a lesson plan (*schéma de classe*), according to which the first ten minutes were to be spent in revision exercises, with all books closed, to be followed by ten minutes of vocabulary work with new words being introduced in illustrative contexts, etc., etc.

Though French teachers have long been accustomed to this kind of treatment and accept it uncomplainingly, it would be wrong to imagine that the Berthoin reforms of 1959 and all the consequences that have flowed from them are in any way popular.

New Directions for a New Society: The French Transformation

On the whole, professional opinion has supported them, but so far as such bodies as the Société des Agrégés are concerned, the prevailing attitude may well invite comparison with that of the Head Masters' Conference to suggestions for the integration of the private sector within the framework of a comprehensive school system in England. Despite this, the transition to a common course of a diagnostic and prognostic nature and covering the first four years of the secondary school's work has been managed very skilfully by means of central direction and control. The transition is, of course, far from complete and much remains to be done before the arrangements for the 'cycle de détermination' are worked out. The intention is that all pupils on reaching the age of fifteen will be allocated either to a 'long' course (15-18) comprising a classical and a modern side of advanced theoretical studies, or to a 'short' course (15-16-17) of general and vocational studies. Since 1963 the pattern for the future has been set by the creation of 'middle' or 'junior high' schools, the Collèges d'Enseignement Secondaires, thus merging the two-track systems which had previously existed side by side, and leaving the *lycée* to function somewhat on the lines of a sixth-form college.

The baccalauréat remains the main avenue to success in a meritocracy, but the range of options has been widened to include science, economics and technological studies, though all candidates are required to satisfy the examiners in at least one foreign language – a concession to the unwavering faith in *culture générale*. The numbers of candidates have increased very considerably and the proportion of those failing has simultaneously been reduced. As a consequence, the pressure of demand for university places has led to an explosive situation as the events of May 1968 testified. For those not eligible for the university, there is now an extensive provision of further education courses and the so-called University Institutes of Technology, created since 1966, are proving so popular that most of them are overcrowded within a year or two of their being built. They are in effect commercial colleges and offer an intensive two-year course of vocational training in which roughly 35 per cent of the time is devoted to general education and the rest to practical and theoretical studies in economics, management and industrial techniques. They are lavishly equipped and use the most *avant garde* methods – language laboratories, teaching machines, closed circuit television, etc. – and rely to a great extent on continuous assessment (a kind of up-dated version of the American credit plan) which ensures that nearly everyone passes. They started by admitting all applicants, but already they are becoming much more selective and, with the pressure of demand growing at the rate it does, it looks as though few applicants who do not have a first-class (A) baccalauréat will be accepted in future.

But if the Institutes of Technology mark a new departure and if the structural changes in the schools are far-reaching, some of the most important reforms have been effected in less spectacular ways. As part of the overall strategy in the democratization and modernization of French education, it would be hard to think of a more significant innovation than the *conseil de classe*. First mooted in a Ministerial circular dated 25 October 1952, this was to take the form of a regular exchange of information between teachers so to provide the basis for continuous assessment of each pupil's scholastic progress and personal development during the critical, formative period between the ages of eleven and fifteen. As such, the class council is not to be thought of as being the same as an informal staff meeting. In order to make the best use of the collective observations, all the relevant information has to be synthesized in a *dossier scolaire*, a document which corresponds to the pupil's record card in Britain, only vastly more detailed. This, it was felt, would enable teachers to see at a glance all the essential facts about a child's physical, moral and intellectual development, and would be invaluable in helping to place him in the right kind of course once the stage of guidance ('orientation') had been reached. Originally, it was suggested that the council should meet at least thirteen times a year, but in practice this proved to be so time-consuming and onerous that the number of meetings was reduced to nine. Following the circular of 23 September 1960, all schools were required to organize class councils. Principal teachers who are responsible for the administrative and clerical work involved in calling meetings and in keeping dossiers up to date receive substantial extra payment for their services. Since the circular of 17 February 1961, anyone who takes part in a class council must be paid.

In the old-style *lycée* it was customary for the *professeur* to deliver his lesson in much the same way as a university lecturer delivers his lecture, formally and without getting to know his pupils individually. As for finding out what his non-graduate colleagues (if they could be called that) had to say, it rarely or never entered his head, for usually he and they were not on speaking terms. Not any more! Like it or lump it, the *professeur* who teaches, say, five different classes now has to attend forty-five council meetings each year and pool his ideas and opinions with the rest of the staff.

Not only with the staff, either. Parents, too, are represented on these councils, and as an indirect result of the events of May 1968, the right of pupils to be represented has been granted. The link between school and home is taken very seriously, just how seriously can be gathered from the form issued to all parents by the Ministry of National Education. By any standards, this is an exhaustive questionnaire which parents are asked to complete 'avec précision' in the interests of their children. Among other things, it asks from what illnesses the child has suffered, what time he gets up and goes to bed, what are the ages of his brothers and sisters, whether he gets on well with them at home, whether he prefers to play with friends or by himself, whether he is well behaved, whether he is extravert or introvert, whether his homework is supervised, whether he is in the habit of working on his own or of asking for help, whether there is a table for him to do his homework on, whether he settles down to do his homework quickly and voluntarily or whether he leaves it until the last moment, whether he is anxious about examination results, whether he is easily discouraged by setbacks, whether he likes his school, whether he talks about what goes on there, how he spends his leisure time, how often he goes to the cinema or the theatre, whether he has joined a sports club or a youth group, whether the parents have thought about the kind of career for which he seems best suited and so on.

All this information, along with the child's medical history and his school record, is compiled and summarized in the *dossier scolaire*. The thoroughness with which the latter is completed is best appreciated by examining its contents. The first page of the booklet gives the pupil's medical history – physical fitness, auditory and visual acuity, after-effects of any illnesses, absences from school, etc. – in the second, fourth and sixth years of his secondary school life, with passport-size photographs of him at different ages. The second page gives details of his physical development and his temperament. His attitude to physical activities is rated on a 5-point scale (bold, rash, nonchalant, diffident, timid) and so is his attitude to group participation (self-effacing, ready to take the initiative, responsible, emulative, team-spirited) – again at three different stages. Pages 3–4 have to do with his scholastic performance during the 'cycle d'observation', i.e. the first two years of the secondary school course. The grade placings (A–E) in the first-, second- and third-term examinations in the various subjects are recorded, as are the considered opinions of the class council and its chairman, the principal teacher. Pages 5–6 similarly record the pupil's performance and progress in the third, fourth and fifth years, together with the general appraisal of the principal teacher and the head-teacher. Pages 7–8 deal with the crucial sixth year when the pupil is due to sit for the baccalauréat examination, pages 9–10 with the terminal class when he is ready for university entrance or the *concours* for a coveted place in the Grandes Ecoles. At the end of the dossier two tear-off pages give the final verdict of all those who have been concerned in passing judgement on the pupil – his teachers, the principal teacher, the head-teacher and the president of the jury (an external examiner, usually a representative of the university).

It may be thought that this elaborate procedure is not very different from the practice of keeping files with which teachers in Britain are only too familiar, and that in any case it has little connection with what actually goes on in the classroom. The great virtue of these class councils resides less in what comes out of them in the form of a dossier than in what goes into them in the form of joint consultation and collaboration between teachers of unequal professional status, social workers and, not least, parents. If only as a means of closing the gap between the *professeur* and the *instituteur*, and the gap between school and home, it would be hard to think of a neater device for ensuring liaison. In addition to those already mentioned, the class council can call on the advice of the school psychologist and the guidance specialist. Resident school psychologists were first appointed in Paris in 1952, and although they are by no means universal they are now to be found working alongside teachers in many of the bigger provincial secondary schools. So, too, are the guidance specialists who are trained under the auspices of the Bureau Universitaire de Statistique or the Centre d'Orientation Professionelle et Scolaire and whose role in the schools is far from being limited to that of a careers master.

The paradox of French planning is that it begins by being autocratic and doctrinaire and ends by being both democratic and practical. When Langevin and his fellows envisaged the first four years of the secondary school as a period of observation and guidance they could hardly have dreamed of its being expedited by so simple a device as the *conseil de classe*, nor could they have guessed that continuous assessment would go so far as it has to humanize the examination system, to foster new styles of teaching and to revitalize the curriculum. The fact that Latin was abolished in the first and second years of the secondary school course in 1969 is only one measure of the triumph of child-centred practice over discipline-centred theory. *Agrégé, instituteur, psychologue, conseiller* and parent may not always see eye to eye and may occasionally find themselves at loggerheads, but at least they are brought together as a common interest group. Head teachers may, and frequently do, protest that they are no longer masters in their own house, that they have no final say in decision-making, that their vote counts for one like everyone else's and can easily be overruled. No matter: they have no choice but to comply with the regulations of the New Society which is determined to translate the principles of liberty, equality and fraternity into a working reality. To this end, as the French see it, a schools council in every school is as reasonable as it is desirable.

SIGNIFICANT DATES IN POST-WAR DEVELOPMENTS IN FRENCH EDUCATION

1945 Liberation.
1946 Commissariat Général au Plan established.
 First national economic plan began.
 Classes Nouvelles introduced in selected schools.
 Langevin Plan published.
1951 Le Gorgeu Commission began work.
1952 Conseil de classe recommended in Minister's circular, 25 October.
1953 Second national economic plan began.
1954 Dien Bien Phu.
1956 National Institutes of Pedagogy (Sèvres, St Cloud) established.
1958 Fifth Republic inaugurated 13 May; De Gaulle became President.
 European Economic Community founded.
 Third national economic plan began.
1959 Berthoin reforms; school-leaving age raised to sixteen; observation and guidance to last two years in secondary schools.
1960 Conseil de classe became official.
1962 Algeria became independent.
1963 Common courses adopted in Collèges d'Enseignement Secondaires.
 Observation and guidance extended to four years.
1964 Raising of school-leaving age postponed to 1972 at the earliest.
1966 University Institutes of Technology created.
 Fifth national economic plan began.

1968   May–June revolt of university students.
1969   Pompidou became President.
       Latin abolished in first and second years of the secondary school.
       Sixth national economic plan began.

REFERENCES

1 W. H. Halls, *Society, Schools and Progress in France* (Oxford, Pergamon Press, 1965), p. 5.
2 ibid., p. 2.

CHAPTER FIVE

Authors, Authorities and Authoritarianism

'Why should I?'
'Make me!'
'Who do they think they are?'
The defiant stance adopted by some teenagers appears to be becoming commoner; and the age of protest, like the age of puberty, seems to be growing earlier and earlier in its onset. While it would be unduly gloomy to think that many teachers are faced with imminent mutiny, or that our secondary schools are potential centres for riotous upheavals on a par with those which have occurred at the London School of Economics and elsewhere, the rumblings of discontent are not to be taken lightly even if, for the time being, they are heard only faintly and surreptitiously. It would be wrong, too, to suppose that the rumblings are confined to an awkward squad of troublemakers, and that the best way of dealing with the problem is to catch a few ringleaders and make examples of them. Although this is the line which the authorities are almost certain to take – the only one open to them, many would say – it is ill-advised and liable to precipitate the kind of head-on collision which it seeks to avoid.

In a way, it is possible to admire the insubordination of the youth who refuses to come to heel, and who is not prepared to accept school regulations willy-nilly. It takes enormous courage, a strength of mind akin to genius, to stand out against the powers-that-be. The individualist is the exception which proves the rule –

the rule being that the vast majority of human beings are easily browbeaten or cajoled into follow-my-leader frames of mind. From Galileo and Copernicus to Marx and Darwin, the innovator has always been cast in the role of a rebel, a divergent thinker who was not afraid of ridicule or martyrdom, and not to be deterred because, to begin with, he was in a minority of one. The whole course of modern history, indeed, can be viewed as a progressive extension of the right and duty of private judgement, beginning with the querying and rejection of ecclesiastical authority in Reformation times, carrying over into the querying and rejection of established political, legal, scientific and economic authorities during the eighteenth and nineteenth centuries and culminating at present in a permissive society in which authority in any shape or form can be called in question. Whether or not we agree with Auden that

> Accurate scholarship can
> Unearth the whole offence
> From Luther until now
> That has driven a culture mad[1]

the trend of events is easily discerned. Luther's 'Here I stand, I can no other', Descartes' 'Accept nothing as true that it is possible to doubt', Einstein's 'I did it by refusing to accept an axiom' – these are the typically fearless utterances of men who thought and lived dangerously. The fact that the opprobrium they had to endure has been replaced by admiration and gratitude for the leadership they provided should not be allowed to obscure the general rule – that the original creative thinker tends to be actively disliked by most of his contemporaries. Persecution of the odd man out is as common in the human species as it is among the birds and beasts of the field. Ideas which are now regarded as having universal validity began life by being seen as sheer lunacy and treated accordingly.

In short, the Copernican Revolution, in removing one of the linchpins which held the medieval world order together, triggered off a chain reaction of heresies which eventually came to be accepted in the guise of new orthodoxies. Seeing that the rise of popular education was implicated in the process from the start, it is not surprising that education has both hastened and confirmed the trend towards self-assertion. After all, the more informed a person is, the less amenable is he likely to be to received opinion and the dictates of conventional wisdom.

Anarchists apart, everyone agrees that it is wrong to suppose that individuals can ever be free to act as they please: think as they please, possibly, but do as they please, never. The paradox of freedom can only be resolved by saying that it involves the recognition of necessity. Since education serves to bring about changes in the behaviour of the learner (including changes in his attitudes and desires), some power has to be invoked whereby some human beings – teachers – exercise legitimate control over others – pupils. Control, in turn, implies the need for constraints and rules. Wherein does this power reside?

The concept of authority is strangely elusive, being apt to escape the mesh of legalistic and philosophical definitions alike. To call it 'legitimate power' may satisfy the politician and the sociologist, but immediately raises questions regarding the ways in which that power is made legitimate. To say that it consists in the ability of one man (or group) to compel others to comply with his (its) wishes and see that they are carried out raises the same questions concerning the fallibility of man-made authority which prompted Luther's protestantism.

In the past, Authority, usually with a capital A, has been variously invested in God, in the State, in Reason, in the General Will, in economic necessity and, latterly, even in 'sensitive attention to the expectations of contemporaries'. Once it had ceased to be thought of as stemming from a supernatural source, as happened during the heyday of Papal infallibility and the Divine Right of Kings, it came to be identified with a supra-personal entity. Absolute power, formerly attributed to the deity, was annexed and institutionalized in political and social forms. These forms are at present being assailed by the same spirit of scepticism which led to the erosion of religious belief and the downfall of church overlordship.

Today the inclination is not to look for definitions of authority but to ask, 'By whose authority?' This is particularly true in the case of education where everyone feels entitled, and qualified, to voice his own opinion, and where the feeling is that the experts, if indeed there are any, cannot be trusted. As standards of educational attainment improve, and as levels of aspiration, expectation and self-awareness rise, we can be sure that this drive in the direction of shared decision-making will gather momentum. At the same time we can also be sure that it will meet with stiff resistance and that there are many forces at work in the opposite direction – that is, towards more centralized planning. The construction of computable models of the education system is as yet in its infancy, but the tools for such construction are already being fashioned and sharpened in readiness for use in the not so distant future.

Although the model can be enriched by the introduction of structural relationships, causal connexions and decision variables, it is still possible to adopt a naïve view of its relation to decision-making. It is still possible to estimate the current state of the system and the values of all parameters of the model from past data, and, by describing a proposed educational policy in terms of values of the decision variables, to make projections of the future state of the system under this policy. Consequently it is possible to cling to the idea of the model as a mere machine for producing 'maps' of the future without ever becoming aware of its potential for more profound and penetrating use.

On being provided with a projection for which he had called, the decision-maker might consider that it indicated an undesirable future, and he might conclude that this was not a good policy to pursue. He might then devise another policy in the hope that it would show improvement. By expressing this policy in terms of the decision variables, the model could again be used to provide a new projection which would be passed back to the decision-maker. If he did not like this new projection, he could devise another policy and the process could be repeated until he found a projection and a policy which he thought acceptable.[2]

Is it naïve to ask who is 'he' in all this? The Secretary of State for Education and Science, perhaps? The prospect before us, it seems, is that of an all-powerful benevolent despot armed cap-à-pie with techniques which no one else will be able to command. Technocracy or democracy – which is it to be?

In transitional periods such as the one we are going through, conflict between institutionalized authority – the Establishment, as it is commonly called – and the up-and-coming claimants for control of the new order inevitably gives rise to battle of wills and wits. It is a struggle between conservatism and radicalism, between those who are in authority and more or less pledged to maintain the *status quo* and those who, to begin with, can only exert their influence through dispersed pressure groups. Each side does its best to disarm and to discredit the other. In the educational field, the curriculum naturally finds itself in the thick of the fray, being as authoritative an element as any in the school's activities.

Management of conflict, accordingly, is the first prerequisite for effective curriculum development in which the crucial problem is that of securing co-operation between seemingly irreconcilable viewpoints and interests. The first step is to find out how the education system in the country concerned operates. Is the decision-making process in the system autocratic, bureaucratic or democratic – centralized or de-centralized? Is there a pecking order and, if so, who is its Big Brother? Who orders whom to do what, and under what conditions? Are there any breaks in the channels of communication between different parts of the system? Where are the lines of demarcation drawn between central and local government administration, between directors of education and head teachers, between head teachers and their staffs, between teachers and parents? How is the system related to the society it serves? Above all, what is the state of the system – dynamic equilibrium, unstable equilibrium, metastable equilibrium or steady state? These are some of the questions which the investigator has to try to answer.

Unfortunately, it is not long before he discovers that the necessary information is hard to track down, that some of it is deliberately withheld, and that most of it is too scattered to permit firm conclusions to be based upon it. Everyone likes to think that the way the education system operates is plain sailing: on the contrary, the truth is that its operation is so intricate in its complexities that nobody really understands it, not even those who are charged with the responsibility for 'running' the system. This is one area of investigation which calls for independent research – independent in the sense that it needs to be undertaken by people who have no interest whatsoever in the maintenance of the system. So far as England and Wales are concerned, the various sectors of the educational services have been exhaustively surveyed in a series of major and minor official reports, but to date little or no attempt has been made to review the administrative set-up as a whole. It is even questionable whether the various sectors (including the independent one) do, in fact, constitute a system. 'However well the country may have been served by the largely uncoordinated activities and initiatives of the past, we are clear that from now on these are not good enough –' the Robbins Report declared, 'the needs of the present and still more of the future demand that there should be a system'.[3] As a declaration of intent, this has led to significant developments in the field of higher education, with repercussions which have been felt at the lower levels, but it has yet to be implemented in the form of a national plan. The same is true of Scotland, which has its own separate system, in many ways a more homogeneous and more manageable one than England's, but in this case any separate identity is offset, or at any rate complicated, by its being partly dependent upon political decisions made at Westminster.

But if the ways in which the education system of a country operates remain unclear, and while a reliable analysis of the state of the system is awaited, it is still possible to distinguish in a general way between the forces of innovation and tradition. If management of conflict is to lead to co-operation, the tactics of any group involved in the work of curriculum reform must be to find out how and where the lines of force are drawn so as to be able to steer a course between them. In practice this is one of the most fascinating aspects of the business, and boils down to a kind of cops and robbers game in which the secret of success is to be quite sure who is friend and who is foe. It is a game that is full of surprises and unaccountable let-downs. It calls for a degree of shrewdness in judging personalities and weighing up chances which is not given to many. As often as not, the individual who is outwardly forward-looking turns out to be the kind of person who privately wants to keep things as they are at all costs.

To begin with, then, it may be useful to compare the roles of innovator and traditionalist with those of 'authors' and 'authorities'. The author of a book is more or less free to express his own ideas and is responsible to no one, except indirectly to his publisher and his readers. Because of this relative lack of constraint, he is in smaller or greater measure an originator. This, incidentally, is the original meaning of the word: to be an 'auctor' was to be a pioneer, an inventor, one who exercises the right and duty of private judgement. By definition, therefore, the 'author' represents a growth-point; and, as we have already argued, the querying, rejection, eventual overthrow and subsequent renewal of established authority throughout the ages has to be traced to this source. Against this, it has to be recognized that the 'author' has no authority, only the hope of influencing other people by persuasion or by personal example. Even when he has earned a reputation for himself, as happens, say, when a scholar is recognized as an 'authority' in a special field, he is still not 'in authority' and is called upon in a consultant capacity by those who are. The latter are the appointed representatives of a decision-making process which is at once more ancient and more powerful than any that can be accomplished in the lifetime of a single individual – in short, the cultural tradition. In the realm of ideas, the author-innovator can afford to be several jumps ahead of his contemporaries – so far as educational theory is concerned, Comenius, for example, may be reckoned to have been born at least three centuries before his 'suitable time' – but the world of affairs is prevented from moving ahead with anything like the same speed and boldness.

To some extent, then, those who are 'in authority' are the prisoners of their office. If 'authors' are unacknowledged legislators of the world, 'authorities' are its acknowledged executives. Whereas 'authors' are accorded the right to pronounce on this or that as they see fit, and enjoy influence without actual power, 'authorities' are charged with responsibilities which leave them much less room for manoeuvre: they have to see that regulations are carried out, that records and accounts are kept, and generally ensure that the services under their charge are maintained as going concerns. In the case of education, this is not to say that the administrator's functions are restricted to the appointment of staff, looking after stocks and stores and similar routine chores, nor to deny that a new-style educational administrator who is actively engaged in the management of curriculum projects is emerging here and there. To be 'in authority', however, to some extent presupposes the acceptance of a role which is hedged about with precedents and pledged to preserve the system in a steady state.

For their part, 'authors' have nothing to fear in urging the need for sweeping reforms and ambitious experimental projects: rocking the boat is the least of their worries. This is why, normally, they are the ones who occupy relatively subordinate positions in the chain of command – assistants rather than head teachers, local authority advisers rather than chief education officers, young H.M.I.s rather than old ones, college and university lecturers rather than principals and heads of departments. Being free lances, they may supply the cutting edge that bites into the cake of custom, the zest of adventure which prevents custom from going stale, but in vying for a place at the head table theirs is essentially a waiting game.

'Authorities', on the other hand, need to be more circumspect. Any move that is liable to cause instability has to be guarded against and, if necessary, blocked. J. G. Owens makes the point that to change the curriculum is neither simple nor safe:

> To organize an interplay between the local education authority and the community is part of the prescribed function of local administration: to organize an interaction open enough to allow society's

values to have a weight in the choice of what is taught and to encourage that interaction to the point of bringing change about is to go beyond the prescribed function. But to create a situation which is so open as to bring instability to the organization of a local education authority is a risk which any organization must face which needs to maintain itself in a steady state. To encourage change which directly affects teachers and which, later and less directly, affects pupils, parents and employers (as well as other users of education) means awakening a response. This response to change should affect the subsequent activities of the administrator. If the feedback cannot be controlled within the norms of administration, disruption follows (and, since the norms are not generally dictated by the need for innovation, this is a real risk). Both the efficiency and the morale of the administrator might be badly damaged.[4]

The relationship between 'authors' and 'authorities', then, is one of permanent tension, a ceaseless struggle between emergent influences and established power. The latter, having been built up and during a period of relative calm, seeks to retain the upper hand when faced with what, to it, looks like the growing threat of the forces of innovation. Once established, power tends to become entrenched and those who wield it act on the assumption that it is pyramidal: that is to say, a few 'top people' make all the important decisions. The education system, accordingly, is conceived of as a hierarchy with a single, supreme authority at the head of affairs and different levels of lesser authority in each of which, as the saying goes, the editor's decision is final. Thus, policies agreed at the ministerial level dictate policies at the local education authority level; directors of education hold the reins over the teachers they employ; heads of schools have ways and means of making life difficult for members of staff who look like failing to toe the line – all of which leaves the pupils at the receiving end of a vertical chain of command against which there is no appeal.

For the most part, this is still the way in which the education system operates. At the same time, there is the growing recognition that decision-making needs to be more widely shared than it has been hitherto, and that in practice as well as in theory it is necessary to think of authority as being dispersed throughout the system. The idea that there has to be a *primum movens* is illusory and mischievous. Despite the activities of such bodies as the Schools Council there must always be a sense in which it can be said that 'Minister knows nowt about t' curriculum'.

'Systems analysts emphasize that information within and between organisms is never linear (cause and effect on two variable systems) but variable, reverberating, circular transactions establishing complicated chains of causation in which all effects become causes and vice versa.'[5] Where this is denied, the interaction between the different parts of the system, which alone ensures that authority is constantly being re-allocated and redistributed, becomes blocked and the system relapses into a condition best described as authoritarian.

What happens is only too familiar. Assistant teachers who find that even when they band together the headmaster refuses to accede to their proposals and requests; headmasters who are under starter's orders issued from the County Office; student teachers who fear that they will be black-listed if they do not do exactly what their supervisors tell them to do; undergraduates who adapt their examination answers to the known views of professors and lecturers who are going to mark them. Who can doubt that pockets of authoritarianism can be found wherever one cares to look? They are to be found wherever those who are answerable to their immediate superiors cannot answer back with any hope of changing decisions which have been made over their heads. In this situation knuckling under may be tolerable for a time, but in the long run its pent-up frustrations are bound to show themselves in low morale, if not in open resentment and revolt. As a society becomes more egalitarian – alternatively, as standards of education rise – the number of those who are disposed to ask 'By whose authority?' increases and the containment of 'authors' by 'authorities' becomes correspondingly more difficult. One of the biggest obstacles in the field of curriculum development arises from a reluctance of those in authority to admit that leadership *rotates* and that no single person or body can claim to be the final arbiter. There are still far too many autocratic directors of education who insist on keeping tight control of everything touching the work of the schools in their area, this despite the twenty-odd-year-old comment that 'one must ask whether the administrator, removed from the actual business of teaching for a more or less considerable time, and concerned inevitably with a variety of problems far removed from the curriculum, is really competent *qua* administrator to speak with authority on the content of the education that he helps to provide.'[6]

There is no easy way out of the conflict between 'authors' and 'authorities' by saying that both parties are in the same boat and that therefore they should work together on the understanding that neither of them can profess to know all the answers. Techniques for bringing about this harmonious state of affairs – systems analysis, role theory, organization theory and the rest – are at best rudimentary and their applications not as obviously helpful as they might be. When all is said and done, the force of individual personalities is as important a variable as any.

No less important is the force of inertia which creates invisible barriers within and between institutions and between different levels of the educational system. Broadly speaking, 'boundary maintenance' means much the same as lines of demarcation do in industry. Disputes about who-does-what are as troublesome and infuriating in educational establishments as those which break out periodically on the factory floor. Whether we ascribe them to vested interests, to puerile jealousies or to empire-building, every institution surrounds itself with its own tariff walls and protective shell. The more firmly established the institution is, the more difficult it becomes to penetrate this shell since the intense we-feeling engendered within its walls tends to make its inmates more or less hostile to outsiders. As a result, policies framed by the institution are treated as if they were a purely internal affair. In one sense, every institution behaves as if it were autonomous and to that extent shuts itself off from the wider system: in another sense, the protective shell is needed if the institution is to preserve its identity and its sphere of influence intact, not to mention the need to carry on its business without undue interference. It was only by incorporating itself in this way that the medieval *studium generale* was able to place itself on a permanent footing as a university. Where, as at Salerno, the *studium* failed to take the precaution of legalizing its existence, it usually disappeared from the face of the earth. To this day, universities provide the classic example of an educational institution adopting a closed-shop policy for the sake of its own autonomy and survival. Granted, no educational institution can ever operate as a closed system, but, as everyone knows, universities are not easy places to get into and what goes on in their innermost courts and senate chambers is not divulged to the common gaze.

While it is not impossible to move across the barriers which serve to keep institutions apart from each other, relatively few people are free to make the attempt. Those who elect to do so, moreover, sooner or later meet with an impasse: parents who sense that they are not welcome when they seek an interview at schools attended by their children; researchers who are denied access to documents which are locked away and filed as Top Secret; press reporters who are turned away from committee meetings which take place behind locked doors; teachers who only hear the headmaster's voice over a public-address loudspeaker and rarely meet him face to face from one month's end to another; neighbouring schools which are not on speaking terms; members of one professional association eyeing askance members of rival associations; academics who regard this or that administrator as a stick-in-the-mud and administrators whose opinion of this or that academic is no less contemptuous – these are typical instances of the way in which 'boundary maintenance' can blight any move designed to bring about closer co-operation.

To complicate matters, the blend of rights and duties varies from role to role. It goes without saying that Everyman in his time plays many parts. As a citizen he likes to think of himself as his own boss. But what he feels free to say and do as a private individual very often does not square with what is expected of him in his tenure of a public office. In the latter capacity, his rights and duties are prescribed for him by the position he occupies: in greater or lesser degree he has to act as an 'authority'. Politician, administrator, teacher, academic, H.M.I. – each has his ethic, his sense of loyalty to the demands of his office, his identification with the public interest: in short, a pattern of values and beliefs which acts as a constraint on his personal opinion. What he says and does may be largely decided for him by his awareness of the kinds of behaviour – protocol, decorum, 'rules of the game' – expected of the role he plays and the position he occupies. The extent to which he is obligated varies, of course, but it is always there, being defined and legitimized by a consensus of attitudes which give rise to the role expectation. The individual's behaviour as head of a family, clearly, is not the same as his behaviour as head of a school, still less as head of a government department. Institutions, therefore, are not alone in erecting invisible walls to protect themselves: in a bureaucracy nearly everyone is wearing a mask.

Moreover, the set of roles which decides who-does-what also helps to decide who-speaks-to-whom. Indeed, the social distance created by institutional barriers may be less inhibitive than the status barriers which effectively prevent individuals even in the same institution from being on speaking terms. All institutions, and the education system as a whole, are hierarchical in their structure – without office-bearers they would be unable to function at all – but where this structure becomes so stratified that channels of communication between the various levels and sectors are blocked, decision-making is monopolized by a high-status clique and the result, once again, is a form of authoritarian rule. In other words, leadership ceases to circulate from member to member, individuals are relegated to the role of cogs in the machine and outlets for 'authors' have to be sought outside the institutional framework.

'As long as man assumes that the evils of this earth have their causes in the specific failures of individual persons and individual institutions, he still remains at the stage of intellectual childhood',[7] we are warned. It is with this in mind, no doubt, that the systems analyst insists on the need to take into account *all* the contextual factors and variables involved in the decision-making process, or at least to identify (and if possible quantify) those which are important. Only in this way can an overview of the ways in which the system operates be obtained. For those engaged in curriculum development the attempt has to be made if there is to be any chance of steering a course between the rocks and shoals which make theirs so risky and dubious an enterprise.

As an exercise in tracing the lines of force and the interactions between four groups of personnel – professional administrators, local education authority representatives, teachers and pupils – Eggleston's model provides an interesting aperçu[8] (Fig. 2). It shows that decisions emanating from one source, in this instance the local education authority, are countered by responses from the schools, and that eventual decision-making takes place in a central area of conflict or co-operation in which no single group or individual can be said to be dominant. It also illustrates the constraints on the various groups – 'boundary maintenance', role expectations, status barriers, etc. – referred to in the previous discussion.

The trouble with this, as with all flow diagrams, is that it is not animated. What happens when a ruthless director of education is determined to have his way? What happens when an obdurate head teacher falls foul of his own staff? What happens when a hot-headed youth raises his fists to a teacher? No diagram can help to answer such questions. In this case, too, it may be thought that the forces engaged are grossly misrepresented in so far as the diagram depicts them as being between two equal sides and between four groups of equal status. Even so, if it lays itself open to the criticism that it makes the decision-making process appear to be less one-sided than it normally is, the model serves admirably as a schema for looking at the process objectively, 'the viewing of a situation in its entirety, with all its interior interactions, with all its exterior connections, and with full cognizance of its place in its context'.

Suppose, now, that a schema is drawn to represent the Scottish

Social context of school

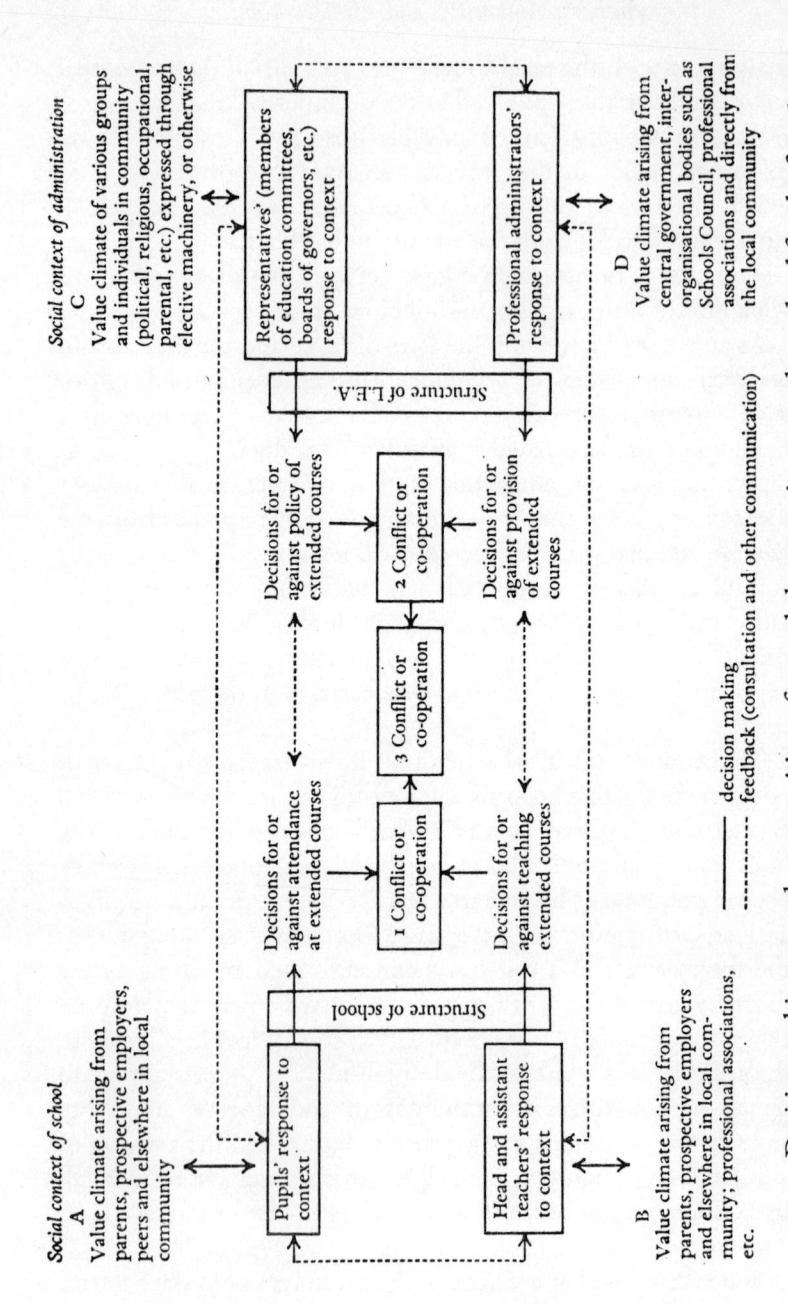

A
Value climate arising from parents, prospective employers, peers and elsewhere in local community

B
Value climate arising from parents, prospective employers and elsewhere in local community; professional associations, etc.

Social context of administration

C
Value climate of various groups and individuals in community (political, religious, occupational, parental, etc.) expressed through elective machinery, or otherwise

D
Value climate arising from central government, inter-organisational bodies such as Schools Council, professional associations and directly from the local community

FIG 2 Decision-making procedure: provision of extended courses in a secondary school for the first time

system of education, a system which is many respects more formal and more centralized than that of England and Wales. Oversimplified it must be, but to the extent that institutional and status barriers undoubtedly exist it is not inappropriate to represent them as closed 'boxes' as in Fig. 3.

From a casual inspection of the diagram it appears that there are a number of points in the network where channels of communication are either tenuous or non-existent. This in itself is a fact worth noting. The more isolated a component of the system is, the greater the likelihood of its behaving as if it were self-contained. Who-says-what-to-whom, likewise, will tend to be restricted to within-institution discussion and may be unresponsive to any wider cross-fertilization of ideas.

PROCEED WITH CAUTION: THE SCOTTISH SITUATION

Take teacher training. In Scotland, where there are no institutes of education to co-ordinate it, this side of the work is reserved to the colleges of education which can pursue their own policies more or less regardless of what the universities in their constituent areas may think about them. Because the two institutions are financed from different sources and ultimately responsible to different departments of the central government, there is little or nothing to prevent either of them ignoring the other's existence if it pleases to do so. Since the inception of the B.Ed. degree, which is awarded by the university although the bulk of the teaching is done in the colleges, this lack of contact has been remedied to some extent, but in practice such interaction as occurs depends far more on tacit goodwill and the diplomacy of individuals than upon any formal channels of communication. Where the key individuals concerned have shown themselves to be incompatible it has happened more than once that diplomatic relations have been broken off between a college of education and its neighbouring university; and even where friendly relations are maintained it is still true that members of the staffs of the two institutions rarely or never meet each other.

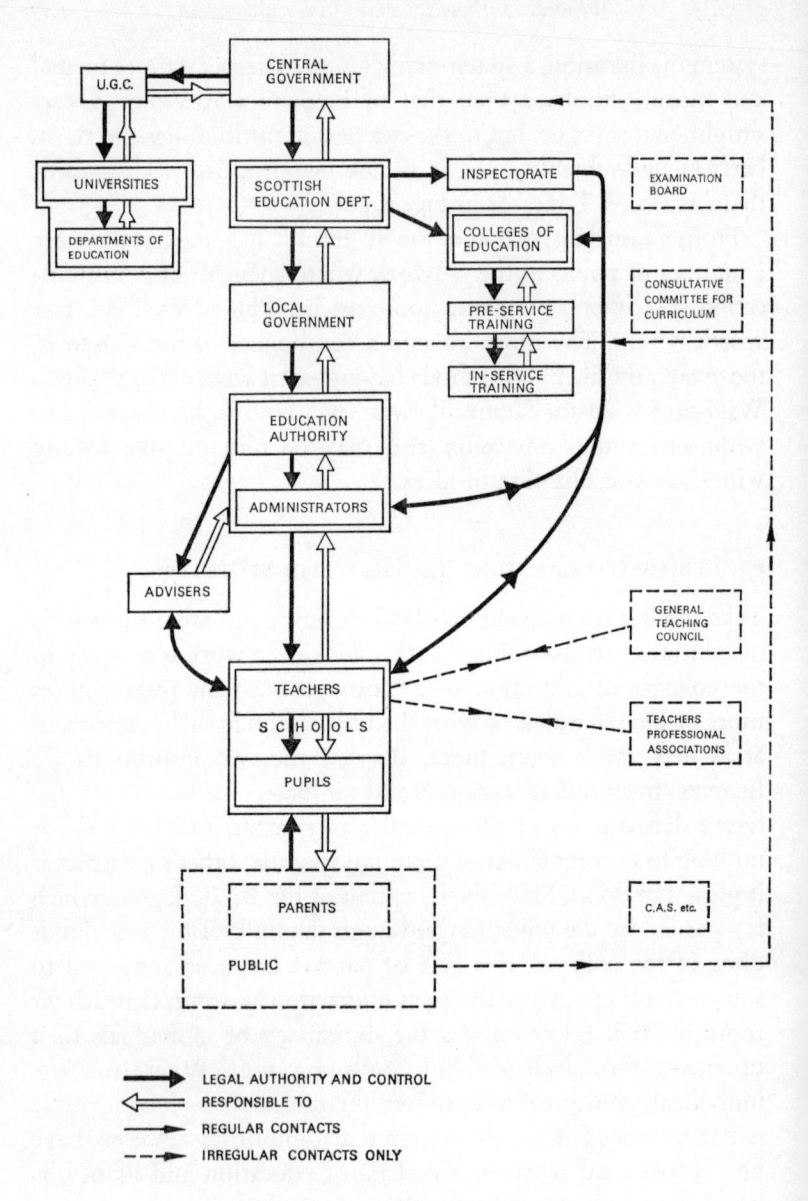

FIG 3   The Scottish Education System

The extent to which departments of education in Scottish universities (excluding Stirling, a new foundation which offers a concurrent course of training for graduate teachers) have been left out on a limb is far from being misrepresented in the diagram. Status-wise, they are by no means impotent, but any advantages they may possess so long as higher education is organized on 'binary' lines are offset by the sheer size of the colleges of education. Not surprisingly, therefore, questions about who-does-what give rise to a certain amount of duplication and, occasionally, friction. Broadly, the lines of demarcation laid down indicate that anything which comes under the heading of professional training ('methods') lies within the province of the colleges, whereas anything of a more academic nature belongs to the university department of education. Like the distinction between 'education' and 'training', this division of labour has become so blurred as to be unreal. The division remains clear enough at the more advanced stages of post-graduate study where students are following the Master of Education course or engaged in work leading to a research degree. At this level the university department's sphere of influence is undisputed. It is at the lower level that the division of labour is merely divisive. For example, if the university department offers an academic course for undergraduates, as it is clearly entitled to do, and a year or so later the college complains that students who have taken it are asking to be exempted from virtually identical courses, how is the disagreement to be composed? Should it be left to the individuals responsible for the planning of such courses to sort out the rights and wrongs of the matter between themselves? Why no Joint Board of Studies?

In general, it has to be said that relations between the Scottish colleges of education and the university departments of education are somewhat distant, coolly polite, verging at times on the frigid. Having regular contacts with the schools, and a large staff of well-qualified lecturers, the colleges are jealous of their prerogatives and are apt to fight shy of any move on the part of the university department which looks like poaching on their territory.

Again, who says what to whom? In Fig. 3 it will be seen that 'boundary maintenance' is represented by a double-line enclosure in some cases, in others by a single line or a dotted line. This is an arbitrary, symbolic way of delineating possible breaks in the two-way flow of information in the system. If only in the sense that schools, education offices, colleges, universities and government departments are housed separately, there are physical barriers between them, but these are insignificant compared with the social and psychological barriers arising from the differing role expectations and status rankings of the people who work inside their walls. Thus, an assistant teacher may have few opportunities of expressing his views outside the staff room, and fewer still of finding out what his colleagues are doing and thinking in other schools. Thus, working-class parents in particular find it difficult to talk to teachers on anything like equal terms, and for the most part never come in contact with them from the day a child's mother takes him to school for the first time to the day he leaves it ten years later. Not only working-class parents, either. It is symptomatic of the Scottish climate of opinion that parent-teacher associations do not flourish, that the man in the street, often with good reason, is inclined to look upon the school in much the same way as he does a police station or a hospital – as a place to be avoided. Or consider the gap between teachers and administrators. In many Scottish education authorities it is still the case that head teachers have no say in the selection of their staff, that unless he is extremely personable and sure of himself a head teacher cannot confer as man to man with his director. Autocratic directors of education are, of course, by no means peculiar to Scotland, but the state of the system being what it is, they are not uncommon. As for academics, what else can they do but live in their own little community?

Of all the personnel involved in the system, it would seem that Her Majesty's Inspectors are the luckiest ones, the ones who have a roving commission and are free to move across the board at will. Having access as of right to the various sectors, they are well placed to act as go-betweens. As leaders of the curriculum reform movement, several Scottish H.M.I.s have earned for themselves a national reputation: indeed, the new physics and chemistry syllabuses, now in general use, were framed more or less singlehanded by men like Donald McGill and A. J. Mee at a time when the reformist cause was nothing like so popular as it is today. The example set by them was infectious.

> McGill came to the inspectorate at the comparatively late age of forty-nine, and was soon leading a small group of teachers in pilot studies designed to work out a more modern approach to physics teaching. The result was an alternative (i.e. new) syllabus in physics, published in 1962. College of education courses were run for teachers in the summer of that year, displaying the new methods and apparatus, and many teachers became very enthusiastic, starting work in the following session on the new syllabus, the keynote of which was the understanding of concepts through personal discovery, in place of the old reliance on the memorization of facts. Since 1962, the enthusiasm for the new syllabus in physics has grown so fast that the great majority of schools are now following it, and the old one is being abandoned in session 1971-2.[9]

McGill's tenure of office as a Scottish H.M.I. was a brief one, lasting from 1959 to 1962, when he was seconded to the Nuffield Science Project. He died in 1963. The speed with which significant changes were effected as a result of his initiative is, perhaps, the best proof that large-scale innovation is a manageable proposition in a country like Scotland. It has led to a series of similar, but more broadly based movements in other subjects, first in chemistry, then mathematics, modern studies, modern languages and English. The lone wolf venture has given way to the working party and the steering committee composed of teachers, college of education staff and academics and, since 1966, to the next-best-thing to a programme of research and development in the teaching of English. Teacher-led study groups have sprung up in many parts of the country. Although no longer alone in making the running, Scottish H.M.I.s continue to play a prominent part in the work of curriculum renewal. That they are supremely well placed and well qualified for the task of disseminating new ideas, and for arranging get-togethers between the interested parties, cannot be doubted.

The same might be said as regards the work of local authority advisers and organizers, all of whom, presumably, owe their appointment to a distinguished record as serving teachers. Their position, however, is slightly anomalous, being midway between the administration and the schools – which means that they may enjoy the best or the worst of both worlds depending upon the latitude they are given. In Scotland, the local education authority has greater power to determine the curriculum than its English counterpart, drawing up schemes of work in consultation with head teachers which have to be submitted for the approval of the district inspector of schools. This means that the work of advisers is largely restricted to the supervision of probationary teachers and the organization of courses of in-service training. The job carries decidedly less prestige than that of an H.M.I., and the adviser's influence is correspondingly limited. Nevertheless, it would appear from Fig. 3 that H.M.I.s working hand in hand with advisers provide one of the main spearpoints for innovation in the Scottish system at the present time.

What other agencies are to hand? There is in existence a national Consultative Committee for the Curriculum, composed mainly of education department officials, H.M.I.s and senior representatives of the teaching profession which has delegated to it powers formerly discharged by the central department alone. The committee has published a number of valuable working papers and organized numerous regional and local sub-committees up and down the country, all of which are actively engaged in discussing the pros and cons of curriculum revision and in conducting a variety of pilot schemes. It is no reflection on the efforts that are being made, however, to say that the Consultative Committee remains a shadowy body, still dominated by civil service administrators. Moreover, it lacks the financial resources of the Schools Council in England, and is for that reason alone somewhat remote from the rank and file of serving teachers.

Yet, in the last resort, no curriculum project can hope to succeed unless it received active, informed participation among the rank and file. The rapid spread of study groups and working parties which has taken place since 1962 speaks well for the willingness of hard-worked teachers to devote themselves to this kind of activity; the question is whether or not, in doing so, they are always as well informed as they might be. To date, comparatively little interest has been displayed in new methods of assessment, in the moderating of internal examinations, in team teaching, in attempts to break away from 'subjects' – mainly because Scottish teachers have had few opportunities of reading about them and fewer still of encountering them in practice.

Although in law the H.M.I. and the education authority have the final say on what is taught in schools, the detailed arrangements of timetabling and the drawing up of schemes of work is normally left in the hands of the head teacher, acting in liaison with his deputies and principal teachers of specialist subjects. In theory, then, it would seem that there is nothing to prevent a progressive head teacher from acting as an 'author' in trying out new methods or schemes of his own. In practice few Scottish head teachers find it worth their while to be nonconformist. The outstanding exceptions, like R. F. Mackenzie (whose Braehead School is now closed down and whose book, *A Question of Living*, remains vibrant in the memory of all who have read it), tend to figure as rogue elephants and sooner or later are roped in with their tamer fellows.

Within the four walls of the classroom, all the same, the assistant teacher is the one who is as free as any to 'have a go' if he chooses. True, there are massive constraints on his freedom, not least examination requirements, but experience shows that time and again the original mind has the strength of will which finds a way to overcome the obstacles placed in its way. Of all the major curriculum projects now under way in other parts of the world there is not one which cannot be traced back ultimately to the inspired 'authorship' of individual teachers. Here, again, the record shows that the Scottish culture pattern leaves its 'authors' as misfits and drives them into exile – A. S. Neill to Suffolk and the many nameless ones who down the years have emigrated to

Canada, New Zealand, Australia and other parts of the world. Where, it may be asked, are Scotland's Susan Isaacses, Marion Richardsons and Sybil Marshalls? Where, for that matter, are its Homer Lanes and Henry Morrises?

In the slow thaw which has been felt in the climate of social and professional opinion in recent years, it is conceivable that a new generation of adventurous-minded teachers is emerging. For the young assistant, certainly, the penalties for stepping out of line are not so severe as they were. If he finds that his colleagues agree with him in thinking that isolation within the classroom cramps his style and that something needs to be done to break down the rigid compartmenting of subjects in the timetable by a team-teaching approach, he can at least enter into negotiations with them, though not, be it said, behind the head teacher's back. Admittedly, he and his colleagues may not gain the necessary consent to go ahead with their plans, but provided he goes about it diplomatically there is nothing to stop him trying. Being so close to the rock face, unfortunately, he is unable to see what is going on elsewhere and so take the larger view which might help to convince him that the moves he wants to make are justified and deserving of approval. He may have heard about team-teaching, programmed learning, closed circuit television, open plan and other new-fangled techniques, but more often than not he knows precious little about them. It is hard for him to keep track of all the latest developments, virtually impossible to make much sense of the findings reported in educational research; he has few opportunities of attending demonstrations of modern aids and equipment, fewer still of learning how to use them effectively. Much easier, and safer, to stay in a rut. Even if he happens to be a would-be leader, with ideas of his own, there are so many sanctions to deter him that in the ordinary way he finds himself quickly checked and concludes that he is getting nowhere.

Moreover, with teachers in short supply, some authorities have to think twice before releasing staff for courses of in-service training. As the main providing bodies for this type of course, the colleges of education already have their hands full with the job of pre-service training and cannot always meet the additional demands now being made upon them. At the moment, the Secretary of State for Scotland is setting up a Committee for the In-service Training of Teachers which is going to plan the administrative machinery for co-ordinating this side of the work on a regional basis. The governing bodies of Jordanhill, Moray House, Dundee and Aberdeen Colleges of Education are being asked to form regional sub-committees, composed of representatives of the colleges, education authorities, teachers' associations and other constituent interests. A member of the inspectorate will serve as an assessor on each of these regional committees. Not surprisingly, only one member of the academic staff from each university in the area is to be nominated. Besides serving in an advisory capacity, the committees are to have the power to arrange for in-service programmes at the request of their members in order to supplement existing courses. All of which sounds promising. But Scotland's habit of hastening slowly is nicely illustrated by the National Committee's decision that the introduction of this co-ordinating machinery must precede the deliberations of a policy sub-committee for which, in turn, a working party has been appointed to 'consider in the light of the existing provision how best a future efficient pattern of in-service training might be planned and introduced to meet local, regional and national deeds'. So the wheels of bureaucracy creak on their cumbersome way of going through the motions of reform. The Scots, it seems, have no liking for crash programmes. Meantime, the hungry sheep look up and are not fed.

Meantime, too, educationists in the universities are left chafing in their ivory towers, cut off from the mainstream of events and powerless to intervene. They are the ones who are supposed to be well versed in the methods and findings of research, in the latest developments in theory and practice. Above all, they are the ones who are, or ought to be, knowledgeable about techniques of organization and management, about the analysis of structure and sequence in courses of instruction, about curriculum developments in other countries, about assessment and evaluation, and about the applications of educational technology, none of which can be counted on as being within the competence of teachers, administrators or even H.M.I.s. Without necessarily setting them up as philosopher-kings, they have a contribution to make. So long as the special relationship between the Scottish Education Department and the colleges remains as close as it is, it is not obvious how that contribution can be made. Except indirectly through their students, the university departments of education have so few formal links with the rest of the system as to be left waiting on the sidelines. Indirectly, of course, their influence is considerable; their M.Ed.s occupy many of the key positions in the colleges, in administration, in the schools and in the inspectorate as well, to say nothing of the large and growing numbers of graduate teachers who take the Diploma in Education course at the university. Why not be satisfied with this, it may well be asked? Why pretend to take on outside commitments, seeing that the departments have only a small staff and are hard put to meet the demands of teaching and research as it is? If they are interested in curriculum development and methods of teaching, would they not be well advised to offer their services to other departments in the university where the need for innovation is arguably greater than it is in the schools?

Good questions, all of them. All the same, it is not easy to see how a further withdrawal into isolationism can prevent educationists in Scottish universities from becoming more inbred than they are at present. As it is, such 'authorship' as is open to them has to be addressed to their fellow educationists at home and abroad, and finds exiguous expression in the learned journals. To add to their quandary, they are themselves inmates of an institution which has always been the last bastion of traditional-mindedness and which to this day remains one of the chief stumbling blocks to innovation by refusing to budge an inch over its entrance examination requirements.

This gap between university departments of education and the rest of the system may or may not be considered disadvantageous; in any case, there are others – between central and local administrations, between primary schools and secondary schools, between teachers and parents, between the electorate and central and local educational officialdom and between rival professional associations, each of which creates its own hiatus in the flow of information in the system. The recent unpleasantness arising from the setting up of General Teaching Council, hailed initially as a charter of professional rights, is all too typical of the Scottish genius for fostering bad human relations. The spectacle of teachers who opted out for reasons of conscience being forcibly expelled from their posts is, to say the least of it, not pretty. Might it not have been avoided if the constitution-makers had gone about their business in a less heavy-handed fashion?

What, then, of the state of the system? In the past, and until quite recently, Scottish education was organized on more authoritarian lines than those which England and Wales were accustomed to, at any rate prior to 1944. Memoranda and circulars issued from the central office in Edinburgh were always taken much more seriously, and observed more obediently, than the lucubrations of the old Board of Education ever were. If they did not have the force of law exactly, the pronouncements of the Scottish Education Department were scarcely in the vein of gentle homily, so nicely exemplified in *A Handbook of Suggestions for the Consideration of Teachers*. At no time was the pretence entertained that teachers were at liberty to teach what they pleased or how they pleased. The master-servant relationship permeated the system from top to bottom. Head teachers who wanted a say in the appointment of staff were told that this was none of their business. Principal teachers, in turn, handed out schemes of work which their assistants were expected to carry out regardless of what they might think about them. Assistants who asked for a staff meeting to be called were liable to be sent away with fleas in their ears. Not unnaturally, the master-servant relationship carried over into the classroom, where the luckless pupils bore the brunt of it from strap-happy teachers.

It should not be forgotten, either, that the master-servant relationship affected the local administration of education also.

The education authority in Scotland has had a much shorter history than in England, where the *ad hoc* principle was abandoned at the turn of the century and where the mutual partition of power between central and local government was affected by a kind of gentlemen's agreement, a partnership between equals. Dating from the Scottish Local Government Act of 1929, the all-purpose education authority was born in rather different circumstances and in its early days remained firmly tied to the apron strings of the central office. The latter, incidentally, had held the whip hand ever since 1872, when the Scotch Education Department was formed with the express purpose of welding together both parochial and independent schools into a coherent system, some thirty years, that is, before England's Board of Education came into existence. The fact that the balance of power has swung to the side of the central government, leaving England and Wales with a virtually all-powerful Secretary of State, while the Scottish Education Department has been steadily moving in the direction of delegating some of its powers to other bodies, should not be allowed to obscure the differences in the evolution of the two systems. Outwardly, the only discernible difference is one of nomenclature – 'education authority' in Scotland, 'local education authority' in England and Wales – but in practice the outcome has been two distinct *styles* of administration. According to one observer,

> In Scotland the tendency is towards specialization of function. The job of the teacher is to teach, and until recently teachers have not sat on education committees at all. The job of administrators is to administer, and an education department which does not get down to the task allotted to it is an anomaly. To an English observer this looks like authoritarianism. It is merely a different way of doing things.[10]

As to that, the only pertinent comment must be that what looks like authoritarianism in one country is the same the world over, and that where Scotland differs from England and Wales is in its passive acceptance of, and liking for, allotted tasks. What will happen when, and if, the Maud and Wheatley proposals for the reorganization of local government are adopted remains open to conjecture.

Nationalism, too, is an important factor which has to be taken into account, although one which cannot be pinned down by the systems analyst. The Scots are a proud folk, hanging on like grim death to institutions and traditions which proclaim their separate identity. Of these, none is more cherished than their education system, which in many respects certainly was superior to that of England during the nineteenth century. Being proud, the Scots are also inclined to be irritable. They have been irritable off and on ever since the Act of Union and to this day go on carrying some hefty historical chips on their shoulders. They nurse their nostalgia for the 'Auld Sang', and they have never quite forgiven the auld enemy. Nothing to them is more hurtful than criticisms which dare to suggest that they may be living in the past, nothing more galling than the suspicion (or is it the realization?) that education, like golf, is a game in which they no longer figure high in the world rankings. 'They say. Let them say', 'Here's tae us. Wha's like us' – these are their mottos.

At the same time the Scots are canny – their own word for shrewdness combined with caution. Not given to rushing in where angels fear to tread, they prefer to wait and see others, best of all Sassenachs, make fools of themselves before deciding on a course of action. In the field of education this has the effect of making Scotland appear to lag behind the times. Thus, the 'activity and experience' curriculum advocated by the Hadow Committee's report on the primary school in 1931 had to wait until 1965 before it received official assent in the Scottish Education Department's memorandum. Innovation, like Spring, comes slowly in North Britain. Change for its own sake is rightly abhorred; the trouble is that change of any sort tends to be distrusted and resisted. However strongly national sentiment may be affronted by political decisions taken at Westminster, therefore, the feeling that they are being dragged along on England's shirt tails does not really bother the Scots unduly so far as the provision of education is concerned. Why worry if the announcement of the decision to go comprehensive came first from a London-based Ministry and was followed by a similar announcement from Edinburgh? Why worry if an Education Act (Scotland) invariably follows an Education Act (England and Wales) as night follows day? Has it not always been a case of England's doing today what Scotland comes round to doing next year or the year after? After all, is there not a certain virtue in believing that the tortoise gets there in the end, despite the hare's showy turn of speed? Judging by the false starts and the difficulties encountered in high-powered curriculum projects in other countries, is not Scotland's wait-and-see policy a sound one?

This willingness to follow a given lead, once it is seen to be reliable, is characteristic of the Scots. Like the French, a nation with which they have recognizable affinities as well as historical links, the Scots look to their strong men, heads of state whose word is virtually unquestioned. From the days of the clan chieftain to the present time this boss mentality has been a feature of Scottish life and affairs. With it goes a certain *incivisme*, the conviction that 'they' (the Establishment) are responsible for all the important decisions, and the fear that any headless organization will flap about like a decapitated chicken. The resignation of the masses in the face of decisions which have been taken over their heads and without their being consulted can be illustrated in several ways. One which visitors, and especially Americans, never fail to remark on is the meekness with which parents tolerate the cavalier treatment they and their children receive at the hands of the school authorities. Another is the docility, if that is the word, of Scottish teachers who had little or no say in the formulation of plans leading to Circular 600 (the equivalent of the English Circular 10/65) – plans which they were expected to implement. Yet another is that quaint relic, the 'class ticket', a document which certifies that students in Scottish universities have dutifully attended lectures, satisfied the requirements of their professor and paid their fees, and without which they cannot gain admission to the examination hall.

Curiously enough, this reliance on 'use and wont' (which in

more permissive societies interprets itself as 'don't and won't') is accompanied by a sneaking ambition to play the pacemaker. Latterly, the log-jam of traditional attitudes has been loosening, and the feeling that 'things are on the move' has been growing, and with it a more widespread recognition of the inevitability of change. The smoothness with which the transfer from the old to the new syllabuses in physics, chemistry and mathematics has been accomplished is frequently pointed to as evidence of Scotland's businesslike approach to the problem of up-dating the curriculum, and it is even claimed that the country now leads the rest of Britain in the teaching of modern studies. Too often, however, these claims are advanced in a spirit of complacency which suggests that things have only to move an inch or two to revive the old-timers' boasts about Scottish education being second to none. In some respects, such claims are well-founded, in others hollow. There is, as yet, little understanding of what a co-ordinated, phased plan of campaign of curriculum development entails; instead, the prevailing view seems to be that all that needs to be done is to redraft syllabuses without much or any provision for the preparation, testing and production of suitable learning materials, aids to teaching, etc., to go with them. To date, indeed, most of the major innovations in Scottish education have been dumped on the school's doorstep without much in the way of prior notice or by-your-leave. Except indirectly, teachers have not benefited from the resources for learning which have been made available by large-scale projects in other countries. The significance of these, whether in England, Sweden or the U.S.A., resides less in a change-over to new content than in a shift in the role and attitude of the teacher.

> Changing the content is only a vehicle for trying to deepen teachers' understanding of the teaching process (in the opinion of John Banks, Project Officer of the Schools Council). The function of the new teaching materials is however not an unimportant one. It could be argued that there is a tendency for directors who omit to produce an adequately specific statement of their project's aims also to tend to the belief that a project can be effective without producing teaching

materials. One might suggest an explanation of this; it is difficult to translate into guidance material for teachers a concept which you have not formulated sufficiently precisely yourself. In more personal terms, any project team who believes that specific educational ideas can be transmitted by word of mouth (by means of courses) from team to teachers (and by those teachers to other teachers), and that this will yield results which are significantly comparable with their original intentions, are almost certainly in for a rude shock. If it were possible to organize educational innovation in this way, the whole conception of 'package' curriculum development – centring a complex of pedagogic and organizational support round a collection of printed material – would be unnecessary. The temptation to take this wrong turning is perhaps all the stronger in the present phase of British educational innovation when, as we have noted, the importance of *what* you teach is being de-stressed, and the importance of *how* you teach it exalted.[11]

To say that Scottish teachers have been granted precious few packages and that they are desperately short of 'pedagogic and organizational support' is to put it mildly. In general, it has been a case of old dogs being left to learn to perform new tricks as best they can. Although the number of local and regional study groups and working parties has increased, it remains the case that professional participation is minimal, and that initiatives in the schools are kept on a tight rein by administrative authority. It is probably true to say that this state of affairs suits the temper of the rank and file, most of whom are so inured to doing what they are told as to take it lying down.

In so far as the state of the system can be gauged, then, the indications are that it is far from being as dynamic as some of its leading spokesmen like to think it is. Certainly it has not yet reached the stage when it can be said to be 'going critical'. All that can be said is that the atmosphere is a good deal more relaxed than it used to be a decade or so ago, that the situation is rather more fluid, albeit one in which individual freedom of action is not as great as might be desired.

Scottish education has long prided itself on being democratic and so, up to a point, it is. Edinburgh apart, it has no use for swank and is much less bedevilled by petty class distinctions than English education. But this democratic aspect is largely superficial. The internal organization of schools, their external relationships and their ethos are normally the reverse of democratic. Moreover, if its structure as outlined in Fig. 3 is at all accurate, it seems that the system is designed to promote conflict rather than co-operation. The lines of force pointing downwards from the top are vastly more powerful than those pointing upwards from the grass roots. The links which might convert a vertical-linear chain of command into a circular one have yet to be forged. If the necessary lead were forthcoming from St Andrew's House, there would be nothing to prevent Scotland from embarking on an all-out systems approach to the problems of research and development, as Sweden is currently doing, but there are no signs of such a lead being given. Such research as is being carried out in the universities and colleges is for the most part undertaken from motives of private ambition (i.e. for the sake of gaining an academic award) and is not geared to on-going developments in the schools. The same might be said of most of the investigations sponsored by the Scottish Council for Research in Education.

Neither is there any prospect of the impetus being created by the kind of get-together so admirably exemplified by the Woods Hole conference in the U.S.A. One of the main impediments to innovation is the difficulty of finding a neutral ground where the various parties entitled to discuss curricular problems can meet as equals, forgetting the cares of office and the institutional and status barriers which keep them cornered in fox-holes during the greater part of their working lives. The difficulty is accentuated by the reluctance, inability or downright refusal of those who are in positions of authority to admit that this is possible without serious loss of face. In the uneasy transition from absolutism to devolutionism, there is naturally a great deal of uncertainty about the different levels and kinds of decision-making – political, administrative and purely educational – and so far as the latter is concerned the acknowledgement that teachers, academics and others have an equal right to be heard is either withheld or grudgingly conceded.

The Scottish education system, in short, is still one in which 'authorities' hold pride of place and rule the roost, in which 'authors' languish. What E. M. Forster once called 'the dictator spirit working quietly away behind the façade of constitutional forms' is still there, none the less potent for being so furtive. Being endemic to the culture, it cannot be exorcized; and the realization that this is so is itself discouraging. Nothing, indeed, is quite so depressing than to meet young graduate teacher-trainees who talk as if they were beaten even before they have started on their careers, and who are convinced not only that there is no point in trying to get things changed, but that it pays to leave them as they are.

This veiled authoritarianism is known to all, but because no one dares to call it by that name it can only be referred to obliquely, or laughed off as a bad joke. Adept at covering its tracks, it pursues its own devious ways – the sly intimidation of subordinates, the unofficial witch-hunt, the preferment of protégés and security men, the lulling and gulling of opposition, the temporizing, the clamping down on any move that looks like breaking the lockstep. Until it is exposed for what it is worth, therefore, the verdict of the would-be systems analyst may well be the same as the poet's:

> Yes, it is too cold in Scotland for flower people: in any case, who would be handed a thistle?
> What are our flowers? Locked swings and private rivers –
> and the isle of Staffa for sale in the open market, which no one questions or thinks strange –
> and lads o' pairts that run to London or Buffalo without a backward look while their elders say Who'd blame them –
> and bonny fechters knee deep in dead ducks with all the thrawn intentness of the incorrigible professional Scot –
> and a Kirk Assembly that excels itself in the bad old rhetoric and tries to stamp out every glow of charity and change, most wrong when it thinks most loudly in its most right – . . .

and dissidence crying in the wilderness to a moor of boulders and two ospreys –
these are the flowers of Scotland.[12]

REFERENCES

1. W. H. Auden, '1st September 1939', *Another Time* (London, Faber & Faber, 1940).
2. P. Armitage, C. Smith and P. Alper, *Decision Models for Educational Planning*, L.S.E. Studies in Education (London, Allen Lane The Penguin Press, 1969), pp. 4–5.
3. *Higher Education*, Report of the Committee under the Chairmanship of Lord Robbins, 1961–3 (London, H.M.S.O., Cmnd. 2154), paras. 14–19.
4. J. G. Owen, 'Administration and curriculum change', in G. Baron and W. Taylor (Eds.), *Educational Administration and the Social Sciences* (Athlone Press, University of London, 1969), pp. 140–1.
5. W. Taylor, 'Issues and problems in training the school administrator', in G. Baron and W. Taylor, op. cit., p. 119.
6. Eric James, *Essay on the Content of Education* (London, Harrap, 1949).
7. Günther Blöker, *The New Realities*, quoted by Alan Bold, *Penguin Modern Poets 15* (Harmondsworth, Penguin Books, 1969).
8. S. J. Eggleston, 'The social context of education', in G. Baron and W. Taylor, op. cit., p. 28.
9. T. Bone, *School Inspection in Scotland 1840–1966* (University of London Press, 1968), pp. 231–2.
10. G. S. Osborne, *Scottish and English Schools* (London, Longmans, 1966), p. 40.
11. L. J. Banks, 'Curriculum developments in Britain, 1963–8', *Journal of Curriculum Studies*, Vol. 1, No. 3 (November 1969).
12. Edwin Morgan, 'The Flowers of Scotland', *Penguin Modern Poets 15* (Harmondsworth, Penguin Books, 1969).

Part II

THE MANAGEMENT OF INNOVATION

Theory

CHAPTER SIX

Learning Situations into Life Situations

One of Henry James's shorter novels, *Washington Square*, centres around a young heiress who agrees to elope with her suitor, only to be jilted at the last moment. The heroine is a plain, simple-minded, stay-at-home girl, essentially a weak character. Her father, a doctor, has good reason to suspect that her wealth is the main attraction for the young man, a social climber with expensive tastes and no income of his own. The father attempts to dissuade his daughter, even threatening to disinherit her unless she breaks off the affair, but only succeeds in alienating her completely. With a substantial inheritance of her own to fall back on, she defies him. In desperation, the young couple agree to a runaway marriage; he promises to return at midnight bringing a horse and carriage to take her away from a home which has become hateful to her; but the hour strikes and he fails to appear. The girl is heart-broken. For her father she has now nothing but cold contempt, and spurns his pleas for a reconciliation even on his death-bed.

Some time later the young man turns up like the proverbial bad penny. At first she refuses to see him, then relents. Full of contrition, the suitor pleads his cause anew, exercising all his old charm. The reunion is ecstatic, the two embrace, all is forgiven, and once again they decide to wed in haste. The young man leaves, promising to return within the hour. When he does, he finds the door locked and bolted against him. The debt has been finally paid, and in full. The plain, simple-minded girl has turned into a hard-bitten woman with a mind of flint.

There would be no excuse for this scampered précis, which does scant justice to the original, if the only moral to be drawn from it were the one which assures us that Hell hath no fury like a woman scorned. It is introduced here for two reasons; first, because the impasse between father and daughter serves as a paradigm of the generation gap; second, because it illustrates a point which John Dewey never failed to stress – namely, that the really crucial learning situations are always life situations.

Obviously, the heroine in the tale has learned nothing that could ever be communicated by formal classroom instruction: she has been taught a lesson, yes, but what exactly was its 'content'? The logic of her father's arguments, the facts he brought to her notice? Her situation, alas, is such that no amount of rational problem-solving can help: father and daughter cannot see eye to eye, words fail and the outcome is a total breakdown of communication. No less obviously, the young woman has learned a great deal. Her whole character has been transformed. How? 'In such a difficulty always ask yourself: How did we *learn* the meaning of this word. . . . From what sort of examples?' In this instance, unfortunately, it is not much use obeying Wittgenstein's behest: to ask how we learned the meaning of this word 'learn' smacks too strongly of self-contradiction.

'I learned *Kubla Khan* by heart.'

'I learned one thing, I tell you – the fellow's a crook.'

'I learned to drive a car last year.'

'I learned today that I have less than six months to live.'

'I learned the difference between digital and analogue computers.'

'I used to detest modern music, but I've learned to like Stravinsky.'

Apart from the fact that each of these sentences begins with 'I' (which at least tells us that some personal interest is involved), it is not obvious that there is much, or anything, in common between these various activities. It cannot even be said that 'to learn' is invariably an active verb. To say that all of them are connected with a 'change in behaviour' or the 'acquisition of skills' is tantamount to saying nothing at all. Again, to try to differentiate between those learning experiences which are mainly cognitive (memorizing a poem, finding out about computers) and those which are mainly emotional (distrusting a colleague, hearing one's own death warrant) only creates an artificial dualism, seeing that human learning in all its forms arises from the interaction of intelligence and feeling.

If it is true that information is always borne on a marker, it is equally certain that learning cannot be dissociated from feeling. A failure of formal education throughout the ages has been to pay lip service to this fundamental truth while condoning practices which deny it. Its rewards have always been reserved for those pupils – 'scholars' – whose frame of mind was attuned to the school's narrow purposes, whereas those who did not fit in with its Procrustean requirements were given short shrift. 'Procrustean' may seem too harsh an adjective to apply to the efforts of teachers who were well-meaning, kindly souls, but not of an educational process which checks so many outlets for the learner's personal satisfaction at the source. In the same way that the early Impressionists had to form their Salon des Refusés in order to win recognition, so most of the innovations in the curriculum have been compelled to find a place for themselves outside the inhospitable confines of school-bound learning. The latter, like the father in the story, 'knows all the answers', supplies all the reasons and the sound arguments, then wonders what has gone wrong when the pupil throws over the traces and refuses to listen. The failure of the educational process has always been its inability to cope with the surge and sweep of human hopes and desires. Thus, the girl with the transistor gets no credit whatsoever for being able to name the Top Ten in the charts at the drop of a hat and is adjudged to be quite unfit as a candidate for an O-level pass in music; and the lad who cannot bring himself to wade through *Julius Caesar*, *Vanity Fair* and all the other prescribed texts ('What a bloody way to grow up!') but who knows the film-of-the-book like the back of his hand is deemed to be in need of remedial treatment. Instead of taking it for granted that the standards and values imposed by school-bound learning are necessarily binding, it would help enormously if our ideas about what constitutes 'learning' were more whole-hearted than they have been so far. At a time when the display of strong feelings is manifestly on the increase, curriculum theorists cannot afford to be cold fish – though it is to be feared that most of them are.

In nursery and infants' classrooms, and to some extent throughout the primary stage as a whole, sympathetic understanding of the problems of growing up, and informed attention to the affective side of learning have become the hall-marks of enlightened teaching. But even here the belief that the school's chief business is formal instruction persists, and so does the conviction that the sooner pupils put away childish things and settle down to serious study the better. Which would be right enough were it not that, for many, 'serious study' is at odds with their hopes and desires during a formative period of growth. The adolescent feels this acutely. Despite the applications of developmental psychology, secondary school practice is as far from adhering to the principle that 'Nature observes a suitable time' as it was in Comenius's day; it insists as severely as ever on the virtues of 'stretching' the intellect, of memorizing useless information, of absorbing and reproducing inert ideas. The idea that the affective life can be left to look after itself at the very time when it is most turbulent and impulsive is worse than dangerous – it is criminal. Yet a combination of pressures – economic, technological, as well as social – makes it more and more probable that the educational process will interpret itself as a ribbon-development of the roof-brain, and that less and less attention will be paid to the learner's personal life. With so much knowledge to be mastered, so many skills to be acquired, so many examinations to be passed, the chances are that the one dimension of learning at which the school has always excelled will become so prestigious as to be beyond challenge. As it is, for an educationist to question the supremacy of the cognitive faculties is bound to seem akin to lèse-majesté, a relapse into romantic anti-intellectualism quite out of keeping with the temper of the times, not to say in poor taste.

It may be thought that, in any case, the argument is making mountains out of molehills since schools engage in far more than formal instruction and cater for a wide range of extra-curricular activities, sports, religious and moral training which affect the learner's character and personality. Has not the English tradition in education always followed John Locke's advice in placing 'virtue' and 'breeding' above 'learning'? In the public schools, and to a lesser extent in the grammar schools, no doubt it has, though always on the understanding that, in Locke's words, 'The great principle and foundation of all virtue is placed in this, that a man is able to deny himself his own desires, cross his inclinations, and purely follow what reason directs as best, though appetite lean the other way.' This Spartan ethic was never without influence on the future man of leisure, the professional man and the scholar, but it had no appeal for an improvident working class destined to earn its living by the sweat of its brow. In the nineteenth-century elementary schools such character-training as was attempted was at best incidental to the inculcation of the Three Rs; and in the day schools of the twentieth century character-training has receded farther into the background as the demand for cognitive skills has increased. The backlash against the sloppiness of 'Life Adjustment' courses in American high schools and the determination to replace them by a 'discipline-centred' curriculum indicate the way things are moving. Curriculum development in this country will almost certainly follow the same direction – that is, towards a closer identification of learning with higher thought processes, the so-called 'things of the mind'. Modern education, for the most part, has no place for the emotions, no time for sentiment. This, in an age when nervous energy is more high-pitched than ever before and young people are all agog for full-blooded leisure pursuits, augurs ill for the rat race in the schools.

But, then, the educational process has always been uneasy in the presence of the stronger emotions. What becomes of ecstasy and grief when the educational psychologist gets hold of them is only too clear: they become a clinical entity called 'affectivity'. What becomes of them at the hands of the taxonomist, who seeks to arrange the emotions in a hierarchy, like so many dried specimens docketed for future use, is worse than ludicrous. Bloom's classification of educational objectives in the cognitive domain being one of the most prestigious documents of our time, it may be rash to characterize the follow-up to it as a sorry mess, misconceived in its attempt to apply the same analytical techniques to human feeling as those which had been serviceable in the realm of human knowledge. *Handbook 11, The Affective Domain* kicks off confidently enough:

1.0 Receiving (attending)
1.1 Awareness
1.2 Willingness to Receive
1.3 Controlled or Selected Attention
2.0 Responding
2.1 Acquiescence to Responding
2.2 Willingness to Respond
2.3 Satisfaction in Response . . .

at which point (the first, incidentally, involving 'a feeling of satisfaction, an emotional response, generally of pleasure, zest, or enjoyment') the authors confess to a sense of loss:

> The location of this category in the hierarchy has given us a great deal of difficulty (they write). Just where in the process of internalization the attachment of an emotional response, kick, or thrill to a behaviour occurs has been hard to determine. For that matter there is some uncertainty as to whether the level of internalization at which it occurs may not depend on the particular behaviour. We have even questioned whether it should be a category. If our structure is to be a hierarchy, then each category should include the behaviour in the next level below it. The emotional component appears gradually through the range of internalization categories. The attempt to specify a given position in the hierarchy as *the* one at which the emotional component is added is doomed to failure.[1]

Hard to say which is the quainter – the idea of an emotional response being attached to a 'behaviour' like a lump of putty stuck to a wall, or the idea that the emotions can be arranged in ascending order like so many Chinese boxes. Doomed to failure and no mistake. As for the contribution of learning theory, the less said the better. The trouble is not simply that there are almost as many theories as there are psychologists – Thorndike, Pavlov, Ebbinghaus, Kohler, Koffka, Hull, Hilgard, Watson, Piaget, Skinner, Tolman, Guthrie, Spence, Bruner, to name but a few – nor that each of them has been over-zealous in generalizing about the applications of his particular prototype, but that between them they have indirectly helped to perpetuate practices in the schools which are none the better for being given an aura of scientific respectability. The wiser the researcher, one cannot help remarking, the greater the likelihood that he will disclaim any responsibility for offering tips to teachers. It is a sign of grace, therefore, to find Gagné writing in the Preface to his recent book *The Conditions of Learning*:

> It will be evident that I do not think learning is a phenomenon which can be explained by simple theories, despite the admitted intellectual appeal such theories have. Although many people, including me, have tried for years to account for actual instances of learning in terms of a small number of principles, I am currently convinced that it cannot be done. To the person who is interested in knowing what principles apply to education, my reply is: The question must be asked and answered with consideration of what kind of capability is being learned. The answer is different depending on the particular class of performance change that is the focus of interest. There are no 'general' rules of learning known at present that can be used as guides in designing instruction.[2]

This forthright avowal is so becoming that it may seem uncharitable to wish that Gagné had left it at that. Better, surely, to 'sit down in a quiet ignorance', as Locke recommended, than to go on to propound a hierarchical theory which places problem-solving at the top of the tree. Certainly a theory which views problem-solving as the outcome of a network series of subordinate capabilities arising, in turn, from an understanding of principles, concepts, multiple discriminations, verbal associations and stimulus-response connections is an improvement on the cruder prototypes which it seeks to displace. It is at least gratifying to be assured that there are at least eight varieties of learning, that they occur at different levels and that each of them depends upon its predecessor. As he says, it is valuable to know how they operate in everyday situations in the classroom. The practical implications for the management of certain kinds of learning, more especially those which allow of the task's being broken down into its elements, are far-reaching. In any case, Gagné is suitably modest in recognizing the limitations of his model, taking pains to point out that:

> The reader needs to be made aware, also, that there are some problems of great importance to education which *cannot* be solved by applying the principles of learning as they are here described. For example, there are many aspects of the personal interaction between a teacher and his students that do not pertain, in a strict sense, to the acquisition of skills and knowledges that typically form the content of the curriculum. These varieties of interaction include those of motivating and persuading, and the establishment of attitudes and values. The development of such human dispositions as these is of tremendous importance to education as a system of modern society. In the most comprehensive sense of the word 'learning', motivations and attitudes must surely be considered to be learned. But the present treatment does not attempt to deal with such learnings, except in a tangential sense. Its scope is restricted to what may be termed the intellectual or 'subject matter' content that leads to improvement in human performances having ultimate usefulness in the pursuit of the individual's vocation or profession.[3]

This is where we came in, it may be thought. The admission that school-bound learning and techniques for making it more efficient are the main business of education is at least honest, as is the admission that equivalent techniques for the establishment of attitudes and values are currently not available. In an age in which economic motives are uppermost, we can be sure that any theory which promises improvement in the learner's vocational-professional performance will be seized on, and that in practice any concern for the formation of attitudes and values will continue to receive no more than lip service. To that extent there is nothing for it but to resign ourselves to the admission that the educational process is nothing else than a special kind of mental training, and that the dispute which began with Socrates' quarrel with the Sophists has finally been resolved in favour of the latter. If there is one crumb of comfort to be derived from the widespread unrest among students today, however, it is the fact that it is they, not their mentors, who are convinced that 'ultimate usefulness' is not to be found in intellectual expertise – and that Socrates was right, after all, to insist on the need to 'care for the soul'.

Gagné's definition of learning is as serviceable as any: 'A change in human disposition or capability, which can be retained, and which is not simply ascribable to the process of growth.'[4] At any rate, this is more acceptable than the usual behaviourist definition, which is content to equate learning with any change in behaviour. By itself, the proposition that learning implies a change in behaviour is less than meaningful, and becomes utterly meaningless when turned the other way round (if a man succumbs to the flu germ, runs a high temperature and becomes delirious, his behaviour is changed and no mistake, but does it make sense to say that he has learned anything?).

At the same time, Gagné's definition remains essentially behaviourist in that it sees learning taking place only when the individual can *do* something afterwards which he could not do before. In other words, he is primarily interested in *capabilities*, and only secondarily concerned, if at all, with *dispositions*. Broadly speaking, capabilities are overt, measurable in terms of the learner's gains as regards information, skill and other cognitive attainments, whereas dispositions tend to be more covert and elusive, having to do with the way the individual feels. For the behaviourist, any elucidation of what happens when the individual learns has to be treated as a 'black box' problem – i.e. as an external observer he has to reckon with an input (stimulus), an output (response) and a functioning process in between which is in the nature of things invisible. Because he refuses to have any truck with what goes on inside the organism, the behaviourist can only judge learning by its effects; its effectors and its affectors are forever excluded from his terms of reference. What goes on inside the black box is not admissible as evidence in his view; it remains a mystery, not a problem.

Unlike Skinner, Gagné recognizes this, of course, but he is obviously more interested in capabilities than in anything else, and fights shy of dispositions not only because they are so intangible but also because they do not fit in with a hierarchical schema. This leaves us with a learning theory which regards problem-solving as its *summum bonum*.

For those types of problem-solving which the theory has in mind the appropriate tools are formal logic and mathematics, both triumphs of abstract reasoning. They demand high levels of conceptualization and the manipulation of symbols, and presuppose a gradual ascent from sense impressions to a grasp of higher-order principles. Whether we follow Bruner in calling the lowest the 'enactive' level, or Piaget in calling it the stage of 'concrete operations', the infant's intuitive learning is firmly rooted in first-hand experience. To begin with, it cannot even be verbalized. Before he can count or name them, he needs to handle, taste, see and smell the objects around him, including the parts of his own body. He has to feel in his bones, as it were, how the see-saw operates and the ways in which his playthings give pleasure. At the 'iconic' level, this free play gives way to rule-bound play in which first-hand experience is to some extent detached from the senses. Now that he knows their names and has the glimmerings of number concepts, things begin to be arranged in his mind in a more orderly fashion than was possible in the blooming, buzzing confusion of early infancy. He can see how the see-saw works by looking at a picture or a diagram. Eventually this detachment from the senses becomes total and he attains the 'symbolic' level where he is at last free to enjoy the combinatorial power of rational thought, to inhabit a stratosphere where all the baser passions have been left behind, and where all his subjective hunches are transcended by his mastery of the strategies of problem-solving.

This onward and upward progress from sense impressions to a zenith of pure intellect has been the ideal of educationists from Plato to the present day. It is so universally approved that any criticism of the ideal stands virtually no chance of gaining a hearing. Nevertheless, it contains a flaw which needs to be exposed.

In those kinds of problems which do not admit of logical-mathematical solutions – being existential, they are more properly referred to as life-and-death issues – the learner's need to 'feel in his bones' can never be discontinued. It is not obvious, for example, how the genius of a Pisano or a Van Gogh could ever mature by rising to the symbolic level. It is not evident that the imagination of a Keats ('O for a life of sensation rather than of thought!') is in any way comparable with the calculation of an Einstein; the latter's is entirely an affair of the roof-brain, the other's much less exclusively so. Judging by the kind of evaluations which have gained the upper hand in educational practice, it appears that artist and poet have to be ranked well below the scientist and the mathematician as 'problem-solvers'. No less apparently, their cast of mind, though lofty, remains embedded in the wonder and delight of sense experience, and shares that same intensity of feeling that characterizes the child's learning at the 'enactive' and 'iconic' levels.

There need be no suggestion that at this point the argument is going to shade off into the hazy ground where creativity takes off from intelligence, nor that it intends to obscure the issue by dragging in a pseudo typology of convergent and divergent thinkers. All it asserts is that what goes on inside the 'black box' cannot be accounted for satisfactorily in terms of cognition alone. Even when the strategies for mathematical-logical problem-solving are fully worked out, the task analysis complete down to the last detail, and the structure and sequence of the course to be followed tolerably well known in advance, the fact is that each and every individual has his own preferences. The destination may be the same for all, but the routes leading to it are in greater or lesser degree a matter of taste. If this is true of symbolic procedures, it is reasonable to suppose that it is true to an even greater extent in those mental activities where mathematical-logical strategies either do not apply or prove unhelpful. What goes on inside the 'black box', in other words, is more a matter of likes and dislikes than of rational cogitation. Introspection, a source of evidence which cannot be ignored, suggests that the operations of our minds, far from being mechanistic, are energized in the blood and first break surface in the consciousness in the form of emotion. It is their *élan* that prompts the search for strategies.

And what of the outputs from the 'black box'? Like three-card tricksters, the behaviourists would have us fasten our gaze on what the learner is doing. But the effects of learning do not display themselves solely, or mainly, in this kind of capability. They show as enthusiasm or boredom, in fits of spleen or bouts of euphoria, in self-assurance or inferiority complexes, in couldn't-care-less outlooks or the determination to persevere in the face of adversity. How a man feels is arguably as important as what he thinks. And this is why for most people, most of the time, life as it is lived is much more like painting a portrait than devising a theorem.

So long as we are committed to a theory and practice of education which is so much more adept at training 'capabilities' than it is at fostering 'dispositions' we must anticipate a further widening of the rift between school-bound learning and the individual's everyday experience. The demand for specialist techniques being so great in the modern world, learning theories of the Gagné type are certain to be adopted on the widest scale, and to confirm the trend towards methods of teaching which concentrate on 'problem-solving'. The prospect held out is that of an educated society composed of experts and trouble-shooters.

Trouble-shooters who are secretly troubled, all the same. For what is to happen if this highly organized public knowledge is purchased at the expense of a private life which is so disorganized as to be a disaster? Realism, not romanticism, demands a much closer investigation of the affective side of learning than we have been prepared to undertake hitherto.

At long last, the groundswell of discontent is beginning to make itself felt. As yet, its ripples have scarcely reached the schools, but the after-effects of the educational process can be seen in a society in which disaffection cuts right across the spectrum from the professional classes to dockers and dustmen. The disaffection, needless to say, is by no means peculiar to Britain, and cannot be attributed solely to a defective education, but there are reasons for thinking that it will prove to be particularly acute in this country because of the arrears of neglect during the past hundred and fifty years. As Max Nicholson puts it, 'Never in history have so many been messed about by so few.' How much longer will they stand for it?

> Secessionism is a course of action, or rather a series of alternative similar courses, brought about by a profound lack of confidence in, or disagreement with, the basic ends sought and means adopted by authority on what are regarded as vital issues. The lack of confidence or disagreement takes shape first, and, after discussion and dissemination, begins to crystallize into an attitude. This then becomes shared by a broadly recognizable although possibly quite unorganized group of like-minded persons. Unless this dissident attitude is met in time by a suitable response from authority, or unless the issue itself dissolves or recedes into the background, some form of secessionism is bound to grow, either subtly and obscurely, or openly and aggressively as with the Dutch Provos.
>
> It is now becoming evident that modern affluent societies are peculiarly susceptible to secessionist protest, not least because they are so blind to the entire process, until it goes to extreme lengths. Britain today is riddled with it, at various stages, and in many forms.[5]

Faced with warnings of this kind, educationists are worse than blind: they simply do not want to see. To their way of thinking, the schools are doing a magnificent job; and any undesirable after-effects can be blamed on conditions of life in a society variously described as 'affluent', 'permissive', 'other-directed', 'centrifugal' and 'technological', for which they are not responsible. As for the traumas induced by compulsory school attendance, is it not too late now to resurrect the 'unwillingly to school' plaint? Are not any fears on this score immediately dispelled by a visit to the entry class in any infants' department, and is it not the case that the great majority of pupils, even the C and D streams in secondary modern schools, are happily engaged most of the time?

Yet there is an inherent irksomeness in modern education which cultural anthropologists have not failed to notice. Says Kneller:

> One of the most striking differences between education in primitive and in advanced societies is the shift from the need of an individual to learn something that everyone agrees he wishes to know to what Margaret Mead calls 'the will of some individual to teach something that it is not agreed that anyone has any desire to know'. The primitive child goes to a relative or perhaps to an expert in his tribe to learn all that he can about some particular activity, such as hunting, fishing or trapping, and its significance in the lore of his tribe. He learns not only because it is universally agreed that there are certain things he should know, but also because he himself, seeing their immediate relation to his present and future life, wishes to know them. He learns, in short, in order to survive – learns, for instance, which paths to follow and which to avoid, which berries are edible and which are poisonous. Accompanying his father, the son learns to hunt by actually killing animals, and his sister learns to bring up a family by sharing the household duties with her mother. The modern child's apathy toward education has precisely the opposite cause – his inability to connect the information he acquires in school with what he must know in order to work productively and enjoy himself in the course of his life. Whereas the primitive child is always in close touch with the adult version of the skill that he is learning, the modern pupil generally is physically and psychologically removed from the offices and factories that will use the knowledge and skills he is taught. Failing to see any immediate practicality in school learning, he often becomes listless and unruly. Indeed, this indifference to education is the mainspring of the pervasive indiscipline of American schools; if children could see more immediate value in what they were learning, they would be more eager to learn it.[6]

Dewey's progressivism, project methods, Winnetka Plan, 'Life Adjustment' and so on in the U.S.A., Hadow's curriculum in terms of 'activity and experience' in England, Khruschev's 'Life and Work' reforms in the U.S.S.R. and 'work-based' courses of the Brunton type in Scotland can all be seen as attempts to remedy this situation. None of them has proved to be conspicuously successful. One by one, they have come under attack from the traditionalists. It seems that there is something in the nature of the school as an institution in advanced industrial societies which is inimical to any child-centred theory and practice, and which violates some of the basic principles of developmental psychology. No matter how gently the five-year-old is initiated into the formal learning process, it is not long before shades of the prison house begin to close around him. Herded with inmates of his own age-group, supervised by a teacher who is *in loco parentis*, he is effectively cut off from home and neighbourhood for the greater part of his waking life, and has to adapt himself to a kind of vicarious existence. In the early stages, no doubt, the social benefits from organized play-way activities with children of the same age far outweigh those provided even in the best of homes. But as time goes on (and by then the youngster is conditioned to learning *in statu pupillari*) the substitution of a self-contained set of procedures for the on-going social life outside the school becomes more and more contrived. The 'divorce from life', as it is often called, is more marked in Britain than it ever has been in the U.S.A., the reason being that

> because of the way in which the school system developed, its slow expansion to meet the educational requirements of the mass of the population in a manner largely determined by ruling élites, the involvement of the church, and the type of multi-purpose authorities that control education at the local level, the school is to some extent isolated from the community.[7]

The difficulty of reconciling the child's spontaneous interests and felt needs with those which the education system decrees to be in his best interests in the long term is compounded by a certain duplicity which ensures that adult society invariably has the better of any arguments concerning the relationship between freedom and authority. In a revealing passage in *Ethics and Education*, R. S. Peters seeks to justify the imposition of adult authority ('the will of some individual to teach something which it is not agreed that anyone has any desire to know') thus:

> In the normative sense 'interests' is used both in a legalistic sense to speak of spheres of action or activity to which a person has a right, and in a more general sense to speak of those things which are both worthwhile and in some way appropriate for the individual in question, i.e. beneficial to him. When we speak of considering a person's interests we are using 'interest' in this latter normative sense. This is the sense of 'interest' which is being used when it is said that the school must be concerned with the interests of individual children. A teacher like a guardian in relation to a ward, who is mindful of children's interests, is not necessarily exercised about what they actually want or are interested in, or in their hobbies; he (or she) is concerned either about protecting them in what he thinks they have a right to pursue or with ensuring that they pursue what is worthwhile and suitable for them, i.e. beneficial for them. He therefore has to consider not only what in general is worthwhile pursuing but also what the potentialities and capacities are of the particular children for whom he is responsible.[8]

The reasoning here is as astringent as it is seemingly realistic, and most people, parents as well as teachers, would agree that it is the only possible line of thought to take. For all that, it exposes itself as a bleak doctrine. It boils down to saying that, when all is said and done, adults know best what is good for the child. For practical purposes there would be nothing to prevent the acceptance of this argument as incontrovertible were it not for the fact that experience shows the adult's claim to 'know what in general is worth pursuing' to be as ill-founded as his assessment of the child's 'potentialities and capacities' is more often than not grievously at fault. The admission that the teacher 'is not necessarily exercised about what they actually want or are interested in' is, to say the least of it, damaging.

Learning Situations into Life Situations

This ascription of the teacher's role may be normative in the legalistic sense, but in every other sense it must be reckoned arbitrary. It denotes a restrictive concept of the educational process which has already been found wanting, and which is heading for serious trouble if it is allowed to go unchallenged. As it is, adequate outlets for personal satisfaction are denied to many pupils in the school-learning situation with the result that alternative outlets are being sought. The vacuum in the affective life is being filled for better or for worse by the gutter press, by the not-so-hidden persuaders in the world of advertising, by profiteers in the pop music racket, by the mass media and other agencies. To protest that it is being exploited unscrupulously when the schools are prevented from doing anything about it by a theory and practice which debars them from trying is worse than ineffectual: it is ludicrous.

By our educational system we compel active children into passive adults. Numerous schools systematically (if unknowingly) destroy a living world of experience and substitute in its place an impressive, but dead, graveyard of facts. And why does this happen? It happens because we endeavour through education to preserve the *status quo* – and the *status quo* demands a certain sort of man: a man who strives after things, who is acquisitive and knows how to win: a man who is centred on Having not Being: who recognizes facts but is blind to experience.

It is true that before eleven in the nursery and primary schools, we allow the children their freedom. Education *really* begins in the secondary schools. Here the children are encouraged to discard their games and fantasies – and identities. They must now become serious. They must learn discipline, the ability to sit silently at a desk and take in the facts that the teachers give. In the evening the facts must be memorized or applied to small problems which can be marked and assessed the next day. Of course, the facts are important; armed with them the children stand a chance of winning, of beating their opponents and gaining the teacher's and parents' approval. And finally – after five years – there are the objective examinations which will objectively inform the children whether they have passed or failed, won or lost. . . . But either way, it doesn't matter, because, at the top or bottom, *success or failure*, the schools have succeeded in breaking them into the *status quo*. We have turned them from children into adults. The system has worked.[9]

How much longer will it take to convince curriculum planners that the education system now has to function under conditions very different from those for which it was designed? Today's adolescent feels older than his years. Rightly or wrongly, he resents being told what to do and when and how to do it. As never before, he knows a great deal more about what he wants – and where to get it. Increasingly, his is a do-it-yourself mentality. Accordingly, compliance with the requirements of school-bound learning does not come as easily as it used to. Ordered to get his hair cut by an irate headmaster, the contemporary youth's immediate reaction is apt to be one of defiance. Dumb insolence is on the way to becoming articulate. 'Why should I?' is fast becoming the kind of question which is seen to be not improper, admitting as it does of more than one answer. The 'lateral' transmission of culture by agencies outside the school has an enormous appeal out of all proportion to that of the 'vertical' transmission for which the school is responsible. As the young see it, the one stands for the pleasure-principle, the other for pain: the one is all for their delight, the other offers them promissory notes in return for a self-denying life of hard mental labour. Left to their own devices, marking time in an education system which deliberately defers their admission as full members of adult society, young people nowadays are creating their own initiation rites and ceremonials, hiving off in a separate culture, a culture which carries the placard 'ADULTS NOT ADMITTED', and whose motto is, 'Trust no one over the age of thirty'.

Time now to ask whither the argument is leading. Thus far it seems to be steering perilously close to the winds of anarchy and irrationalism. This is not its intention. Clearly, there is no excuse for any advocacy of 'thinking with the blood'. On the other hand, a curriculum which is designed to manipulate only the *external* conditions of learning for the sake of achieving a bloodless expertise lays itself wide open to the charge that it leaves too much to chance. At the cognitive level, of course, the teacher–pupil relationship admits of little or no equality; it is at the volitional level that the clash between the learner's legitimate interests and those which are held to be 'in his own interest' is liable to be most pronounced. At this level there *is* no inequality; if anything, the adolescent feels things more strongly and more acutely than does the adult. Without necessarily agreeing that childhood is the sleep of reason, there is a sense in which it can be said that this sensitivity and nervous energy supplies the driving force for learning in all its many forms. Where it is fully harnessed, the learning situation transforms itself into a life situation; what is learned is not only unforgettable but is so assimilated into the learner's personality as to become part of him. Where nervous energy is left running in neutral, however, it is dissipated sooner or later. This may not happen during the learner's school life, but eventually disillusion sets in and the seeds of anxiety are sown.

There are many ways in which school-bound learning can be seen to be anxiety-prone. One of them concerns the conflict set up between the learner's aspirations as an individual and those expected of him as a member of a group. In recent years, changes in organization and methods of teaching have brought about a significant shift away from competition in the classroom and more of a stress on the virtues of co-operation between pupils. Most educationists would agree that these changes are salutary. But although the shift has not gone anything like so far as the collectivism that is favoured in communist theory and practice, and although it has been accompanied by an insistence on the need to cater for individual differences, the effect, inevitably, has been to engender a near-schizophrenic state of mind as regards the aims of education. In Britain, more so perhaps than in other countries in the Western world, this split personality needs to be taken just as seriously as do the rival claims of general and special education or those which, a few years ago, occasioned the Two Cultures debate.

What is at stake is nothing less than the type of personality we want to see emerging, the British equivalent of the New Soviet

Man. Until we have made up our minds about *that*, none of the other objectives specified by the curriculum-makers will fall into place: as a nation, we shall be left threshing around in search of a role. One of the axioms of contemporary curriculum development asserts that the selection of objectives comes before the selection of subject-matter: in other words, the question 'What outcomes are desired?' necessarily precedes the question 'What are we going to teach?' Unfortunately, it is all-too evident that we have not made up our minds. We can only temporize, waiting for Godot or an ideology.

Meantime the young are left to sort things out for themselves in a tangle of school regulations which constantly leaves them in two minds. On the one hand, the pupil is sent to school to 'pay attention', to 'do his best' and get 'good marks', and is encouraged in all this by a system of rewards and punishments which emphasizes the need for ruthless competition. Passing the 11-plus examination may no longer be quite the terrifying hurdle it used to be, but its equivalents are still there in the shape of internal and external examinations which monitor the learner's cognitive progress from term to term and from year to year. Moreover, the pressures on him to 'do well', and the penalties for failure, become progressively more intense as he grows older.

On the other hand, the learner's role as a group-member calls for the wearing of a very different kind of face. Any pretensions to one-upmanship he may have as a scholar have to be dropped in favour of showing himself to be a good mixer. Instead of striving to outsmart his fellows, he is expected to cultivate team spirit, to accept decisions arrived at on a consensus basis, to lend a helping hand to his weaker brethren and even to follow the leadership of those who are his intellectual inferiors. In short, he has to come to terms with an entirely new set of incentives. That the latter are affective rather than cognitive can hardly be doubted, for all techniques for the investigation of the dynamics of interaction within groups, psycho-analytical as well as sociometric, agree in emphasizing the emotional components.

But the conflict between the individualistic and collectivist motives is insignificant compared with the major conflict between 'cerebral' and 'sensational' learning. Long latent, the latter has been activated – electrified – by the new technologies of communication which have opened up realms of experience previously inaccessible to the masses. This 'sensational' learning, and the culture to which it is giving rise, is in many ways more vivid, more immediate and more impactful than the 'cerebral' learning which is recognized in the schools. It exists in its own right, and vies with the other for equal recognition. So long as that recognition is withheld, however, the educational tug-of-war remains one-sided; the pupil's sense of duty in keeping his intellectual nose to the grindstone is all the time impaired by side-long, half-guilty glances at the goings-on around him.

The upshot of it all is a state of suppressed anxiety which gets worse as the pupil grows older. To begin with, admittedly, 'anxiety' is too strong a word: to talk of the 'prison house' seems manifestly absurd in view of the readiness with which most children take the primary stage in their stride. It is only at the secondary stage that anxiety becomes even faintly perceptible. Everyone is familiar with the all-too-common change of attitudes which occurs between the ages of eight and fifteen, the sad contrast between pupils who are as frisky as lambs and those who are as doughy as sheep, whose taste for school and all it stands for has somehow turned sour.

Never let it be forgotten that the word 'curriculum' is a derivative of 'curro' – 'I run'. He who runs may read, but does he have to follow a track which suits a few agile minds and provides heavy going for most of the others in the field? Does he have to abide by one set of rules? Does he need to apply a local anaesthetic to his senses? Keep his feelings in cold storage? Believe that his potentialities and capacities are strictly limited – intellectual and nothing more?

In each case, custom answers 'Yes'. No wonder that, as time goes on, the runners lose their freshness and many fall by the wayside. From start to finish they are dogged by fear – fear of losing face in the eyes of their whippers-in, fear of not being able to stay the pace or last the course, fear of not being able to take it, 'it' being a process of intellectual stretching to the point where it hurts. It is not surprising that so many decide that the game is not worth the candle and call it a day. If this is what lifelong learning means they have had their fill.

T. S. Eliot's *caveat* against the illusion of thinking that education makes people happier should not prevent us from asking whether it necessarily makes them positively miserable. Just how deeply the morale of the British people has been eroded as a result of the treatment they have received in schools during the past century and a half is anybody's guess. As Dr Wall has observed, 'Anxiety seems to impair performance more in complex than in simple tasks. The fear of failure inhibits search and may prevent it altogether.'[10]

At the risk of labouring the point, the greatest failing in the provision of education hitherto has been its wilful disregard of the learner's dispositions. Far from promoting the at-ease frame of mind which characterizes the typical American high school graduate, British education has had the effect of undermining confidence and belittling self-assurance. Without being so rash as to say that it has left us a nation of nervous wrecks, the damage done has been very considerable and possibly irreparable. How to cope with uncertainty, how to adapt to continuously changing circumstances, how to find worthy causes for strong feelings, above all, how to think well of oneself – these are some of the life-situations which children have to face now, not in the near future. As things stand, the education system is incompetent to deal with any of them, and lets them go by default.

Attempts to convert learning situations into life situations by simulation and gaming go part of the way, but nothing like far enough. Airing problems by playing with them has a therapeutic value, but in the last resort is bound to lead only to next-best-thing solutions. In any case, it is not evident how the lessons learned through simulation exercises, no matter how realistic these may be, can be transferred and applied in the contexts of life as it is lived. To say this is not to disparage the growing use of simulation techniques in the classroom, simply to insist that more fundamental approaches will be needed if there is to be any chance of pupils feeling in their bones that what they are learning is vital and worthwhile.

Then how is it to be done? So long as the prevailing climate of opinion is that things are not half so bad as the argument alleges, it cannot be done. If there is to be a change of heart, it is not likely to occur in educational thought, which remains as obdurate as it is complacent; it can only be effected by the young people themselves. Their drive, their zest, their aggressive independence afford the best hopes for the overthrow of the age-old monopoly of 'cerebral' culture. As it is, any fundamental reform of the curriculum has to be ruled out as being practically unthinkable. Unthinkable, for example, that most of the trouble in school-bound learning emanates from the teacher himself; unthinkable, too, that the educational services are over-staffed. Unthinkable only because vested interests brainwash public opinion into thinking that there is a chronic shortage of teachers. Referring to the largely unquestioned assumptions made by those who are in charge of the educational services, Dr Briault notes that

> It is the basic assumption of almost all concerned, at any rate with school education, that there should be more teachers and smaller classes. The worst anathemas are reserved for those few education authorities who save money in hard times by cutting down on the number of teachers they employ. Yet how far can and should and need the pupil/teacher ratio be improved? In the area of my Authority in primary schools it is already one to 26·8 and in the secondary schools one to 16·6. I suspect that in the sixth forms up and down the country as a whole the actual pupil/teacher ratio, counting simply the numbers of pupils taught and the teachers teaching them in the sixth forms, is as favourable as in the universities. At some point – though we have certainly not reached this in the primary schools – a judgement will have to be made that enough is enough.[11]

Another assumption which is more vain than valid concerns the over-possessive 'me and my children' attitude shared by most teachers. Yet another might be called the 'me and my subject' complex. So far as the majority of non-academic pupils are concerned, it appears that none of these assumptions holds good any more in the secondary school. If so, the prognosis for future development must be in the direction of the school as a resources-for-learning centre in which teachers will be content to remain discreetly in the background, if not to absent themselves altogether.

Given the requisite grounding in literacy and numeracy in the primary school (where more teachers *are* needed) and a generous provision of high-quality learning materials and equipment it is possible to envisage a secondary school organized on open-plan lines in which pupils would be free to come and go and take their pick more or less as they pleased. An à *la carte* curriculum, then? With teachers reduced to the roles of youth leaders? Offensive as the suggestion is to the wiseacres, we might do worse than agree that the young are as capable of judging what is good for them as we are, and that the time is coming when there may be nothing else for it but to give them the tools and leave them to get on with the job of learning which our pussyfoot practice has so consistently bungled.

REFERENCES

1 K. R. Krathwohl, B. S. Bloom and B. B. Masia, *The Affective Domain*, Taxonomy of Educational Objectives, Handbook 11 (New York, David McKay, 1964).
2 Robert M. Gagné, *The Conditions of Learning* (New York, Holt, Rinehart & Winston, 1967), Preface.
3 ibid., p. 23.
4 ibid., p. 5.
5 Max Nicholson, *The System: The Mismanagement of Modern Britain* (London, Hodder & Stoughton, 1967), pp. 350-1.
6 George F. Kneller, *Educational Anthropology* (New York, Wiley, 1965), pp. 75-6.
7 W. Taylor, 'Learning to live with neighbours', in W. R. Niblett (Ed.), *How and Why do we Learn?* (London, Faber & Faber, 1965), p. 125.

8 R. S. Peters, *Ethics and Education* (London, Allen & Unwin, 1966), p. 168.
9 Peter Abbs, *English for Diversity* (London, Heinemann, 1969), Introduction, p. ix.
10 W. D. Wall, 'Learning to think', in W. R. Niblett, op. cit., p. 74.
11 W. H. T. Briault, National Council for Educational Technology, Occasional Paper No. 2 (1969).

CHAPTER SEVEN

Aims and/or Objectives?

DEATH IS THE ONLY TERMINAL BEHAVIOUR

It may be thought that the previous chapter made heavy weather of an argument which was stated much more eloquently and convincingly in the Harvard Committee's Report, *General Education in a Free Society*:

> Education must look to the whole man. It has been wisely said that education aims at the good man, the good citizen, and the useful man. By a good man is meant one who possesses an inner integration, poise and firmness, which in the long run come from an adequate philosophy of life. Personal integration is not a fifth characteristic in addition to the other four and co-ordinate with them; it is their proper fruition. The aim of liberal education is the development of the whole man; and human nature involves instincts and sentiments as well as the intellect. Two dangers must be mentioned. First, there is the danger of identifying intelligence with the qualities of the so-called intellectual type – with bookishness and the manipulation of concepts. We have tried to guard against this mistake by stressing the traits of relevant judgement and discrimination of values in effective thinking. Second, we must remember that intelligence even when taken in its widest sense, does not exhaust the total potentialities of human nature. Man is not a contemplative being alone. Why is it, then, that education is conceived as primarily an intellectual enterprise when, in fact, human nature is so complex? For instance, man has his emotions and his drives and his will; why should education centre on the training of his intellect? The answer is found in the truth that intelligence is not a special function (or not

that only) but a way in which all human powers may function. Intelligence is that leaven of awareness and reflection which, operating upon the native powers of men, raises them from the animal level and makes them truly human. By reason we mean, not an activity apart, but rational guidance of all human activity. Thus the fruit of education is intelligence in action. The aim is mastery of life; and since living is an art, wisdom is the indispensable means to this end.[1]

If the style of writing in this passage now strikes us as being slightly dated, and the vein of thought a shade too rhapsodical, it is because the trend of events during the past twenty years has brought about a rather different persuasion. It is no accident that phrases like 'mastery of life' are now regarded with suspicion, that words like 'wisdom' are shunned, and that it has become fashionable to denigrate such statements as 'Education must look to the whole man'. In the same way that philosophic thought went through a period of linguistic analysis in which the perennial questions concerning the nature of man and the universe were jettisoned as being unanswerable, so educational thought is at present in no mood to settle for nebulous aims. Unsure what is meant by the 'good man', or even the 'good citizen', it would rather set its sights on more obviously tangible accomplishments. In short, aims are 'out', and objectives are very decidedly 'in'.

This way of looking at educational problems is becoming increasingly popular and seems certain to become predominant in an age which takes its cues from the achievements of scientific technology. When John F. Kennedy made the decision which led to the first moon landing he was, however unwittingly, lending his support to an educational theory and practice which had been gaining ground both in the fields of curriculum development and programmed learning in the U.S.A. The spectacular success of the Apollo missions is, of course, only one example of the way in which technological expertise is coming to be seen as a miracle-worker, but if only because it is fresh in the memory the reasons for its spellbinding appeal are worth considering.

In fact, Kennedy's decision provides a perfect illustration of how to state a clearly defined objective. The outcome, placing a man on the lunar surface within the space of ten years, was plainly visible. The means of achieving it were known and allowed of the necessary prediction and control. Once the decision had been taken, all the available resources of brainpower, equipment, skills and money could be harnessed in a nation-wide combined operation which had this single end-point in view. The result, as the world knows, was an impressive demonstration of the ability to tackle seemingly impossible tasks. Critics who complain that space exploration represents a colossal waste of resources which might have been devoted, instead, to cancer research, say, or to alleviating hunger and disease in the underdeveloped countries, are barking up the wrong tree – and might as well bay at the moon. Why so? Because even if the same resources *had* been diverted to such deserving, humanitarian causes, there is no guarantee that any clear-cut solutions would have been forthcoming. On ethical grounds this may be no justification of the rightness of the decision; on pragmatic grounds it is easy to see why the temptation to go all-out for an objective which was clearly achievable and promised a handsome pay-off in terms of national prestige proved to be irresistible.

At the outset, however, it is necessary to distinguish between those kinds of problem in which the solution can be foreseen and defined in terms of actual performance, and those in which it is not possible to satisfy either of these conditions. In the one case, objectives can be stated so specifically as to leave no room for doubt as to what has to be done and how it is going to be done; in the other, because of the huge uncertainty principle involved, aims can only be expressed in terms of faith, hope and charity. In the one, the terminal behaviour, if not exactly known, can at least be envisaged; in the other, there is no closure to the problem which remains permanently open-ended.

Teachers, like politicians, prefer policies which look like leading to clear-cut solutions. Like politicians, too, they spend most of their time in procedures which seem to be getting nowhere and which bring no visible returns. Any technique of instruction which holds out the prospect of yielding measurable results, therefore, is bound to be appealing, as is a learning theory which delivers the goods in problem-solving.

But the distinction drawn between problems which have a definite end-point and those whose nature is indefinite mirrors the distinction between training and education. Training can be completed. Its criteria are satisfied once the learner is seen to be capable of performing tasks which were not within his competence at the beginning of the course of instruction. Education, on the other hand, must always be an unfinished business for which death is the only terminal behaviour.

The current vogue for stating educational objectives in behavioural terms has arisen from a number of widely separated sources. The first of these may be located in the work of educationists like Ralph Tyler in the U.S.A. which stresses the need for accurate assessment and measurement of the information, concepts, skills, etc., acquired by pupils as a result of following courses of instruction. A second source can be traced to an economic-industrial base where it finds its expression in a whole range of input–output techniques – cost-benefit analysis, operational research, systems engineering, job evaluation *et al.* – all of which require that the end-point (objective) be known before the problem can be formulated. Not surprisingly, in view of the size and complexity of the educational services, there is a growing demand for the application of the same techniques which have been found to be effective in the management of other large-scale enterprises. As the author has written in another context,

> Education is *the* great service enterprise, if only we could bring ourselves to see it that way. To the extent that it brings about changes in people (leaving aside for the moment what these changes are and how they are brought about), it is productive in precisely the same way as any other service – or for that matter any manufacturing process – is said to be productive. Children enter the school system at five and emerge ten, fifteen or twenty years later after undergoing a process of formal instruction and social training which affects them

in a variety of ways. To declare that we have no way of assessing these effects is tantamount to saying that we do not know what we are trying to do.²

A third source, and the one which has probably been most influential in popularizing 'objectives' at the expense of 'aims', is to be found in the movement launched in the 1950s under the name of programmed learning. The movement, which quickly became world-wide, has had its vicissitudes and several of the so-called basic principles enunciated by its early proponents have had to be quietly shelved in the light of research findings. The need for small steps, for write-in responses, for low error rates and for self-pacing – these are only some of the features of programmed learning which have been scrapped. 'A programmer, nowadays, seeks to arrange an environment within which learning activities appropriate to the programme's objectives are provided',³ we are informed – which sounds pretty amorphous to say the least. In practice, however, the mapping out of objectives is anything but amorphous; the more carefully it is done the less room it leaves for uncertainty in the minds of instructor and pupil alike. As Mager puts it:

> A statement of an objective is useful to the extent that it specifies what the learner must be able to DO or PERFORM when he is demonstrating his mastery of the objective. Since we cannot see into another's mind what he knows, we can only determine the state of his intellect or skill by observing some aspect of his behaviour or performance (we are using the term behaviour to mean overt action). Now, the behaviour or performance of the learner may be verbal or non-verbal. He may be asked to respond to questions verbally or in writing, or be asked to demonstrate his ability to perform a certain skill, or be asked to solve certain kinds of problems. But whatever the method used, you (the programmer) can only infer the state or condition of his intellect through observations of his performance.
>
> Thus, the most important characteristic of a useful objective is that it *identifies the kind of performance* which will be accepted as evidence that the learner has achieved the objective.⁴

Aims and/or Objectives?

In so far as a statement of objectives makes it plain what the learner is expected to do, well and good; Mager is right in insisting that the contract between instructor and pupil ought to be a two-way affair; right, too, in thinking that, more often than not, the teacher's avowed aims only serve to keep pupils guessing or utterly in the dark. Again, he is within his rights in warning against the use of equivocal words and phrases – words like 'understanding' and 'appreciation', phrases like 'the ability to think for oneself', 'the habitual vision of greatness' or that old favourite 'educating the whole man' – which, however well-meaning, are not readily verifiable in practice. Thus, instead of saying that the aim of a science lesson is 'to develop a thorough understanding of the theory of combustion', the teacher is recommended to list his objectives as a set of operations which the pupils will be able to carry out under given conditions, for example:

1] Tell one way that a scientist might attempt to answer the question, 'What is necessary for combustion?'
2] Demonstrate how water can be made to boil in a dish made of paper without burning the paper.
3] State several hypotheses (guesses) as to why the paper will not burn in the demonstration.
4] Conduct experiments to determine which hypothesis is correct.
5] Tell how a scientist might explain the results of the experiments which you have conducted.
6] Tell how the findings of your experiments might be put to practical use.

This operational approach has many advantages, not least in checking the pupils' progress and ensuring that they are, in fact, learning what they are supposed to be learning. It lays down guidelines which are so well delineated as to leave no one in any doubt about the way ahead. It provides an exhaustive inventory of the course's content and hence facilitates the testing of pupils both during the course and after its completion.

With behavioural technology pressing its claims, a hardening of this conviction that teachers had better cut their losses as regards any profession of ultimate aims has to be anticipated. Increasingly, the advice proffered is that summarized by Derek Rowntree:

> State your objectives in *concrete* terms. *Specify* the *behaviour* that you require from your student. Tell him what you want in terms of *observable, measurable performance*. Give him actual examples of the kind of situation he'll be able to deal with successfully (i.e. the criterion test).
>
> Only with your objectives stated in precise, measurable terms can you ever demonstrate whether you've succeeded in teaching what you set out to teach. Saying that your student will 'have a flair for', or 'acquire a deeper understanding of' will help no one (not even you) unless you go on to say just how you'll recognize it once you've got it. *If you find this difficult to do, you may be getting close to discovering why students find the subject difficult.*[5]

So far as short-term practice is concerned this advice is sound enough. It is all to the good that the teacher and his pupils know exactly how they stand, where they are going and how to get there at the end of the day. The trouble begins when it comes to transferring from immediate, concrete objectives to higher-order ones which are not so amenable to prediction and control. As Rowntree says, these may include such objectives as, 'That the student will remain interested in the subject', 'That he will continue to be confident and at ease in handling it', 'That his confidence will help him to get on better with his colleagues', 'That the experience of successful learning will help him in other attempts to learn', 'That his loyalty will increase' and so on – all of which, significantly, he calls 'hopes'.

The cat is out of the bag at last, it seems. For while it may be true that the difficulty of stating higher-order objectives with the same clarity and certitude that characterize short-term ones does not absolve the teacher from the duty of trying to find ways and means of achieving them, it is a fallacy to suppose that this is always possible. Pask and Lewis rightly make the point that the specification of a terminal behaviour (that is, listing the observable capabilities which the learner is expected to acquire) is naïve, since what is required is, rather, a whole repertoire of behaviours. This being so, 'an optimal teaching system must frequently operate at several levels of discourse at once. And the model or theory which specifies the teaching routine accordingly must have the same multi-level structure.'[6]

Fixing higher-order objectives and devising criterion tests for them is somewhat easier in mathematical, scientific and technical subjects than it is in the humanities, which explains why nine out of ten programmes and most of the major curriculum development projects to date have dealt with the former group. The question arises as to whether the difference between the two fields of inquiry (and the difference between tightly stipulated objectives and loosely worded aims) is a difference in kind or only one of degree. When it comes to discriminating between *Geisteswissenschaften* and *Naturwissenschaften* is it a case of oil and water?

One of the cherished beliefs of the discipline-centred school of thought is that every branch of study has its own distinctive 'logic' or 'grammar'. The prescription is summed up in Bruner's oft-quoted assertion that 'the curriculum of a subject should be determined by the most fundamental understanding that can be achieved of the underlying principles that give structure to that subject'.[7] In the voluminous literature of curriculum theory it would be hard to think of a sentence which has been more widely acclaimed or more influential than this. If its advice is sound, the first duty of the subject-specialist and the curriculum-maker (ideally one and the same person) is to analyse the particular branch of knowledge with which he is concerned so as to make explicit its conceptual and procedural character; in other words, to lay bare its substantive content, types of proposition, tests for truth, criteria for evidence and methodology which give the subject its distinctive explanatory power. Having done this, he can determine the contribution his subject is likely to make to global educational objectives (personal satisfaction, social competence, occupational skills, etc.) and then proceed to select a sequence of appropriate learning experiences which will achieve these objectives.

What seems to have escaped notice is the fact that Bruner's advice contains a number of anomalies. In the first place, it is not clear what has to be inferred from the idea of 'underlying principles', or whether the 'principles' adduced, say, by a physicist hold good for a historian – or, for that matter, a chemist. In the second, any 'fundamental understanding' of the nature of a particular branch of knowledge is arrived at as the culmination of long years of study; it is not something which can be given to the learner ready-made at the start of his career. True, the learner is less likely to be bewildered and daunted by the difficulty of the subject if he is provided with a skeleton framework on which the multifarious bits and pieces of knowledge can be arranged and seen to have related significance. Admirable as the intention may seem, however, the suggestion that young children should learn history or physics by being introduced to the ways in which the research scholar and the trained scientist go about their business is essentially reactionary; it violates the 'principles' of developmental psychology. For all its fine airs, this policy of making explicit the conceptual framework of the field of study is no more than a revised version of Herbartian pedagogy; it is emphatically not the kind of policy which has generated a sense of purpose and creative energy in child art. Innovators of the calibre of Marion Richardson and Robin Tanner were not the kind of teachers who wracked their brains in search of 'underlying principles' which would serve as guidelines for the young artist-craftsman. On the contrary, Marion Richardson suggested

> that the children should be allowed to paint what they liked and not be given subjects or models. The results of this, as it then seemed, wildly revolutionary policy was that young children began to produce paintings which many adult art critics found very exciting. They typically set about painting a picture without a moment's pause, with extraordinary confidence and apparently with a clear purpose in their minds.[8]

Thirdly, the notion of 'structure' calls for closer scrutiny than it has yet received. If the assumption is that it is static, like the ground plan of a house or an engineer's blue-print, then it has to be rejected as misleading. The notion of 'structure' as frozen process is invalid. It may be the case that the internal logic of mathematical, scientific and technical subjects can be reduced to a set of rule-of-thumb statements, but this cannot be done, or cannot usefully be done, in fields of knowledge where the 'structure' is dynamic. It may be relatively easy to jot down what trigonometry is about on the back of an envelope, but to do this for English literature is rather like saying that *Moby Dick* is about the killing of a whale.

The discipline-centred approach, programmed learning, task analysis and techniques for problem-solving all abjure the muddling-through, by-guess-and-by-God methods of traditional practice, and agree on the need to state objectives in behavioural terms. In doing so, however, it seems that they are bound to foster convergent habits of thinking and convergent frames of mind. An objective, by definition, is an end-point which admits of no divergence if it is to be attained. If the current trend towards a deterministic theory of education is to be arrested, the conclusion must be that the difference between *Naturwissenschaften* and *Geisteswissenschaften* really *is* one of kind. And the corollary must be that a distinction has to be drawn between statements of objectives and statements of aims.

Behavioural technology, like any other technology, is amoral. It may provide answers as to what can be done in education, but can never pronounce on questions regarding what ought to be done.

> Questions regarding the aims or objectives of an educational system are like those regarding a specific program. They are not questions of scientific fact. They are questions in the area of the philosophy of education. No matter how much information we acquire about the control of human behaviour, there are important non-scientific questions concerning who should exercise control and the purposes to be realized by that control.

The distinction I am making works both ways. Empirical scientific investigation of the factors influencing behaviour does not settle scientific questions about the aims of education. Nor does philosophic inquiry about the aims of education settle any questions of fact regarding the most efficient method of attaining those aims.

The view that man's behaviour is determined is an important premise to work with, but it does not settle any of the important questions in philosophy. Among other things, a philosophy of education will specify the aims of an educational system for individuals who are to learn certain ways of behaviour, and are to learn certain subjects. The individual being educated makes many responses to stimuli, but the individual is not a mere aggregate of stimulus-response connections. It is not responses that go to school but individuals who make responses. The philosophy of education requires a more satisfactory concept of the individual than we obtain simply by studying stimulus-response-reinforcement patterns. Of course, the science of behaviour also requires some such concept.

The study of astronomy is quite different from the study of the behaviour of astronomers. The satellite Mariner was not sent around the world to examine the behaviour of astronomers. It was sent up to examine the behaviour of Venus. Our knowledge of astronomy is certainly created by the efforts of astronomers. But the subject of astronomy cannot be reduced to the astronomers' behaviour any more than a piece of beefsteak can be reduced by the act of chewing. In short, the philosophy of education must go beyond the science of behaviour in formulating a concept of the subject to be taught to individuals.[9]

Were it not for the growing tendency to see education as a practical activity which is preoccupied with techniques derived from the social sciences, it would scarcely be necessary to remind ourselves of the cogency of this viewpoint. Far from commanding universal assent, however, the assertion that empiricism is essentially neutral and to that extent subordinate to value-judging, now finds itself assailed on all sides.

Yet, while acknowledging that the widespread impatience with woolly theories and muddled practice is well-founded, there *is* something to be said on behalf of loosely expressed aims. As R. S.

Peters avers, 'On occasions there is point even in enunciating tautologies such as "the function of government is to govern"; so the fact that "education is of the whole man" is a conceptual truth imprecisely expressed is not necessarily a reason for avoiding such a remark.'[10]

What could be more dismal than a language of educational discourse which excluded words like 'understanding' and 'appreciation' from its vocabulary: what more arid than an educational practice which found no place for inspired guesswork, for unexpected flair or for acts of faith. Like it or lump it, education is an activity which people engage in without being absolutely sure what it is they are trying to do. It is, therefore, a disservice to planning to pretend that routes leading to desired outcomes can be laid down in advance. It is an even greater disservice to pupils to disguise the fact that the learning process is hedged about with uncertainties, since learning to live with uncertainty may well be reckoned the ultimate aim of education, 'that for the sake of which everything else is done'.

Objectives are like targets. The nearer they are, the easier they are to hit. By taking thought, higher-order objectives are hittable, too, though not so reliably. Where higher-order objectives shade off into ultimate aims, however, visible targets disappear and we are left to gaze at over-the-horizon prospects which are more like Eldorados, Promised Lands beckoning us forwards as mistily as mirages. Route-finding in this situation is much more a matter of creating paths where none exist than it is of firm prediction – more a matter of travelling hopefully than of heading for a known destination.

Hindsight shows that educational outcomes are sometimes the very reverse of what was intended. The generation gap and the drop-outs are only two of the more striking examples of outcomes which were not bargained for by the planners. The recent 'swing' towards arts courses in universities at a time when the country's need for skilled scientific and technological manpower was acute is another; the drift towards agnosticism, despite the provision of compulsory religious instruction in schools, yet another. It is now generally agreed that the most sophisticated economic and demographic projections which can be made have enormous margins of error built into them.

Unfortunately, with systems as large, as uncertain and as complex as the economy and the educational system, it is unlikely that any single prediction will be highly accurate and both planning and the use of models is likely to be discredited. In order to overcome this difficulty, alternative plans may be produced corresponding, for example, to several different rates of growth. This is an improvement since it at least admits uncertainty about what is going to happen. However, faced with a number of projections, the planner is confused about what action to take. Consequently one plan is chosen from the alternatives and the uncertainty is effectively eliminated again.

It might be suggested that this approach should nevertheless be welcomed since it is a considerable advance upon previous unsystematic methods of making decisions. However plausible this argument might be, we think it is fallacious to proceed as if the future were certain and as if we must calculate what is going to happen before we decide what to do. We believe that the problem is not to decide what is going to happen in order to contemplate action, but rather to decide what to do knowing that the future is uncertain and that a 'spectrum' of outcomes is possible.[11]

In the opinion of the authors of *Decision Models for Educational Planning*, the necessary conditions for successful planning do not at present exist, mainly because of the lack of any clear formulation of objectives. To what extent this can be remedied in the construction of more refined models which take into account the interrelations and reciprocity between events, information, objectives and decisions remains to be seen.

The fact that things rarely turn out as anticipated is neither surprising nor upsetting. As I write this sentence I know exactly how it is going to end; the interval between its formulation in my mind and the penning of the last word is a matter of moments. I am rather less positive about when or how the next paragraph will be finished, still less so about the ending of the next chapter. There may (will) be interruptions and distractions. I may find myself bogged down in one of those blank periods when the urge to write anything at all deserts me, when words go lame and sheet after sheet of manuscript paper has to be consigned to the waste-bin. In a general sort of way, of course, I know what it is I wish to say, but there is many a slip between wishing, intending, deciding and doing. Even the near future is indeterminate. I acknowledge this when I say that I am 'aiming to' dig the garden at the week-end, that I am 'thinking of' taking a holiday abroad next summer or that I 'have a notion to' take a trip round the world one day. The longer the interval between the decision and its eventual outcome, the greater the gap between certainty and uncertainty becomes. No amount of technological forecasting can change the human situation in this respect. The ideal it is working towards is the well-programmed, predictable man, the astronaut whose position in space-time can be plotted with the nth degree of accuracy on a journey which may take a lifetime, and whose every reaction is as reliable as that of the instruments with which he is coupled. No longer a fantasy of science fiction, this ideal of the man whose life-schedule is controlled by machines is nevertheless remote from reality and needs to be contested.

It is often said that all learning has a future reference. This is a convenient half-truth. It is true from the point of view of instruction and the instructor, not necessarily true of learning and the learner.

> Do we teach algebra, or reading, or logic so that the student can perform these skills *now*, without any concern for the future? When we attempt to impart an appreciation for music, are we only concerned that the appreciation be done *during* the course, during the period of our influence? No. We are far more concerned with influencing how the student is able to perform *after* the course is over, *after* our influence is discontinued. We try to instil an appreciation for music *now* so that the student will behave appreciatively *after* our help has been withdrawn.[12]

This is so obviously the case that there would be no point in querying it but for one thing. From the student's point of view, and particularly the young child's, the essence of the learning experience is its immediacy. Too often, the requirement that he learn A in order to do B only serves to awaken that conflict between *opus* and *labor* which Rousseau was the first to note.

Advocates of child-centred methods of teaching prefer to think that the most effective learning is engaged in for its own sake; they urge the sheer impossibility of educating pupils for a future which cannot be anticipated. 'Life now!', 'Treat the child according to his age', 'the insistent present' – these are some of their well-worn slogans. By contrast, the discipline-centred approach is based on the conviction that children can best be prepared for their roles in adult society by subjecting them to graded courses of instruction, the relevance of which need not depend upon their immediate appeal. Although there are other important differences between the two schools of thought, not least in their incompatible interpretations of freedom and authority, the fundamental difference is between a philosophy which is content to leave the learner's development, as it were, in the lap of the gods, and one which is determined to control that development by all the means at its disposal. It is the difference between being satisfied with a loosely expressed aim and working to a set of predetermined objectives.

To specify an objective is to state in no uncertain fashion what has to be done and what is certainly going to be done, come what may. To profess an aim is more in the nature of an act of faith; it presupposes an intention which carries with it no guarantee of its being fulfilled. In so far as the existence of free will can be posited, and with it the learner's right to self-determination, it seems that the cult of objectives is implicated in a theory of social engineering which treats education, training and conditioning as one and the same process. On the other hand, any reliance on loosely expressed aims seems to be equally remiss in that it leaves the learner to his own devices and hence at the mercy of natural consequences. To be sure, it is never an either-or choice between the two alternatives which the teacher has to make. Nevertheless, when the chips are down, there can be no doubt as to the side on which his commitment has to be made.

Peters aptly remarks that

> To ask for an aim is to ask for a more precise specification of what an action or activity is. We ask people what they are aiming at when they seem rather confused about their purposes or when they are drawing up a plan of campaign and have to formulate what they intend to do in a coherent way. Asking a person about his aims is a method of getting him to concentrate or clear his mind about what he is trying to do. . . . To ask questions about the aims of education is therefore a way of getting people to get clear about and focus their attention on what is worthwhile achieving. It is not to ask for the production of ends extrinsic to education which might explain their activities as educators. Aims can be high level or low level. A teacher can write down in his lesson notes that his aim in the coming lesson is to reach the end of Exercise 6, or to get his pupils to speak some Latin, or grasp something about ancient Rome. Or he may say that his aim is to train their character a bit by making them cope with a difficult unseen. But whatever he says he is aiming at, the formulation of his aim is an aid to making his activity more structured and coherent by isolating an aspect under which he is acting. It is not something which he does in order to explain what he is doing; it is, rather, a more precise specification of it.[13]

It cannot escape notice that there is a world of difference between making sure that pupils reach the end of Exercise 6 and trusting that their character will be trained a bit in the process. It is not simply that the first objective can easily be put to the test and seen to have been achieved, and that the other cannot. It is not simply that the one requires only a short space of time for its completion whereas the other is so much more indefinite. The vital difference lies in the degree of latitude which is granted in a statement of aim and largely denied in a statement of objective. Nothing concentrates the mind so wonderfully as the knowledge that one is going to be hanged in the morning, said Dr Johnson, and by the same token nothing is calculated to focus the learner's attention so surely as the realization that he has no option but to do what he is told. In the sense that something is being done to him which he is powerless to prevent, the child who is in *statu pupillari* is in much the same position as the man who is about to be hanged. That is to say, the clearer and more coherent the teacher's specification of aim becomes, the greater will be his chances of getting pupils to do what is wanted of them. If behavioural technology had its way, presumably, the margin of error between the teacher's intentions and the actual outcomes would disappear, or at any rate be drastically reduced, and the result would be an unashamed process of conditioning.

Mercifully, in education as in life, there are so many loopholes and loose ends as to rule out the feasibility (but not the possibility) of anything so tidy as human engineering. As teachers have learned to their cost, pupils are very far from being defenceless; they have their own escape mechanisms, their own ideas about where they want to go and what they propose to do. They are prepared to submit to discipline (having things done to them) only to the extent that it opens the door to the pursuit of ends of their own choosing. For the rest, education is something they are quite capable of getting for themselves. In the current vogue for behavioural objectives there is a danger of overlooking the truth so pithily stated half a century ago by Sir Percy Nunn: 'Character is largely what a person makes out of his temperament, just as the learning he may acquire is what he makes out of his cognitive abilities.'[14]

But to say that education is full of loose ends is no excuse for relapsing into a happy-go-lucky Micawberism. The acceptance of loose ends is not the same as being at a loose end. It implies a proverbial truth – to wit, that the most that can be done is to lead the horse to the water. What happens thereafter is beyond the teacher's control and strictly none of his business.

In fact, regardless of the subject that is being taught, there is one overriding objective which must always be borne in mind – namely, to leave the learner at least as well disposed towards the subject at the end of the course as he was at the beginning. Unfortunately, all the indications point to the conclusion that this is the one objective which is normally not achieved, thanks to aversive practices which all too often defeat the teacher's high-minded purposes and which make life difficult for himself and his pupils. And yet . . .

> There once was a teacher
> Whose principal feature
> Was hidden in quite an odd way.
> Students by millions
> Or possibly zillions
> Surrounded him all of the day.
>
> When finally seen
> By his scholarly dean
> And asked how he managed the deed,
> He lifted three fingers
> And said, 'All you swingers
> Need only to follow my lead.
>
> To rise from a zero
> To Big Campus Hero
> To answer these questions you'll strive:
> Where am I going,
> How shall I get there, and
> How'll I know I've arrived?'

If only it were as easy as Mager's light-hearted doggerel[15] would have us believe! Even so, he earns credit for pointing out how few teachers recognize an 'approach response' when they see one and how many teachers adopt a style which can only be described as positively discouraging. It needs no detailed affect analysis of everyday practice in British schools to prove that the learning situation is, for many, punitive, and, for some, nothing less than degrading. Corporal punishment may be on the way out, but violence of the tongue still runs rife in our classrooms. For instance:
  'You, there – what do you think you are doing?'
  'You probably won't understand this, but . . .'

'How can you be so stupid?'
'I shouldn't have to tell you that . . .'
'If you don't do better than this at least half of you will fail.' – etc., etc.

No teacher, it may be hoped, is deliberately heartless. Many, it may be feared, give the appearance of being so unintentionally, and go about their business in a manner which is in some way or other hurtful. To be fair, however, it has to be conceded that most teachers nowadays are prepared for far more give and take than would have been deemed proper in the quasi-authoritarian régimes of the nineteenth century. The signs are that they will need to 'give' less and 'take' a great deal more in the future. One of the emergent axioms in curriculum planning which is hard to take affirms that the emphasis is shifting from the teacher as instructor to the teacher as a manager of learning situations. Harder still is the admission that, as manager, he is no longer boss.

In the black-out which has followed the eclipse of a religious view of life it may seem that there is no place for acts of faith in education, and that in the absence of any agreed absolute values there is nothing for it but to cut adrift from starry-eyed ideals and settle for viable objectives. As to that, there can be only one answer:

> That low man seeks a little thing to do,
> Sees it and does it:
> This high man, with a great thing to pursue,
> Dies ere he knows it.
>
> That low man goes on adding one to one,
> His hundred's soon hit:
> This high man, aiming at a million,
> Misses an unit.

Education needs its high men. They are the ones who persist in the search for the Good Life knowing that it is endless, the ones who exhibit the supreme virtue of preserving their minds, and their options, open.

REFERENCES

1 *General Education in a Free Society*, Report of the Harvard Committee (Cambridge, Mass., Harvard University Press, 1945).
2 W. Kenneth Richmond, *The Education Industry* (London, Methuen, 1969), p. 61.
3 G. O. M. Leith, *Second Thoughts on Programmed Learning*, National Council for Educational Technology, Occasional Paper No. 1 (1969).
4 R. F. Mager, *Preparing Instructional Objectives* (Palo Alto, Calif., Fearon, 1967), p. 13.
5 Kenneth Rowntree, *Basically Branching* (London, Macdonald, 1966), p. 83.
6 G. Pask and B. Lewis, 'Theory and practice of adaptive teaching systems', in R. Glaser (Ed.), *Teaching Machines and Programmed Learning*, 11 (D.A.V.I., 1965), p. 237.
7 Jerome Bruner, *The Process of Education* (Cambridge, Mass., Harvard University Press, 1960), p. 31.
8 *Inside the Primary School* (London, H.M.S.O., 1967), p. 112.
9 J. W. Blyth, 'Programmed instruction and the philosophy of education', in G. D. Ofiesh and W. C. Meierhenry (Eds.), *Trends in Programmed Instruction* (D.A.V.I., 1964), pp. 12–13.
10 R. S. Peters, *Ethics and Education* (London, Allen & Unwin, 1966), p. 32.
11 P. Armitage. C. Smith and P. Alper, *Decision Models for Educational Planning*, L.S.E. Studies in Education (London, Allen Lane The Penguin Press, 1969), pp. 3–4.
12 P. Nunn, *Education: Its Data and First Principles* (London, Arnold, 1920), p. 132.
13 R. S. Peters, op. cit.
14 P. Nunn, op. cit.
15 R. F. Mager, *Developing Attitude Toward Learning*, VII (Palo Alto, Calif., Fearon, 1968).

CHAPTER EIGHT

What Knowledge is of any Worth?

Strange bedfellows as they sometimes are, the advocates of educational reform like to think of themselves as forming an *avant garde*. Those who rallied to the banner first hoisted by Skinner under the name of programmed learning, and those who later swelled the ranks of the movement which has gone from strength to strength under the title of educational technology, would be very surprised if anyone queried their claim to be breakers of new ground. Similarly, the followers of leaders like Ralph Tyler and Jerome Bruner might well be taken aback if it were suggested to them that in pressing forward with the work of curriculum development they were bent on pursuing courses which in some respects might be styled as reactionary. Adherents of these allied movements, many of whom have a foot in both camps, never tire of pointing to their achievements. Among other things, have they not demonstrated the importance of defining teaching objectives in operational terms, the importance of analysing subject-matter in order to highlight its conceptual framework and the importance of devising more sensitive and sophisticated assessment procedures than the crude ones which teachers have been content with in the past? Better still, have they not shown that as a result of their efforts both the quantity and quality of learning can be stepped up quite dramatically?

    Some of these demonstrations certainly are impressive. Summarizing the latest advances in the U.S.A., Francis Keppel notes that

> In some schools two- and three-year-olds were being taught to read and write; first graders were being asked to deal with fundamentals of economics and algebra; second and third graders were exploring concepts of relativity physics and learning to write music; fourth and fifth graders were encouraged to 'discover' set theory in mathematics; junior high school students explored anthropological concepts; and high school students studied physics and literature courses formerly taught only in college.[1]

All very gratifying, no doubt. But what would John Dewey have made of these marvels, one wonders? Come to think of it, what is so unprecedented – or so desirable – about these *jeunes professeurs*? By all accounts, seven-year olds were translating and commenting on Cicero's *Verrine* orations in Sturm's Academy at Strasbourg as long ago as the early sixteenth century, yet few educationists nowadays would regard this as a cause for congratulation, still less for emulation. Could it be that this is where we came in? And may it not be timely to remind ourselves of Pestalozzi's wry comment on the well-drilled pupils in the schools of Geneva: 'Sie kennen wiel und wissen nichts?'

What knowledge is of any worth? The Socratic twist to Herbert Spencer's famous question is deliberate, a way of drawing attention to the huge uncertainty principle operating in educational theory and practice at the present time. To pose it is to invite the accusation of being a jesting Pilate (and the world knows what happened to Socrates), yet upon reflection it can hardly be denied that there is a sense in which virtue has gone out of the curriculum, and another in which it is arguable that our ideas about what children should learn have been almost literally turned inside out. It is not simply that the possibility of arranging the various branches of knowledge in a hierarchy of worth, with theology as the 'Queen of the Sciences', as it was in the days of the medieval schoolmen, or with the natural sciences at the top of the tree, as Spencer saw them in his, is no longer conceded; much more troublesome is the difficulty of winning any universal assent to the belief that the intrinsic value of this or that branch of knowledge resides either in its content or in its efficacy as a 'discipline'.

It is true that members of examination boards rarely or never allow themselves to be troubled by this difficulty, and that teachers of specialist subjects tend to dismiss it as merely doctrinaire. They go about their business on the understanding that society's demands for general and special education alike are, on the whole, well enough catered for by the existing range of school subjects. *Ça va quand même* is the sum of their philosophy. Periodically, of course, courses may need revising as regards their content, objectives and methods of presentation; new combinations may be called for to meet the changing requirements of skilled manpower (witness the recent debate over the advisability of discarding O- and A-levels and replacing them with Q- and F-type leaving certificates); but whatever happens the assumption is that the *mappa mundi* will be so drawn as to cover those same areas formerly charted as the seven liberal arts and which the Harvard Committee designated as the humanities, the natural sciences and social studies. A further assumption, so widely accepted that it can scarcely be called in question, is that a broad-based acquaintance with all of these areas of knowledge, however minimal, is essential.

The day of the polymath being over, contemporary curriculum theory is inclined to look to the 'disciplines' as the key to the problem of finding some principle of unity in the diversity of modern knowledge. But what *is* a 'discipline'? Nothing is more likely to bring curriculum theory into disrepute than the loose usage of this term – unless it be its penchant for high-flown talk about 'forms of knowledge', 'realms of meaning' and 'cognitive domains', some of which comes perilously close to falling into the pathetic fallacies of nineteenth-century faculty psychology, and some of which deserves no better than to be called pretentious drivel.

A research discipline or subject is taken to be a coherent and consistent body of knowledge which relates to some particular area of man's concern and which gains its unity from its own inherent logic, in most cases the logic of explanation or exposition.²

Fair enough. But how many school studies can be said to answer to this rigorous definition except at the most advanced levels? Again,

> A discipline is a way of making knowledge. A discipline may be characterized by the phenomena it purports to deal with, its domain; by the rules it uses for asserting generalizations as truth; and by its history. Chemistry deals with chemical phenomena, according to the rules of science applicable to chemistry; both the rules and the domain of the field are in some degree a product of the history of the field. Literature deals with literary phenomena, and literary analysis has its own set of rules and its own history. The same may be said of biology, mathematics, geography, any organized discipline at all. But the physicists, especially, have been telling us that it is possible for children and youth to come to an understanding of physics directly. This approach to a discipline directly, not indirectly, is, I say, the chief meaning of the subject matter projects now being developed with such vigour.
> The idea – that the disciplines may be approached directly – has very great power. It contrasts sharply with the subject-centred approach that we have known. It is not a new subject-centredness; to call it subject-centred is to misname it. It is centred upon an attempt to teach children to grasp the intellectual means through which knowledge is discovered, in the hope that they may thus become active, not passive, learners. The disciplines themselves, understood as ways of making knowledge, offer suggestions about how they may themselves be learned.³

Praiseworthy as the sentiment expressed here may be, the definition of a discipline as a way of making knowledge is less than satisfactory. To say that literature deals with literary phenomena is tautologous. According to this, any body of knowledge which has a semblance of organization can be called a discipline, regardless of the ways in which its organization is achieved.

Such doubts are intensified rather than relieved by the line of thought exemplified in the following argument by Professor Paul Hirst:

> The concepts on which our knowledge is built form distinctive networks of relationships. If we transgress the rules of the relationships which the concepts meaningfully permit, we necessarily produce nonsense. If we talk about magnetic fields being angry, actions being coloured, beauty having weight, or stones being right or wrong, we simply produce conceptual confusions. But not only do we convey meaning by the use of networks or interrelated concepts, meaningful propositions are judged true or false by criteria appropriate to the propositions. A moral judgement is not validated in the same way as mathematical theorem, nor a historical explanation in the same way as theological proposition. There are thus within knowledge a number of distinct types of rational judgement. From considerations of this kind it can be seen that the acquisition of knowledge in any area involves the mastery of an interrelated group of concepts, of operations with these, as well as more general criteria of a reasoning common to all areas of knowledge. Indeed, the objectives of education we have been considering are closely related together as elements of distinguishable cognitive structures, each unique in crucial respects.
>
> Looked at this way, the development of mind has been marked by the progressive differentiation in human consciousness of some seven or eight distinguishable cognitive structures, each of which involves the making of a distinctive form of reasoned judgement and is, therefore, a unique expression of man's rationality. This is to say that all knowledge and understanding is logically locatable within a number of domains, within, I suggest, mathematics, the physical sciences, the human sciences and history, literature and the fine arts, morals, religion and philosophy.[4]

Were it not for the thought that educational theory is not to be validated by propositional logic alone, one might agree with all of this. The great failing of this kind of epistemological argument is that where it is not self-evident it is so dreadfully vague. It is not clear, for example, why, if certain criteria of reasoning are common to all areas of knowledge, it is vital to grasp the distinctive features which mark them off from one another. This may be necessary so long as we stick to the rules of logic, but in our daily lives (still more in the child's experience) we feel free to cross the boundaries between sense and nonsense and see nothing wrong in speaking of actions being coloured, or even in seeing sermons in stones. Again, it is not clear whether the human sciences and history are to be lumped together as constituting a single 'domain', though the punctuation suggests that this is the intention. If so, in what sense can they be said to form a logically distinct area? Or literature and the fine arts (a rare old mixed bag here!)? Do not psychology, sociology, economics, politics and the rest have their own forms of reasoned judgement, and if so, what is to prevent us adding to the list indefinitely? If mathematics is at once a 'domain' and a 'discipline', what is the difference? And if the physical sciences occupy a separate 'domain', why no mention of language? Is it helpful to pretend that a 'cognitive structure' can be found for morals, philosophy and religion – and that it can be made plain to the learner?

Curriculum theorists who take their stand on the 'disciplines' would presumably answer such questions on something like the following lines. First, all human knowledge can be broadly classified under two headings; (*a*) knowledge which is the result of deliberate, systematic inquiry, and (*b*) knowledge which is the residue from ordinary experience. The former is to be found in the various disciplines; the latter is what we normally refer to as conventional wisdom. Each of the disciplines has its own peculiar internal organization or structure. This structure has both a substantive and a syntactic aspect. The substantive aspect includes the subject-matter, key concepts and the kinds of data with which the discipline deals; while the syntactic aspect includes its procedures, methods of inquiry, rules and relationships. Knowledge which comes under the heading of conventional wisdom may have some kind of substantive structure, but lacks syntactic structure because it is not sufficiently well organized.

The 'discipline-centred' school of thought, typified by American thinkers like Phenix and Broudy, would accordingly restrict the curriculum of general education to those studies which clearly exhibit a syntactic structure, leaving special education and technical training to draw on conventional wisdom. This school of thought, not surprisingly, finds a good deal of support in this country where ideas about educational excellence tend to be identified with sixth form work. Its leading spokesmen are highly articulate and highly placed. For all that, the gospel they preach has unmistakable overtones of reaction in it.

We have already commented on the peculiar difficulties raised by the notion of structure as frozen function. As the biologist understands it, 'structure' can best be defined as the static arrangement in space of the parts of an organism (or system), and to that extent is not to be confused with 'process', which is the dynamic flow of matter-energy in the organism (or the information in the system) over time. Quite apart from this – a point to be discussed more fully later – there is the additional difficulty that the so-called syntactic aspect which is alleged to give the 'discipline' its distinctive character is usually apparent only to the mature scholar and as nebulous as a Platonic 'form' to everyone else.

Reliance on conventional wisdom may be abjured in mathematics, logic and the physical sciences, but not in the humanities. The real objection to any move which seeks to exalt those studies which possess a well-defined conceptual framework – 'abstract symbolic systems within which all propositions are consistent with one another' – is not that it is calculated to revive the age-old quarrel between pure and applied studies, nor that it looks like returning us to the state of affairs which existed in the Classe de Philosophie of the pre-war French *lycée* where everything had to be analysed in the light of 'clear and distinct ideas', but that it is guilty of intellectual arrogance. It ignores the fact that human knowledge is never one-dimensional. Broadly speaking, Aristotle's threefold division of knowledge into theoretical, practical and productive categories corresponds to the cognitive, affective and psycho-motor 'domains' of Bloom's taxonomy. To out-Hirst Hirst, if we transgress the rules of the relationships between the 'domains' of thinking, feeling and doing we necessarily produce nonsense – and this is precisely what 'discipline-centred' curriculum theorists are in danger of doing.

In any case, most learning occurs outside the formal conceptual framework of the 'disciplines', and hence is amenable to the general criteria of reasoning which hold good in all areas of learning. Before getting down to the selection of content, says Wheeler,

> it may be pointed out that some behaviour can only be learned through experiences with a particular kind of matter, e.g. mathematics, while other behaviour can be learned through experiences with any number of subjects. This fact serves to divide the behavioural outcomes ... into two broad classes, which are here designated 'generally determined' and 'specifically determined'.[5]

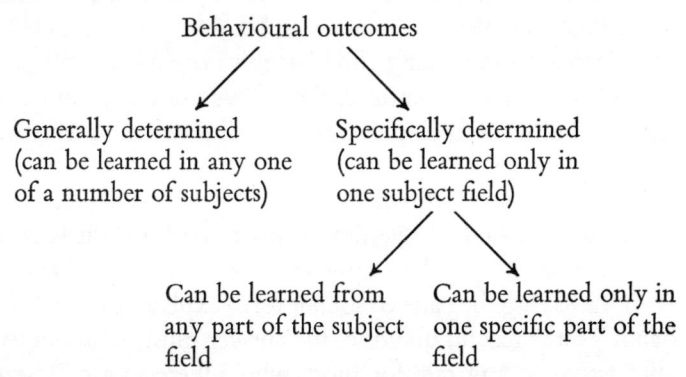

```
                    Behavioural outcomes
                    /                \
    Generally determined          Specifically determined
    (can be learned in any one    (can be learned only in
    of a number of subjects)      one subject field)
                                   /            \
                      Can be learned from    Can be learned only in
                      any part of the subject one specific part of the
                      field                   field
```

While it cannot be proved that educational outcomes, ethical as well as intellectual, are for the most part generally determined, the grounds for thinking that school learning should concentrate on particular 'disciplines' is indeed flimsy. Incidentally, why is it that mathematics is invariably adduced as an exemplar of a coherent and consistent body of knowledge? Could it be because it is the only obvious one? Obviously, if he lived to be as old as Methuselah, the child would never learn how to solve quadratic equations if he were left to his own devices. Given the wherewithal, he *would* learn to express himself through drawing and painting but not through playing the piano! Left to himself, he would probably never learn to read and write, but certainly would be able to use the mother tongue well enough for practical purposes.

> The often unconscious nature of learning structures is perhaps best illustrated in learning one's native language. Having grasped the subtle structure of a sentence, the child very rapidly learns to generate other sentences based on this model though different in content from the original sentence learned. And having mastered the rules for transforming sentences without altering their meaning – 'The dog bit the man' and 'The man was bitten by the dog' – the child is able to vary his sentences much more widely. Yet, while young children are able to *use* the structural rules of English, they are certainly not able to say what the rules are.[6]

If babes in arms have this extraordinary ability, two questions arise. First, is it always necessary to be able to say what the rules are? Second, if the young child has this insightful, intuitive grasp of transformational grammar, should we not credit him with far greater abilities in finding things out for himself than we normally do?

In those fields of knowledge which are generally determined, the answer to the first question seems to be NO – it is perfectly possible for the pupil to appreciate, say, Shelley's *Ozymandias* without having the rules of sonnet form explained to him beforehand. To the second question, the answer must be an unqualified affirmative, at any rate for those who adhere to a child-centred theory and practice. Once the learner has mastered certain specific skills which he cannot acquire by himself, they maintain that self-activity can be relied on to do the rest. To the 'discipline-centred' way of thinking, however, this is rather like saying that formal sex education is unnecessary since the way of a man with a maid has been known for thousands of years without anyone troubling to explain the rules of love-making. Reliance on self-activity leaves too much to chance in their opinion. The fact that the child learns his native tongue incidentally and by natural habit does not relieve the teacher of making plain what would otherwise never become plain to him – that is, the conceptual framework on which language depends.

To gain mastery of this formal symbolic system, students must master the basic sound and visual elements by which the meaning elements are organized into patterns. Consequently, some of the concepts which the curriculum-maker must consider are phonemes, graphemes and morphemes, morphology and syntax, classes of parts of speech and paradigms relating to them, the conventional patterns of expressing meaning and the devices for indicating the particular grammatical structure of the language.[7]

Readers who have not had the benefit of a course of primary school linguistics may like to ask themselves how far their understanding of spoken and written English has been impaired for want of an early introduction to the concepts of phonemes, graphemes, morphemes, etc. Reminiscent as it is of the pedant's insistence that it is not good enough for the Monsieur Jourdains of this world to grow up without ever realizing that they are using prose, the 'discipline-centred' theory nevertheless rests on an argument which would have appealed to Aristotle. Just as the state is prior to the individual, so the validity, authenticity and significance of studies which are vouched for by scholars take precedence over the interests of the learner in deciding the content of education. This argument is elaborated by R. S. Peters in his book, *Ethics and Education*, and finds forthright expression in Wheeler's assertion that 'In so far as learners at different stages of development are interested in certain broad categories of phenomena, these interests should influence the selection of content *after the other criteria have been satisfied.*'[8]

But although the case for thinking that the curriculum should be based on organized bodies of knowledge is firmly established, the reasoning of the latter-day Sophists remains as suspect as it was when Socrates first attacked it. So far as the primary school is concerned, all the evidence suggests that a curriculum conceived in terms of activity and experience, one which takes the learners' interests as its starting point, has done far more to improve the quality of teaching and learning than one which is formally didactic. 'Child-centred' and 'discipline-centred' may be artificial terms, labels which no longer stick, but the issue which divides them hinges upon the extent to which teachers believe that the pupil can do things for himself. It also hinges on the question of how far knowledge is something that can, and needs to be, doled out in neatly prepackaged consignments, and how far it is only meaningful when it engages the learner as an agent rather than as a recipient.

At the same time, it has to be recognized that the drift of educational opinion is towards the kind of curriculum-making which emphasizes the part played by the 'disciplines' in providing the essential blue-prints for knowledge. 'Grasping the structure of a subject is understanding it in a way that permits of many other things being related to it meaningfully. To learn structure is to learn how things are related.'[9]

Instead of accepting this as say-so, it is worth pausing a moment to ask whether it is necessarily true. After all, the pupil may know a great deal about the structure of the sonnet form and still dislike *Ozymandias*. It is possible to comprehend the structure of a symphony and yet remain unmoved by Beethoven's Ninth. This is not to deny that a conceptual framework helps, simply to make the point that more is involved in learning than conceptualization.

It appears that Bruner's hypothesis, and with it a good deal of contemporary thinking about the curriculum, is modelled on Turing's theorem: 'Provided a problem is well defined its complexity can be broken down into a set of simpler operations.' This kind of reductionism works well enough in the solution of problems of a mathematical or logical nature (which explains why most of the successes achieved in programmed learning and in curriculum projects have been in mathematical, scientific and technical fields), but it quickly shows signs of breaking down when it is extended to the social studies and humanities. The reductionist approach leads the biologist, for example, to assume that, whatever the organizing principle in living organisms is, it must be hierarchical: tissues consist of cells, which consist of molecules, which consist of atoms, which consist of fundamental particles . . . at which point the biologist has to confess himself at a loss.

What Knowledge is of any Worth?

In much the same way, the educationist resorts to the kind of reductionism which gives us 'domains', 'disciplines', 'concepts', 'principles', 'facts', etc. For the educationist, as for the biologist, the snag is that the problem is not well defined in the first place. As a result, what was thought of as an interrelated set of *structures* in space turns out to be an interacting pattern of *processes* in time. In other words, the problem answers to the condition of music, not of architecture. Just how its themes are orchestrated is known only to the composer. And this is why a child-centred theory is vindicated in practice – because it locates the form-creating capacity in the learner himself.

The problem is not well-defined for another reason – namely, that there is no agreement as to what constitutes knowledge. For practical purposes most people would say that it has to do with the apprehension of certainty – certainty being that which can be verified. Thus, 'Pekin is in China' and 'All men are mortal' are held to be statements of common knowledge, whereas 'I know that my Redeemer liveth' is regarded as an expression of faith. Strictly speaking, the knowledge that Pekin is in China also depends on an act of faith for those of us who have never been there, only in this instance the circumstantial evidence is so overwhelming that it seems a quibble to say that we only *believe* it to be true. As for the proposition that all men are mortal, it is as certain as anything can be, yet in the ordinary way we behave as if it had no meaning for us; that is, we give it intellectual assent while treating it as if it were irrelevant. To the hale and hearty man and the chronic cardiac case, the knowledge of the inevitability of death has very different implications; the one knows that he must die and carries on as if he only partly believed it, the other knows and believes it, literally, in his heart. What is it that gives the sick man's knowledge its infinitely greater urgency and significance? Not the concept.

Of all civilized peoples, the ancient Greeks were perhaps the least concerned with the content of education and the most concerned with right conduct. Yet even in Athens, the School of Hellas, there were learned men who professed to descry the fundamental principles of knowledge and who undertook to train the minds of the young in the light of them. What their arch-critic thought about their profession may be gathered from one of Dio Chrysostom's *Discourses*, possibly based on a lost work of Antisthenes, in which we seem to catch an echo of his actual words:

> Now Socrates, whenever he saw several persons assembled, would cry out most bravely and frankly with indignant rebuke and censure – 'Whither are you drifting, men? Are you quite unaware that you are doing none of the things that you should do, in concerning yourselves with money in order that you may not only have it in abundance yourselves, but may bequeath still more to your children? Yet the children themselves – aye, and earlier yourselves, their fathers – you have all alike neglected, since you have found no education and no mode of life that is satisfactory, or even profitable for man, which if acquired will enable you to use your money rightly and justly, and to treat without hurt not only yourselves, whom you should have considered of more value than wealth, but also your sons and daughters and wives and brothers and friends, even as they should treat you.
>
> 'But, pray, is it from learning to play the lyre and to wrestle, and to read and write, and by teaching your sons these things that you think that your city will be inhabited by more disciplined and better citizens? And yet if one were to bring together all the music masters, gymnastic instructors and school teachers who have the best knowledge of their respective subjects, and if you should found a city with them or even a nation, just as you at one time colonized Ionia, what sort of a city do you think it would be, and what the character of its citizens? Would not life be much worse and viler than it is in that city of shopkeepers in Egypt? . . .
>
> 'Furthermore,' he would go on to say, 'to be uneducated and to know none of the essential things, and to have no adequate preparation for life, and yet to go on living and to attempt while in that condition to carry on important matters of state – this cannot satisfy the persons themselves; for they themselves criticize the ignorant and the uneducated as not being able to live aright. And by the ignorant I mean, not those who do not know how to weave or how to make shoes, nor the people who cannot dance, but those

who are ignorant of the things one must know it he is to be a good and noble man.'

And speaking in this manner he would exhort his hearers to take care and give heed to his words, and to pursue philosophy; for he knew that if they sought that which he recommended they would be doing nothing else than study philosophy. For if a man strives earnestly to be good and honourable, that is nothing but being a philosopher.[10]

It may be thought that *mutatis mutandis*, the gravamen of Socrates' charge is as well founded today as it was two and a half thousand years ago. At least, however, we can share his annoying habit of asking what education is for, something which until fairly recent times struck most people as being as uncalled-for and as naïve as asking what the sky is for. The Victorians were in no doubt that the stuff of education was to be found in books. 'Sound learning' in traditional Scots parlance meant a thorough grounding in the Holy Scriptures and the Three Rs for all children, proficiency in Latin and Greek for the lad o' pairts. Today, we are more disposed to speak of the conditions of learning, or 'the learning situation' – a semantic shift which is itself indicative of a significant change of standpoint.

The change can easily be illustrated. For example, in Dr Edmund King's opinion,

> Whatever career advantages secondary education has possessed are more likely to arise from the social structure of a country than from anything the schools themselves have done. For example, if Latin and Greek open doors to careers and social acceptability that is a statement about the society where such a thing happens – not a statement about the classics. In Japan until after 1868 it was the Chinese classics that similarly opened doors. In other countries the talisman is, or has been, Sanskrit, Pali or Old Persian – the older the better, in fact, in most cases.[11]

Contrast this with Dr Moberly's unshakeable conviction that classics alone provided the indispensable basis for the education of a gentleman. 'It is plainly out of the question that we should teach chemistry, astronomy, geology, etc.,' he affirmed in giving evidence to the Clarendon Commission. When asked, 'Do you not think that there is a tendency in all knowledge learnt as a boy to fade away – the facts of history, for instance?', his reply was emphatic: 'The difference which I see between these things is, that whilst the one fades away absolutely and leaves nothing behind, the other gives power. All classical learning tells on a man's speech; it tells on a man's writing; it tells on a man's thoughts; and though the particular facts go, they leave behind them a certain residuum of power.'[12]

If modern educationists no longer share this conviction, any more than they accept Spencer's all-out claims on behalf of the teaching of science, the reason is that they have to take into account a host of contextual factors which never entered into the reckoning of the Victorians. It is not simply that subsequent research has put paid to nineteenth-century ideas about mental discipline and the transfer of training. The view expressed by Dr King, fairly obviously, has been influenced by evidence drawn from sociological sources and from comparative studies, whereas Dr Moberly's is much more parochial, not to say opinionated.

So long as educational theory was based on nothing more solid than a set of high-flown philosophical principles, its perspectives were necessarily limited. Though O'Connor's charge that the term 'educational theory' is normally no better than a courtesy title has been angrily denied, it has yet to be refuted, for while there is no lack of theories *about* education it remains true that an over-arching theory *of* education still escapes us. Today, educational thought draws on a wider range of empirical evidence than ever before – cultural anthropology, psychology, sociology, economics, politics, linguistics, technology, as well as philosophy *et al*. In doing so it has broadened its perspectives, but at the same time, in becoming more informed, it has shed many of its traditional dogmas. If we consider only *two* of the many factors which the curriculum-planner has to bear constantly in mind – the one loosely referred to as social class and the intimate connection between language and learning – there is now a prodigious amount of evidence, some of it summarized in official reports, most of it dispersed in an extensive research literature, all of which has the effect of focusing attention on the *circumstances* for success or failure in school learning.

If, then, the potency of this or that branch of study is no longer thought of as inhering in its subject-matter, it is only fair to add that another dogma which has fallen into discredit is the concept of educability as a fixed quantum. Deep-rooted as it is in popular belief, the idea that some children excel at school-learning because they are 'brainy' has been countered by evidence which shows that the secret of success or failure is to be sought less in the pupil himself and more in environmental factors – in the learning situation. Needless to say, teachers still speak affectionately of the high flier, the high I.Q. and the gifted child. No one denies the existence of genetic inheritance and everyone acknowledges differences in ability as one of the facts of life. Nevertheless, such doctrines as the 'limited pool of ability', 'innate intelligence' and the 'constancy of the I.Q.' have taken so many hard knocks in recent years that it seems inconceivable that they can remain intellectually respectable much longer. The trouble with the controversy over the relationship between Nature and Nurture is that it is dead but somehow refuses to lie down; no sooner has one side gained the upper hand than the other rallies to the attack and the old, old, pointless argument is resumed. The Gilbertian situation which would arise if scientists were so foolish as to allow themselves to become embroiled in a debate on the motion that 'This house considers Time to be more important than Space in the conduct of human affairs', is easy to imagine, yet this, or something like it, is the situation from which educational theory has yet to extricate itself. The sooner the Nature–Nurture wrangle is given its quietus and a decent burial the better for all of us.

Latterly, of course, the environmentalists have had the better of the exchanges. Regardless of the final outcome, however, it can be said without fear of contradiction that differences in ability which formerly were held to be so extreme as to necessitate differential treatments for so-called academic and non-academic pupils are now seen to be reducible. One of the lessons learned from curriculum development projects, particularly those mounted in the U.S.A., has been that there is a built-in tendency to underestimate the capacities of the average and below-average child. If the hypothesis that any subject can be taught effectively to any child at any stage of development has not been taken seriously in this country, the reason is not that it is incapable of validation but rather that British outlooks in education remain incorrigibly élitist.

Yet no one doubts that a great deal can be done to minimize difficulties in the learning process by stating objectives in terms which leave the learner in no doubt as to what he has to do and under what conditions, by careful analysis of the task to be performed, by guided discovery rather than by trial and error, and by preparing the ground in advance (Bruner's 'predispositions', 'entry behaviour' in the jargon of programmed learning). Having already cast a jaundiced eye on the formalism which a 'discipline-centred' approach is bound to impose, it may seem that the argument is back-tracking if it goes on to urge the need for analysis of the *substantive* structure in fields of knowledge where the syntactic aspect is so elusive as to disqualify them from ranking as 'disciplines'. In practice, any theoretical problems arising from the concepts of 'structure' (and 'sequence') are outweighed by the obvious advantages to be gained from a well-designed course of instruction. While a fully prescriptive curriculum theory is not yet in sight, the emergence of a methodology which guarantees rising standards of attainment, and which makes it possible for feats of learning hitherto limited to the few to become accessible to the many, if not to all, cannot be gainsaid.

To claim that individual differences in ability are reducible is not to say that they can be made to disappear. What it means is that instead of thinking of children as if some of them were intellectually ten feet tall and others the size of Tom Thumb, the range of mental differences is comparable with that of their physical make-up. More simply, differences in learning capacity which were once thought to be so enormous as to warrant the categorizing of children as if they were predestined to become first-, second- and third-class citizens have come to seem relatively unimportant. Perhaps only the credulous will share the vision of advanced thinkers who look forward to a time when these differences will become virtually irrelevant. Even so, thanks to the amplification of physical power, we live in a society in which it no longer matters whether the person operating a hoist or a self-drive car is a giant or a dwarf. According to the cyberneticist, there is nothing in principle to prevent the amplification of intellectual power. If so, why should it be so ridiculous to envisage a state of affairs in which it ceases to matter whether the learner's measured intelligence is great or small? Either way, he will be capable of performances which are at the moment looked upon as quite impossible.

To those who protest that all this is mere science fiction the retort must be 'Look around you'. In our daily lives we are constantly presented with illustrations of the ways in which the coupling of man and machines has extended the dimensions of human knowledge and experience. The backward adolescent who is 'hopeless' at English and reads and writes, if at all, with difficulty, has seen more dramatic presentations on the television and cinema screens than many a seasoned theatre-goer could have done fifty years ago. To object that what he has seen is mostly trashy stuff, and that 'entertainment' is not to be confused with 'education' (which may have been a valid objection in Newman's time, but not in ours) is to miss the point. The point is twofold: first, that each and every advance in the technologies of communication adds, however imperceptibly, to the inventory of aids to learning and so helps the individual's potential educability to become actual; second, that the advent of new media has the effect of reslanting the learning situation.

> With respect to the student, the difficult point to grasp is that he is not a younger version of the people who run the educational establishment. Not only does he know more, but, more significantly, he perceives the world differently. And this is because he has been conditioned by a different environment.
>
> Take television. Just about all the kids in school today have spent

more time watching television than the total time spent in school. But the more important fact is that the student acquires his information from television in a different way from school. From the former he receives information in fast-moving electronic patterns, but in school he learns at a slow, point-after-point, one-thing-at-a-time pace. Furthermore, information in school is presented in a linear, sequential manner, whereas the television presentation is characterized by discontinuity. Richard Lister said that, 'TV is best at those sudden shifts of reality', e.g. a Viet Nam war item, than a toothpaste ad. and then Gomer Pyle.

Where is the logic, the sequential treatment, the story line (the introduction, development and conclusion which are characteristics of literature culture) in programs like *I Spy*, *The Monkees*, *Mission Impossible*, *Rowan and Martin's Laugh-In*, and, in one of the most significant songs of the decade, *I am the Walrus*? Or, for that matter, in the new so-called television movies? Or in the new trend in advertising?

That's just television. Then there is the ubiquitous transistor, and the phonograph, and the tape recorder, and so on.... The slow and different pace of the classroom is frustrating and confusing to urban students. More and more of them are dropping out, either physically or psychologically, and more of them are becoming antagonistic. The obvious implication, then, is that we must try to see the younger generation in a new light – before it is too late.[13]

The provenance of this kind of statement (from a recent issue of the *McGill Journal of Education*) is easily guessed. It is the kind of statement which can easily be dismissed as exaggerated and unnecessarily alarmist. Sceptics will point out that the few authoritative investigations into the effects of media exposure, Dr Himmelweit's *Television and the Child* for one, and Joseph Trenaman's rigorous research study, *Communication and Comprehension* for another, have revealed little or no evidence of serious disturbance. So long as the emphasis on learning as a cognitive process remains as strong as it is, however, it is hardly surprising that research findings report no significant differences in the amounts of information acquired through reading, listening to the radio and watching television. Commenting on similar findings in the U.S.A. by Wilbur Schramm in his study, *Television in the Lives of Our Children*, McLuhan explains why they were bound to be inconclusive:

> Since he had made no study of the peculiar nature of the television image, his tests were of 'content', preferences, viewing time and vocabulary counts. In a word, his approach to the problem was a literary one, albeit unconsciously so. Consequently he had nothing to report. Had his methods been employed in A.D. 1500 to discover the effects of the printed book in the lives of children or adults, he would have found out nothing of the changes in human and social psychology resulting from typography. Print created individualism and nationalism in the sixteenth century. Program and 'content' analysis offer no clues to the magic of these media or to their subliminal charge.[14]

The ways in which modern instrumentation are altering methods of teaching are readily perceived; much less obvious are the ways in which instrumentation affects the learning situation itself. The extent to which the motivation, outlook and attitudes of children have been re-orientated by exposure to the new media can only be surmised. The *Paris-Match* cartoonist probably showed as shrewd an insight as any in his drawing of a baffled, defiant five-year-old standing in front of a blackboard on which the teacher had chalked the addition sum, 3 plus 2 equals . . . ? The caption read, 'I thought we had calculating machines for this sort of thing?'

McLuhan's remedy may strike most educationists as being as desperate as it is implausible. Broadly speaking, his proposal amounts to dropping the traditional subject-matter in the school timetable altogether and replacing it by a set of investigations into the nature and character of the various media from writing and print to radio, television and computers. Unless and until the ways in which they operate are known, and the 'laws' of communication explained, there will be nothing to prevent the media from being exploited unscrupulously and their effects will continue to be subliminal indefinitely, he thinks:

> In education this means the end of the one-way passing along of knowledge to students. For they already live in a 'field' of knowledge

created by the new media which, though different in kind, is yet far richer and more complex than any ever taught via traditional curricula. The situation is comparable to the difference between the complexity of language versus the crudities of traditional grammars used to bring language under the rule of written forms. Until we have mastered the multiple grammars of the new non-written media we shall have no curriculum relevant to the new languages of knowledge and communication which have come into existence via the new media.

These new languages are known to most people but their grammars are not known at all. We have 'read' these new languages in the light of the old. The result has been distortion of their character and blindness to their meaning and effects.[15]

Unfortunately, apart from one or two practical handbooks – Nicholas Tucker's *Understanding the Mass Media* is a good example – the average teacher has precious little to go on when it comes to interpreting his duties in this novel way. The training he has received unfits him for it. It conflicts with most of the presuppositions he brings to his work. To be told that his mastery of subject-matter and his skill in expounding it count for a great deal less than he has been led to believe seems as much an affront to common-sense as it is to his *amour propre*. 'And gladly would he teche and gladly lerne' may have been a virtue in Chaucer's schoolmaster, but to divest him of authority and expect him to share his ignorance with an awkward squad of youngsters who 'read' the new media as well as, if not better than he does himself – surely, this is asking too much? Things have come to a pretty pass if the secondary school curriculum is to be stripped of its age-old content and the vacuum filled with a media mishmash.

Yet in saying that our ideas about the content of courses have been, as it were, turned inside out we are only acknowledging the existence of a trend which is no less visible in the fields of religion, ethics, philosophy and science. Theology, too, has been largely emptied of its traditional content. From Bonhoeffer to the Bishop of Woolwich there has been a progressive demythologization of established doctrines and dogmas, a trend towards concepts of

Christianity without Christ, of religion without God. From Wittgenstein to Ayer, similarly, there has been a trend towards a genus of philosophies which is more concerned with training a man *how* to think than to tell him *what* to think. Again, in the sphere of ethics, the open disregard of standards of conduct and codes which were formerly thought to be binding on all as having absolute validity is a sign of the times. 'Moral education', we are informed, 'is a name for nothing clear'.[16] Like coal merchants in a smokeless zone, clerics and teachers of R.I. may still hawk their Ten Commandments from door to door, but the people, it seems, are not interested; they live in houses where the central heating is all-electric.

The difficulty of deciding what constitutes religious or moral 'knowledge' is only one instance, though arguably the most important one, of a difficulty which faces the curriculum-maker at every turn. In 1870 the religious issue was political dynamite. Even as late as 1944, denominational niceties were a matter of hard bargaining and everyone, or nearly everyone, was agreed that, whatever subjects might or might not be taught in schools, religious instruction must be one of them. Accordingly, it was made compulsory along with a daily act of corporate worship in the Education Act. This, it may be thought, was the last flicker of England's professing to be a Christian country. Today, it is hard to imagine the religious clauses of 1944 being retained unchanged in any future legislation. In the intervening years, for reasons which have nothing to do with the methods or content of religious instruction in the schools, the issue has been defused with the result that disillusion over the consequences of reserving a special place for religion in the timetable have become more vocal. What is the good, people ask, if at the end of the day the outcome is the very opposite of what was intended, not a generation of God-fearing citizens, let alone Christian gentlemen, but a race of agnostics?

Whether or not we attribute it to ethical pluralism, secular humanism or other-directedness, it appears that contemporary society does not take kindly to authoritative pronouncements and is much more disposed to be choosy in its opinions and beliefs. Student protest, irresponsible as it often is, is symptomatic of a quasi-Cartesian determination to accept nothing as true that it is possible to doubt.

> As free individuals seeking an education for *our* purposes and for a truly free society, we will not subject ourselves to the compulsion which says in effect that you cannot have a degree or attend this university unless you follow this precise set of rules regarding your education and fulfil these obligations. . . . .We question the educational value of competition for marks, written examinations as a basis for grades, and ultimately the utility of any grading system. There is increasing unrest over courses which are often restrictive, often biased, and usually irrelevant.[17]

The fact that this outburst comes from a Canadian spokesman is immaterial. The mood may strike the Committee of Vice Chancellors as aggressive, intemperate, even anarchical, but there is no denying that it is adamant – and that it is infectious. Would it be so adamant, and could it spread as easily as it does, unless it was prompted by a deep-seated and genuine sense of grievance? Though reformist idealism is less fervid in academic circles than it is among hot-headed undergraduates, there has been no lack of agonizing over methods of teaching and assessment in universities and some of the case-hardened assumptions about the essential worthwhileness of the content of degree courses have been shaken. This is true both of science and the arts.

While it remains strong, faith in 'knowledge of words' as exemplifying the best that has been thought and said in the world has been steadily undermined so that the kind of arguments adduced by Matthew Arnold carry less and less conviction. The man of letters, typified by the bookworm in Browning's *Grammarian's Funeral*, could immerse himself in the works of the ancient writers because, for him, essential truth was to be found in the words themselves, in the printed page. Today, with a vastly wider range of learning experiences accessible to all, the diet sheet is correspondingly more varied; if anything, the problem is one of information overload, not of any shortage of supply. So far as the study of English literature is concerned, this leads to a sharpened critical awareness which in turn throws doubt on the assumptions on which the teaching is based and on the information which is being communicated.

> For example (thinks Stephen Spender), a theory which rests on a whole string of dubious assumptions is that of the Great Tradition of English Literature which forms the basis of the teaching of Dr F. R. Leavis and his followers. The basic assumption is that we are living in the modern period in which there has been a complete breakdown of the continuity of tradition in our fragment-society. The tradition existed when there was the unified culture of what is called 'organic community' in which the social order, religious belief, arts and crafts all shared a single view of life. Since this no longer exists the critical reading of such books as crystallize in their vision of life the organic community is the only means by which contemporaries can establish contact with the tradition. These works form the Great Tradition. There follows a great deal of debate as to what works fit into the canon. A theory of this kind can only have force if it is preached as a kind of dogma, subscribed to by disciples who really believe that such an order as the Great Tradition exists and is infinitely superior to vulgar ideas such as the Six Foot Book Shelf or the Hundred Great Books. If they were not prepared to bow their heads in reverence when, for instance, the High Priest of the Cult declares that the only work of Dickens to fit into the canon is *Hard Times*, the whole idea would seem arbitrary and rather silly.[18]

As regards the teaching of science, the doubts go deeper than this, not merely because the problem of deciding what to include and what to leave out of courses is aggravated by the heady growth of new information, but mainly because of the recognition that the findings of science, once held to be 'positive knowledge', are so hedged about with uncertainty as to be, at best, provisional. This explains why in all the recent science teaching projects there has been a marked shift away from methods of teaching which rely on the memorization of factual details and the acceptance of data as given in favour of a more open-ended approach which allows the learner to experience the nature of scientific inquiry for himself. It is almost as if the old tag about religion had rubbed off on to science, the consensus now being that it is caught, not taught.

Whichever way we turn, we find this same transfer of the focus of attention from the content of learning to its situational and contextual aspects. There is more to it than a revulsion from rote methods and the type of instruction so often satirized as capes-and-bays geography. Granted, most academic courses in secondary schools remain largely unaffected by the trend, and the majority of teachers still measure their successes in terms of examination results. As Jevons observes, 'It is not only because of its teachability but also of its examinability that description of nature tends to be disproportionately emphasized at the expense of other facets of science.'[19] Or of any other subject one cares to name, for that matter.

Dwelling on subject-matter is inexcusable for a variety of reasons.

(1) It tends to assume that the subject-matter is worth knowing for its own sake. In doing so, it ignores the alternative assumptions: (a) that subject-matter may not be worth knowing unless it can be put to practical use; (b) that subject-matter may be no more than a medium for inculcating intellectual skills, mental attitudes and ideals. 'Content has no intrinsic worth, indeed no place, until man does something with it as a result of experience in which behaviour is learned', says Wheeler. 'Content is important only in so far as it helps to bring about intended outcomes.'[20] It is a mistake to locate the criteria for selection in the content of courses rather than in the learner's objectives. Needless to say, this is precisely what established practice bids us to do! It is taken for granted that each and every subject in the timetable must be good for something and has its own peculiar contribution to make to the learner's development – otherwise how did it come to be there in the first place? This is the time-honoured Myth of the Disciplines. According to this, Latin and mathematics are supposed to help in promoting logical thinking, poetry in stimulating the imagination and aesthetic

appreciation, and so on. The belief that some studies, like some foods, have a general nutritive value and that when taken in the right proportions they provide a balanced diet, attractive as it is, is almost certainly false.

(2) Concentration on subject-matter inevitably places too heavy a work-load on the learner. Whether the assumption is that it is intrinsically worthwhile and therefore deserving of a place in general education, or that it has practical applications and therefore must be regarded as indispensable for special education, the amount of information which has to be absorbed is necessarily great.

> There is one thing that the subject and career lines of argument have in common. Both concentrate on *what* is taught. The result is that there is a built-in tendency for syllabuses to become overloaded, with all the effects that has on *how* they are taught. As is widely recognized, cluttered syllabuses exert a baneful influence on the quality and style of science teaching.
>
> Yet if considerations relating to subjects and careers could be kept firmly in place *behind* those relating to students, it would become clear that it is the *style* of teaching that is the most vital thing about it. Student-oriented teaching must concentrate not on what the course covers but on what it does to the students; that is, it must attend less to what is taught than to how it is taught. If that could be effectively achieved, the clutter would almost automatically drop out. A student-oriented overloaded teaching programme is a contradiction in terms. If it is successfully student-oriented it cannot be overloaded.[21]

So long as secondary education remained selective, teachers did not have to worry over much about the motivation of pupils, the assumption being that they were interested in scholarship for its own sake and that, in any case, if they were not, the incentive to learn was taken care of by examination requirements. Now that the whole range of abilities has to be catered for, this position is no longer tenable. The Two Cultures controversy which really concerns us is not the one between arts and science but rather between those whom it has hitherto suited us to call academic and non-academic.

For the latter, evidently, an entirely new approach is required. Having said this, it is necessary to add at once that neither British society nor the education system is well enough prepared to make the necessary adjustments. Among the impediments which stand in the way of a new deal for the broad mass of pupils are: methods of recruitment and training of teachers, inadequate facilities for in-service training, lack of suitable equipment and learning materials (and the ability to use them when available), the obsession with external examinations, above all the constitutional and institutional force of habit which makes it virtually impossible for professional and public opinion to raise its sights and believe that something better than a second-best provision can ever be made for the so-called non-academic majority.

Is it going to be possible to communicate the grandeur of Shakespearean tragedy, the high seriousness of Miltonic verse, the beauty of mathematical proof or the significance of quantum theory to such pupils? In the prevailing climate of opinion the question is bound to seem rhetorical. Teachers grappling with the problem of dealing with mixed-ability groups in the comprehensive school may well be forgiven for thinking that in mathematics, foreign languages and science, at least, streaming is the only answer. To be told that it is defeatist to conclude that the Newsom children are incapable of rising to the conceptual levels which great literature and scientific thought presuppose is no comfort to them. Everyone knows that for these children the sense of Shakespearean tragedy is not to be derived from close study of an annotated edition of *Hamlet*, and that the implications of Heisenberg's Uncertainty Principle are not to be culled from a textbook – but what are the alternatives?

Educationists who are never happier than when they are waxing eloquent on the any-subject-can-be-taught-to-any-child theme might do well to hold their peace until they have shown how Bruner's hypothesis can be validated by the average teacher in the average classroom. It is all very fine to stress the exciting possibilities opened up by modern techniques – to affirm, for example, that multi-media presentation *can* translate *Hamlet* from the printed page (where the author never intended it to be in the first place) and restore it to its original channel to bring it home as forcefully and directly to backward readers as the Globe performance did for the illiterate groundlings in Shakespeare's day; but until ways and means of doing it are easily accessible few teachers are likely to be convinced.

In the U.S.A. and in Eastern Europe, where two-track systems of secondary schooling either never existed or have been abolished, this rooted prejudice against the viability of common courses is nothing like so strong as it is in Britain. Ideas born and bred in the bones of the grammar school tradition are not to be sloughed off over night. In view of the fact that teachers in these selective schools are reckoned to be, on the whole, the most knowledgeable and the best trained in the profession, the explanation which follows may seem distinctly odd. Before going on, therefore, the reader is advised to refer to Fig. 4 (reproduced from *The Quality of Education in Developing Countries*), in particular to the characteristics of the third and fourth stages through which school systems, according to Beeby, are said to pass. Although the characteristics listed are drawn from the primary school, there is no reason to suppose that they do not apply equally well to the secondary school.

Bearing in mind the kind of developments which have taken place in English primary schools during the past fifty years, few educationists would cavil with the opinion that *two* of the key characteristics are 'activity methods, problem solving and creativity' and 'internal tests'. To be sure, the former are by no means universal, and the fact that the 11-plus examination lingers on despite its legal abolition indicates that procedures for continuous assessment by teachers are still not the general rule. At the same time, it cannot seriously be doubted that many English primary schools are moving from the stage of 'transition' to that of 'meaning', and that *two* of the reasons for this are in some way connected with the adoption of 'progressive' methods and the gradual release from the pressure of external examinations.

Thanks to the dominance of the grammar school tradition, neither of these characteristics holds good of developments at the secondary stage. As regards the pressure of external examinations, some advances have been made – mainly through the Schools Council's efforts to establish administrative arrangements by which the C.S.E. can be taken internally and moderated by teachers themselves – but for the most part the reliance on the expertise of examining boards remains strong, and as Eggleston and Kerr point out,[22] there is still no nationally-accepted system of examination by assessment. This is partly because the necessary measuring instruments and procedures are still in the process of being perfected and are not widely available, but mainly because of the let's-keep-on-doing-what-we've-always-done attitude which keeps the competence of the average secondary school teacher pegged well below the genuinely professional level. It should be remembered that until quite recently there was a large proportion of teachers in English grammar schools who were totally untrained, and that the notion that 'knowing one's stuff' is the best guarantee of 'getting it across' persists in many quarters to this day. With it goes the conviction that once the teacher has discharged his duty as an imparter of information his job is done, and that, apart from marking papers which place pupils in some kind of order of merit, any final assessment is best left to the arbitrement of outsiders. The effect of all this, inevitably, has been to put a heavy premium on the theoretical aspects of learning at the expense of practical ones, worse still to convert examinations into ends in themselves. This means that methods of teaching are equated with covering the subject-matter of courses, and that learning consists largely of the storing of information for eventual retrieval and reproduction, usually in the form of a written paper.

Dissatisfaction with the tyranny of examinations seems to be growing, but it is no accident that when a Minister of Education publicly announces that the time has come to get rid of it the most violent protests come from teachers. Most of the innovations

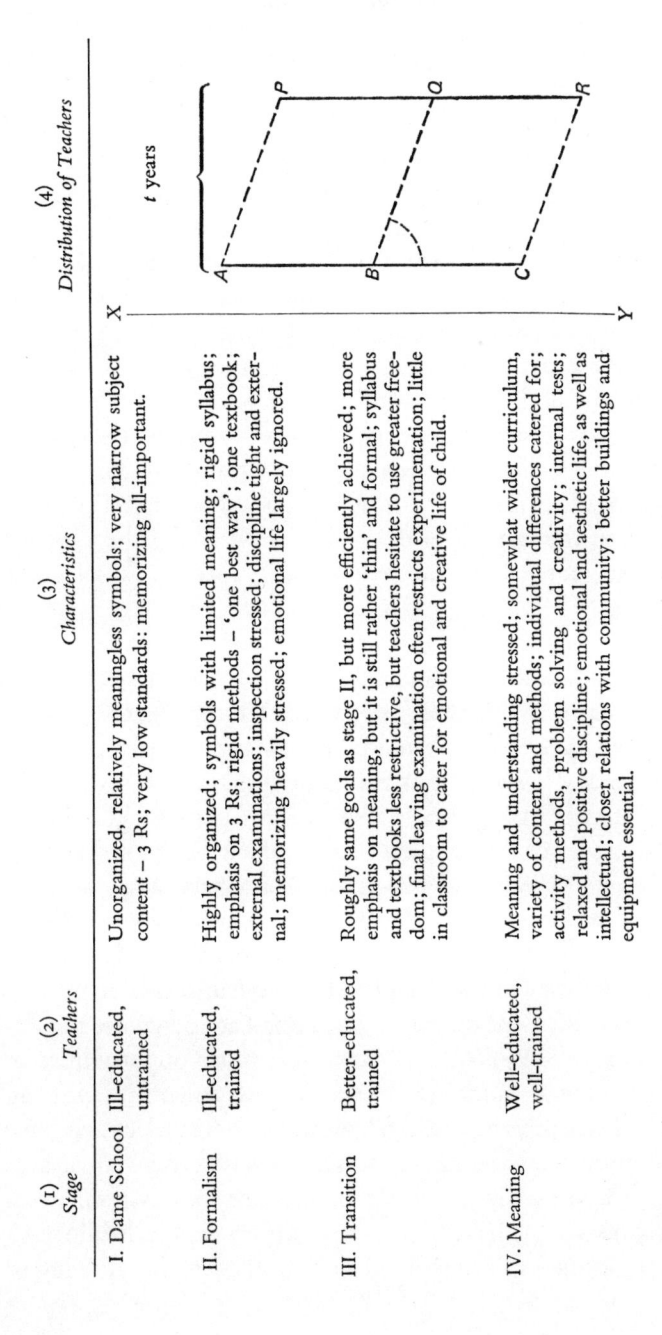

(1) Stage	(2) Teachers	(3) Characteristics	(4) Distribution of Teachers
I. Dame School	Ill-educated, untrained	Unorganized, relatively meaningless symbols; very narrow subject content – 3 Rs; very low standards: memorizing all-important.	
II. Formalism	Ill-educated, trained	Highly organized; symbols with limited meaning; rigid syllabus; emphasis on 3 Rs; rigid methods – 'one best way'; one textbook; external examinations; inspection stressed; discipline tight and external; memorizing heavily stressed; emotional life largely ignored.	
III. Transition	Better-educated, trained	Roughly same goals as stage II, but more efficiently achieved; more emphasis on meaning, but it is still rather 'thin' and formal; syllabus and textbooks less restrictive, but teachers hesitate to use greater freedom; final leaving examination often restricts experimentation; little in classroom to cater for emotional and creative life of child.	
IV. Meaning	Well-educated, well-trained	Meaning and understanding stressed; somewhat wider curriculum, variety of content and methods; individual differences catered for; activity methods, problem solving and creativity; internal tests; relaxed and positive discipline; emotional and aesthetic life, as well as intellectual; closer relations with community; better buildings and equipment essential.	

FIG 4 Stages in the growth of a Primary School System

in secondary schools to date have, in fact, been engineered by the examining boards which have rightly seen themselves as fulcra for bringing about changes in method of teaching which would otherwise have been resisted. As the vogue for stating objectives in behavioural terms becomes more popular, the fetish of external examinations will come to be seen for what it is worth as an outgrowth of mass-production methods and sub-professional standards of teaching. As it is, if we ask what the learner will be doing at the end of the course, the only honest answer is that he will be making marks on paper, sitting alongside a crowd of candidates who are all doing the same. And if we ask him what he is doing it for, or for that matter why he goes to school, the chances are that his reply will be 'To pass examinations'. A Martian observer might well be puzzled to know what possible connection there was between the writing of essay-type answers and the eventual performance for which the examinee's paper work allegedly qualifies him.

If the primary school is now characterized by a more relaxed atmosphere, the most obvious reason is that if its teachers know less in the way of specialist subject-matter they know a great deal more about children than do their colleagues in the academic secondary school. To say that womanly intuition has saved them from the formalism which somehow goes hand in glove with graduate modes of thought may be ungallant but probably true. Without pretending that non-graduate teachers, as a class, are always as well-versed in developmental psychology and its applications as they need to be, there is something to be said for the view that they are no longer preoccupied solely, or mainly, with the cognitive side of learning. Having had to manage mixed-ability classes willy-nilly, they have had more opportunities of exploring the possibilities of continuous assessment, in allowing for individual differences among pupils, and to that extent have become more sympathetic – or at least less defeatist – as regards the feasibility of common courses. In resorting to activity methods they may not always have been as clear-sighted and well-informed in practice as they were supposed to be in theory, but in doing so they helped to create a learning situation which was open-ended, even if at times it gave the appearance of being somewhat aimless (as the Plowden Report noted, some of the best work was being done in primary schools which had no clearly stated aims). If child-centredness often failed to stand up to close philosophical scrutiny, even when it was most muddled it escaped the vice of allowing methods of teaching to be dictated either by the formalism of the 'disciplines' or by the requirements of external examinations. If 'creativity', 'self-expression', 'guided discovery' and all the rest of the jargon which grew up around it sounded rather vacuous, the child-centred approach always kept the balance between algorithmic and heuristic problem-solving.

This last point is crucial.

> A characteristic feature of algorithmic processes is that instructions in the algorithm determine the thinking process completely by defining precisely how and when the learner is to act, and what operations should be performed under certain specific conditions. Since the instructions in the algorithm involve only elementary operations the learner is in no doubt as to the character and sequence of performing the operations. To solve a problem with the help of an algorithm the learner must fulfil accurately what is prescribed by the algorithm without himself introducing anything into the solution. A second feature of algorithmic methods is that the set of objectives for the actions to be performed, and the set of actions themselves, is determined in advance. In solving algorithmic problems the complete field of choice is determined: for example, theorems, rules and so on, as well as the conditions under which they must be used.

By contrast, Landa goes on:

> The necessity to search in an indefinite field is a special characteristic of heuristic processes. The difficulty of heuristic processes is that the conditions of the problem usually suggest the need for search in one area, while the solution lies in another. . . . In so far a genuine heuristics always contain some element of uncertainty and determine the thinking process incompletely, heuristic processes always

allow for independent pupil activity and self-organization. Thus no creativity is possible without independence and self-organization. As soon as you develop an algorithm for some creative process it ceases to be creative.[23]

Without in any way suggesting that the problems facing secondary school teachers are the same as those with which their colleagues in charge of younger pupils have to contend, it can hardly be disputed that to the extent that they 'hesitate to use greater freedom', that the 'final examination often restricts experimentation', and that there is 'little in classrooms to cater for the emotional and creative life of the child' (cf. Fig. 4), most secondary school teachers are still at the stage of 'Transition'. The most promising signs for future development are to be found, first, in the growing recognition of the need for deciding what outcomes are desired before anything else is done; second, in the current interest in new methods of assessment and attempts to find more wholesome measures of attainment than those provided by crude 'marks'; third, in the moves now being made to devise courses of an interdisciplinary nature in which the subject-matter is used to illustrate broad themes, topics, areas of inquiry and issues of immediate interest and relevance to adolescents.

What knowledge is of any worth, then? It is tempting to take a leaf out of Landa's book and conclude that it is the kind which results from 'search in an indefinite field'. To be sure, knowledge gained by following instructions – algorithmic route-finding – is indispensable for the acquisition of specific skills, but, in the last resort, personal knowledge can only come from the act of creating paths where none as yet (for the learner) exist. The stress on drawing valid inferences from evidence, on the framing and testing of hypotheses, on accurate observation, on inductive as well as deductive reasoning, is common to all the new courses. Whether it be physics or history, the objectives are broadly identical, as are the means of achieving them.

What knowledge is of any worth? The Socratic riddle, 'Virtue is knowledge', remains as teasing as ever. Whatever the answer, we can be sure that it varies from individual to individual. Why so? Because, to repeat, the form-creating capacity is ultimately to be found only in the learner himself.

REFERENCES

1 Francis Keppel, *The Necessary Revolution in American Education* (New York, Harper & Row, 1966), pp. 113–14.
2 D. K. Wheeler, *Curriculum Process* (University of London Press, 1967), p. 178.
3 Arthur W. Foshay, 'A modest proposal', in L. H. Clark (Ed.), *Strategies and Tactics in Secondary School Teaching* (London, Macmillan, 1968), pp. 65–6.
4 Paul H. Hirst, 'The logic of the curriculum', *Journal of Curriculum Studies*, Vol. 1, No. 2 (May 1969).
5 D. K. Wheeler, op. cit., pp. 184–5.
6 Jerome S. Bruner, *The Process of Education* (Cambridge, Mass., Harvard University Press, 1960).
7 D. K. Wheeler, op. cit., pp. 190–1.
8 ibid., p. 222.
9 Jerome S. Bruner, op. cit.
10 Dio Chrysostom, *Thirteenth Discourse*, translated by J. W. Cohoon, Vol. 2 (Cambridge, Mass., Harvard University Press, Loeb Classical Library), 16–28.
11 E. J. King, *Education and Social Class* (Oxford, Pergamon Press, 1966), p. 116.
12 C. Dilke, *Dr Moberly's Mint-Mark* (London, Heinemann, 1965), p. 7.
13 W. J. Gushue, 'Marshall McLuhan: educational implications', *McGill Journal of Education*, IV, 1 (Spring 1969).
14 Marshall McLuhan, *Understanding Media* (London, Routledge & Kegan Paul, 1966).
15 ibid.
16 J. B. W. Wilson *et al.*, *Moral Education* (Harmondsworth, Penguin Books, 1969), p. 11.
17 David Zirnholt, 'A student manifesto', in G. F. McGuigan (Ed.), *Student Protest* (London, Methuen, 1969), pp. 57–8.
18 Stephen Spender, *The Year of the Young Rebels* (London, Weidenfeld & Nicolson, 1969), pp. 175–6.

19 F. R. Jevons, *The Teaching of Science* (London, Allen & Unwin, 1969), p. 40.
20 D. K. Wheeler, op. cit., p. 39.
21 F. R. Jevons, op. cit., p. 44.
22 J. F. Eggleston and J. F. Kerr, *Studies in Assessment* (London, English Universities Press, 1969).
23 A. N. Landa, 'The construction of algorithmic and heuristic models of thinking', in W. R. Dunn and C. Holroyd (Eds.), *Aspects of Educational Technology* (London, Methuen, 1969), pp. 136-7.

CHAPTER NINE

'Christ, What a Way to Grow Up!'

THE DROP-OUT GENERATION

In his *Essay on the Content of Education*, published in 1949, Eric (now Lord) James wrote, 'It is necessary to ask ourselves whether we know what the content of education should be for the great majority of children between the ages of eleven and fifteen', and concluded that 'It is, at any rate, doubtful whether it is possible to lay down for the new secondary schools more than the merest outline of a curriculum.'[1] Despite all that has been thought and said and done in the intervening years, it remains no less doubtful today.

That it is impossible to teach without teaching *something* is a truism which does not cease to be true because it happens to have become a cliché. Easy enough to agree that what children learn is at least as important as how they are taught. Easy enough to sympathize with those who complain that education has become so preoccupied with managerial and methodological problems as to rule out much or any serious consideration of its ultimate purposes. In the contemporary situation, unfortunately, the Kantian adage which tells us that 'matter without form is blind, form without substance is empty' seems to have lost its force, and the old philosophical distinctions between means and ends are now so blurred that they are widely held to be unreal.

To complicate matters, the educative society, like society at large, tends to become progressively depersonalized, a lonely crowd in which the individual often feels helpless and lost. As the educational services expand, the energies of those who are responsible for providing them are increasingly absorbed by administrative duties, with the result that the impression given, at times, is that they are engaged in more for the sake of keeping things going than for any better reason. As schools grow bigger, head teachers are kept so busy keeping track of a thousand and one details that they have no time for teaching and rarely meet their pupils face to face. In the multiversity this breeds a sense of alienation, in the secondary school an undercurrent of moody restiveness.

'Sir, why do we have to learn French?'
'What's the point of wearing school uniform, sir?'
'Why shouldn't we let our hair grow long anyway?'

Questions of this sort are being asked more persistently and more querulously than ever before, and though teachers have heard them all before it is no longer quite so easy as it used to be to fob them off with dusty answers. Student protest and the generation gap are only two symptoms of the malaise of a society which is casting about for new values like a dog trying to catch its own tail. What is it all in aid of? Where are we going? If education is a sub-system of the wider socio-economic system must it take its orders from the latter and does it not have purposes of its own? Are human beings no more than cogs in the machine, or, worse, merely raw material for processing in the machine? 'Stop the game if that is the way it has to be played' is the cry raised by the activists. Belated as it is, the fear that things are in the saddle and ride men is by no means confined to the ranks of existentialist intellectuals; it is widespread and vociferous, nowhere more so than among members of the rising generation. For them, as for all, Jacques Ellul's book, *The Technological Society*, may well be reckoned a tract for the times. Its thesis, as abhorrent as it is difficult to refute, is that *technique* (defined as the one best way of doing anything) has now reached the stage where it has become autonomous and can only be controlled by the application of super-techniques. Accordingly, education has come to be seen as part of the man-machine system without which modern

'Christ, What a Way to Grow Up!': The Drop-out Generation

industrial societies could not survive for more than a few hours. Thus,

> Pure science seems to be yielding its place to an applied science which now and again reaches a brilliant peak from which new technical research becomes possible. Conversely, certain technical modifications – in airplanes, for instance – which may seem simple and mechanical, presuppose complex scientific work. The problem of reaching supersonic velocities is one. The considered opinion of Norbert Wiener is that the younger generation of research workers in the United States consists primarily of technicians who are unable to do research without the help of machines, large teams of men, and enormous amounts of money.
>
> The relation between science and technique becomes even less clear when we consider the new fields which have no boundaries. Where does biological technique begin and where does it end? In modern psychology and sociology, what can we call technique, since in the application of these sciences everything is technique?
>
> But it is not application which characterizes technique, for, without technique (previous or concomitant), science has no way of existing. If we disown technique, we abandon the domain of science and enter into that of hypothesis and theory. In political economy (despite the recent efforts of economists to distinguish the boundaries between science and economic technique), we shall demonstrate that it is economic technique which forms the very substance of economic thought.
>
> The established foundations have indeed been shaken. But the problem of these relations, in view of the enormity of the technical world and the reduction of the scientific, would seem to be an academic problem of interest only to philosophers – speculation without content. Today it is no longer the frontiers of science which are at issue, but the frontiers of man; and the technical phenomenon is much more significant with regard to the human situation than with regard to the scientific.[2]

Getting an education or getting to work, making a living or making love – everything we do is dominated by technique, apparently. Today the pill, tomorrow the test-tube baby. Technological advance follows its own immutable laws. There is no stopping it; the system of all the systems has the world in its grip and there can be no turning back nor turning aside from its irresistible logic. Anyone who tries to do so must resign himself to idle speculation about what might have been and shut his eyes to what is certainly going to be.

But Ellul is unduly pessimistic in thinking that his profound disquiet is not widely shared. On the contrary, it is all-pervasive and reveals itself in a host of unlikely places and in unexpected guises. One of these is to be found in the rebelliousness of a sizeable section of modern youth, a phenomenon which is by no means new, of course, but one which affords its own clues to the situation. In turn, the Teddy Boys, the Mods and Rockers, the Skinheads, Hell's Angels and the Hippies have served notice on us that what we have to reckon with is not simply a succession of teenage fadsters but a dissident underground movement which is impatient of the *mores maiorum* and determined to set up its own code of values. The movement cannot be dismissed by saying that as yet these wild boys and weirdies are only a small minority, and that the vast majority are happily conformist. It is a mistake, too, to suppose that because this underworld contains so many raffish elements it can be easily contained. Just how numerous and how well organized are the street gangs in a city like Glasgow is anybody's guess – this is not the kind of problem which the educational researcher normally cares to investigate[3] – but it can hardly go for nothing that pitched battles and large-scale vandalism are still common after a hundred years of compulsory schooling. To be sure, this sort of thing was a good deal commoner in Dickens's London, but that it should continue to flourish as it does in the midst of a welfare state is, to say the least of it, puzzling.

No one wanted the street gangs. No one foresaw the hippies. Academic circles were taken completely off their guard by the sudden upsurge of student power. If this is the terminal behaviour, what was the point of all those lessons on citizenship, all those lectures on the rule of law, and what are we to make of the patient and well-meaning efforts of teachers if, at the end of the educational process, the outcome is so often completely at odds with what was intended?

'Christ, What a Way to Grow Up!': The Drop-out Generation

So long as the groundswell of disaffection is treated with indifference, as if it were too objectionable and too obscene to bear mention, educational policy will find it easier to gloss over its failures than to come to terms with them. As it is, the tendency is to assume that there is nothing very novel or perturbing about the so-called generation gap. What else is it but a twentieth-century version of the time-honoured habit of the old pot calling the young kettle black?

'I would there were no age between ten and three-and-twenty, or that youth would sleep out the rest; for there is nothing in between but getting wenches with child, wronging the ancientry, stealing, fighting,' moans the shepherd in *The Winter's Tale*.[4] Dr Johnson's opinion was no less vehement:

> Subordination is sadly broken down in this age. No man now has the same authority which his father had – except a gaoler. No master has it over his servants: it is diminished in our colleges, nay in our grammar schools.... Why, Sir, there are many causes, the chief of which is, I think, the great increase of money. No man now depends upon the Lord of the Manour, when he can send to another country and fetch provisions.... But, besides, there is a general relaxation of reverence. No son now depends upon his father, as in former times. Paternity used to be considered as of itself a great thing, which had a right to many claims. That is, in general, reduced to very small bounds.[5]

While allowance has to be made for the ah-the-past attitudes of crabbed age towards the excesses of hot-blooded youth, however, it has to be recognized that the outlooks of the older and the younger generation are now so violently opposed that it begins to look as though a total breakdown in communication between the two is threatened. It is not simply that adult authority is openly flouted; much more serious is the failure of nerve on the part of adult authority itself.

Ironically, the term drop-out (meaning an early leaver, one who failed to stay the course at school) was first coined by educationists. Now, all at once, it has ballooned and blown up in their faces. Some of them are worried, as well they may be, for without saying that teachers and academics are responsible, except indirectly, for the growing wave of unrest among pupils and students, there is no escaping the fact that these malcontents are the products of an education system which appears to have gone sadly awry somewhere along the line. It is useless to retort that the drop-outs are just a bunch of long-haired layabouts who ought to know better and deserve a stiff dose of old-fashioned discipline to bring them to their senses. Even more useless to pretend that they can be treated as untouchables, or that their indecencies will cease to haunt us if we ignore their existence. Like the ghost in *Hamlet*, the presence of the drop-outs in our midst is vaguely reproachful, an uncomfortable reminder of the sins of omission of all who profess to be in any way concerned about the quality of life. The tragedy is that now that they have arrived, and in force, their elders and self-appointed betters can only stare at them with blank incomprehension and downright disapproval.

The drop-outs' appearance, certainly, is disconcerting (and meant to be); these young men in fancy dress, attired as if for a walking-on part as Robinson Crusoe, Peter the Hermit (or is it Christ?), the girls frizzed out like sackcloth Cinderellas or medieval pilgrims. Here again, historians of costume may assure us that so far as male fashions are concerned there is little or nothing to choose between the extravagances of 1970 and those, say, of 1770 or 1570. Even so, it can hardly escape notice that the Italianate styles favoured by the first Elizabethans and the frills and fineries affected by the pre-Romantics were themselves indicative of turning points in England's social history which can now be seen to have been epoch-making, though at the time they were laughed at or berated for their foppishness and effeminacy. It may be thought, too, that the contemporary liking for clothes which openly proclaim the difference between young people and the middle-aged, while at the same time minimizing the difference between the sexes, marks a departure from previous fashion trends.

Sociologists have attempted to explain the generation gap, not always very convincingly. That the gap exists and that it is widening all the time can scarcely be doubted. On the whole, nevertheless, informed opinion is inclined to think that the gap is no more than an accentuation of differences between the generations which have always been there, and that there is no excuse for regarding it as unprecedented.

For their part, educationists seem to be keeping their fingers crossed and hoping that the generation gap is no more than a passing phase which will eventually disappear of its own accord. Although to say so is the surest way to lose friends, few of them have felt compelled to engage in fundamental re-thinking about the validity of many of the assumptions that are built into existing theory and practice. There are two reasons for this disability. The first is that anyone who calls himself an educationist cannot even begin to question the first article of his faith, which affirms that education is necessarily a Good Thing. The second is that his modes of thought render him incapable of value-judging other than in terms of language. On both counts he is singularly ill-prepared to understand the cultural upheaval which is taking place.

Ill-prepared because in all our facile talk about the 'education explosion' and the 'explosion of knowledge' we fail to recognize that what we have to do with is a massive release of mental energy on a par with the amplification of physical power made possible by modern engineering. In our daily lives we are constantly presented with nerve-tingling demonstrations of massive physical force – the Bomb, the blast-off, the jet's take-off, even the road drill – but we are curiously unaware of the comparable effects in our psychic life which are no less terrifying in their implications. This is because the energy is not containable in intellectual forms; it does not emanate from, neither does it inhabit the realm of conceptual thought. Not being communicated through the channels of language, which are the ones we have come to rely on more or less exclusively, it tends to be heard only as a distracting noise.

In the same way that it never occurred to Botticelli, say, that he was living in a period which historians would later characterize as the Renaissance, so we are inclined to miss the point when it comes to trying to understand the forces at work in the contemporary world situation. Just why our modes of thought are liable to fail is a question which calls for further elucidation, but for the moment the point to be noted is that all great historical movements have a way of occurring spontaneously and of defying any attempts to control them by rational planning. This was certainly true in the case of the first Industrial Revolution which took place while the governments of the day had their backs turned; and it is equally true of the mutation of sensibility which is taking place at the present time almost without anyone noticing.

Thanks to the presuppositions which he brings to his work, the educationist is often the last person to sense the winds of change and carries on in the spirit of business-as-usual even in the eye of the hurricane. Given the intellectual background and training which have shaped his outlook it would be very surprising indeed if he possessed the insights that are needed when the composure, not only of society but of the central nervous system itself, is being upset as never before. If this sounds unnecessarily cryptic it is pertinent to add that, in any case, British educational thought has never been distinguished for its perspicacity, that its record for being wrong is as inglorious as its predilection for believing itself to be in the right is vainglorious, and that some of its leading exponents today are little emperors without clothes.

It is not as though educationists have been without warnings. With each successive raising of the school-leaving age, the tensions created by the secular trend towards earlier physical maturity have become more acute. No question about it, children are growing up faster, are more knowledgeable, more critical, and more self-assured; in an age in which space travel and electronic communications are rapidly becoming commonplace their ways of looking at the world and the experiences open to them are not the same as they were for children born thirty or forty years ago. This in itself poses problems not only as regards attitudes to school-bound learning and classroom discipline but also as regards the role of the teacher and the function of the school.

'Christ, What a Way to Grow Up!': The Drop-out Generation

In Marsden and Jackson's illuminating study, *Education and the Working Class*, one of the youths interviewed was asked why he had left Marburton College instead of staying on to the sixth form, to which the terse reply was, 'Christ, what a way to grow up!' In the judgement of nine out of ten educationists, it goes without saying that the lad would be classed as maladjusted, deviant, a born wastrel if not a potential delinquent. They might do worse than begin by asking themselves, as we shall, whether his reasons for rejecting an extended grammar school education were perfectly sound.

There is no need to rake over all the arguments relating to the divisive effects and the inequalities arising from social-class at this stage. The point to be emphasized is that the lurking dissatisfaction with the secondary school cuts right across the academic/non-academic apartheid which we are trying to get rid of in the current reorganization on comprehensive lines. It is an illusion to suppose that it stems only from the have-nots who failed the 11-plus examination. Many a hippy, it seems, has gained his handful of A-level passes and, as vice-chancellors have learned to their cost, student protest is just as rife, more so if anything, among those who are intellectually gifted as among those who are not. The causes, therefore, must lie deeper than those which appear on the surface. They are connected with that massive release of mental and nervous energy referred to earlier, the dynamics of which are partly understood by the media men and the vendors of pop culture, and scarcely at all by educationists.

It is here, perhaps, that techniques drawn from the social sciences – in particular organization theory, communication theory and systems analysis – may prove helpful. In the last resort, admittedly, the necessary insights cannot be guaranteed by any techniques, but in the first instance some attempt has to be made to expose the flaws in established theory and practice. For this purpose, systems analysis has at least the virtue of emphasizing the need for a contextual approach, taking into account the inter-relationships between the variables, *external* as well as *internal*, which determine the state of the system. As things are, educational decision-making operates in a world of its own. To some extent universities, colleges and schools function as if they were closed systems with regulations which are more calculated to preserve them in a steady state than to maintain the kind of dynamic equilibrium demanded by continuous adaptation to change. Without regulations, of course, no institution is able to carry out its day-to-day business in an orderly fashion, or secure itself on a permanent footing. So long as these regulations are seen to be necessary there is no question of dissent; it is only when they come to be seen as unresponsive to changing circumstances that they are apt to be resented. When that happens, regulations come under attack on the grounds that they no longer serve the best interests of members of the institution concerned, and that they are retained more for the sake of perpetuating the *status quo*, or for administrative convenience, than for any better reason. It seems clear that for well over a hundred years rates of change in society at large have so far outpaced those in the educational sphere as to create not only a serious cultural lag but also a credibility gap between the two. While there is no warrant for jumping to the conclusion that the situation is so bad that secondary schooling has become for many, most of the time, an irrelevance – a 'disaster area' as one American writer sees fit to call it – a preliminary systems approach immediately raises a number of awkward questions. For a start:

> Over the years educators have given a great deal of attention to this matter of process, including such problems as those of curriculum, method, evaluation and promotion, but all efforts have been circumscribed by the assumption that the teacher-class subsystem is necessary. It has been taken as axiomatic that one teacher teaches a 'course' or 'grade', the content of which takes a year (or term) to complete, and that all students should begin and end it together. Some of the greatest scientific discoveries have been made when investigators have dared to question an axiom. And if one follows their example and questions the validity of the teacher-class axiom, he soon realizes that it is actually more mechanical than the innovations that might supersede it. The methods of assigning marks is an escape, a

'Christ, What a Way to Grow Up!': The Drop-out Generation 239

rationalization in the psychological sense of the term. It projects the failures of the system on the children and young people, giving low or failing marks to those who have not been properly classified or adequately taught, and at the same time giving rewarding marks to those who do well, some of whom may not even have needed the instruction.[6]

Much the same point of view is expressed in Peter Abbs's polemic, *English for Diversity*:

> The petty tyranny that goes on in so many of our schools at the moment needs to end for there is no good reason why children should be made to wear uniform or made to wear their hair short. The uniform is often an excuse to make teenage girls and boys experience themselves as more childish than they are. Children should be allowed to express themselves in the styles they wish – in accordance with their real age. . . . The fierce competition engendered by marks, positioning, internal examinations, external examinations and streaming should be finished with, for the competitive system is bound to create children who experience themselves as failures. For each smug child at the top there is an insecure and hostile child at the bottom. Any system that is responsible for the creation of such emotions can only be considered inhuman.[7]

Educationists are not to be blamed for refusing to be swayed by emotive pleas of this sort. They have always distrusted the impassioned geniuses of their profession, wayward thinkers like Rousseau who have hinted at the dog beneath the skin of rationalism. Today, however, when the moulds of rational thought are being broken by a new wave of romanticism, it is their misfortune that in at least one sense, one which is all-important, they are out of sympathy and out of step with the march of events.

As propounded so far, the argument cannot be expected to carry much conviction. On the face of it, it appears to be a wholly undeserved attack on the competence of a body of professional men and women – teachers, academics, administrators – whose integrity deserves better than to be libelled in this way. But it is not a question of integrity. In Victorian times, men like Robert Lowe ('The lower classes ought to be educated to discharge the duties cast upon them') and the Rev. James Fraser ('I venture to maintain that it is quite possible to teach a child soundly and thoroughly, in a way that he shall not forget it, all that is necessary for him to possess in the shape of intellectual attainment, by the time that he is ten years old') were presumably not lacking in integrity, yet in retrospect it is only too obvious that this did not save them from being purblind. The fact that their opinions were widely acclaimed did not prevent them from being pronounced wrong in the judgement of posterity. Is it not just as likely that opinions about the educational process which are firmly held today will suffer the same fate?

Conceivably, the argument can be made to appear less truculent by taking its cue from the communication theorist and asking:

1] Who
2] says what
3] through what channel
4] to what audience
5] in what context
6] with what effect?

As Schramm explains,

> The problem of 'who' is the problem of source, and how it operates in encoding the message. 'What' is the problem of content, its symbols, themes and form. 'Channel' introduces problems of the differences between the media as carriers of messages. 'Audience' research is concerned with the description and enumeration of receivers of messages. 'Context' with the worlds of the sender and receiver at the time of sending and receiving, including ... their group relationships. 'Effect', of course, implies a study of the responses to messages.[8]

Suppose, now, that we apply this simple model to the transmission of culture as it has operated in the education system hitherto:

1] Adults (mainly parents and teachers) were the prime source of information by virtue of their greater knowledge and experience.

'*Christ, What a Way to Grow Up!*': The Drop-out Generation

2] A selection of this information embodying the social mores and know-how was handed down from the old to the young in the form of school-learning, its content remaining more or less constant so long as society remained stable.

3] The normal channel of communication was language – chalk and talk, supplemented by reading from books in the case of school-learning.

4] Since the young depended upon their teachers to supply the information they needed, the audience was largely a captive one; it could, of course, ask questions and answer back, but it was in no position to query the supremacy of adults as the source and senders of messages.

5] So far as school-learning was concerned, however, these messages always had a rather limited context in that they were addressed mainly to the acquisition of cognitive skills – literacy and numeracy. Because adults could count on the children's acceptance of established norms and codes of behaviour, emotional and moral training tended to receive less attention and were inculcated either incidentally or by example.

6] School-learning was formally tested by examinations, which were used to select those who showed themselves to be proficient in decoding the messages transmitted verbally by adult society, and who, in turn, were given the job of encoding and transmitting similar messages to the next generation.

This vertical flow of information took the form of a closed loop which can be crudely represented in a diagram (Fig. 5).

In the new-style transmission of culture hardly any of the conditions which assured the cosy, self-contained state of affairs depicted in Fig. 5 holds good to anything like the same extent as it did formerly. With a whole range of alternative channels at their disposal, the young are much less dependent upon their parents and teachers; they are born into an environment that is teeming with information, most of which is non-verbal, and most of which is transmitted *laterally* by a process of continuous creation. The young do not need to wait until they are grown up before they count themselves as equals with adults: in some respects they are one jump ahead of their mentors simply because they are less inhibited by convention and 'read' the messages transmitted from

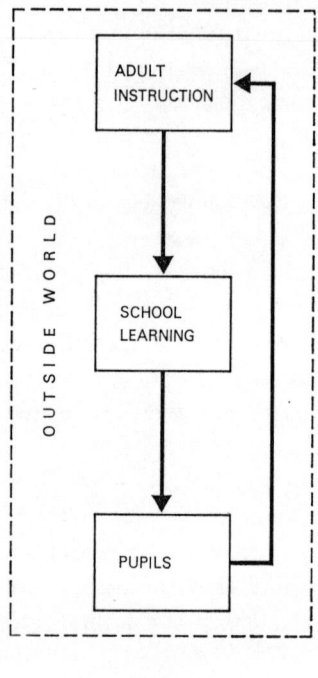

FIG 5

other sources more easily and fluently. Information is no longer hard to come by; their daily experience is exposed to a saturation bombing campaign from the new media. When it comes to asking 'Who says what?', teachers and parents have to confess that their monopoly has gone. A great deal of communication now stems from sources which are not within the control of the education system, and many of the messages transmitted run counter to those which find their currency in school-learning.

'Christ, What a Way to Grow Up!': The Drop-out Generation

It can safely be said that a child probably derives more of his ideas of environment, more of his sense of values and his knowledge of roles, from outside the classroom than from inside it. Furthermore, there are likely to be notable contrasts and conflicts between the classroom and the outside world – popular art as against classical art, peer-group values as against older-generation values, violence in the media as against restraint in school, etc. To the communication researcher this seems a fact of major importance. What, he asks, does it mean in terms of curriculum-making and educational policy? For one thing, how can the school make use of the great wealth of communication that the student receives outside? Are there some parts of this outside communication which are so rich as to replace some of the classroom work and free the class for more advanced things? On the other hand, what can the school do to guard against possible ill effects of this outside communication, and to make sure that the student selects well from what he has available?[9]

As before, the ways in which the traditional, vertical transmission of culture in schools is being disturbed by the non-stop cross-fire of information from the outside world may be crudely represented in a diagram (Fig. 6).

The extent to which adult instruction has been left high and dry, so to speak, and the extent to which formal school-learning has been swamped by communications from the outside world may be somewhat exaggerated in Fig. 6, but what cannot be exaggerated is the tension and disturbance set up within the education system.

Through what channels? We have still to ask the key question on which the entire argument depends. In the past, our frames of reference in educational thought have been so strongly conditioned by the use of linguistic codes of communication that we find it almost inconceivable that other codes could be equally meaningful and serviceable. Literacy is still our first priority. Thought and language have come to be so mutually linked that the idea of thought without language tends to seem as absurd as the idea of water without wetness. Without language, we say, none of the triumphs of abstract conceptual thought would ever have been possible. Moreover, we say this without fear of contradiction, unmindful of the fact that it is flatly contradicted by our experience with such art forms as music, dance, sculpture and painting. In the language of educational discourse, for the most part, we hear only the traffic of words. The rest is 'noise'.

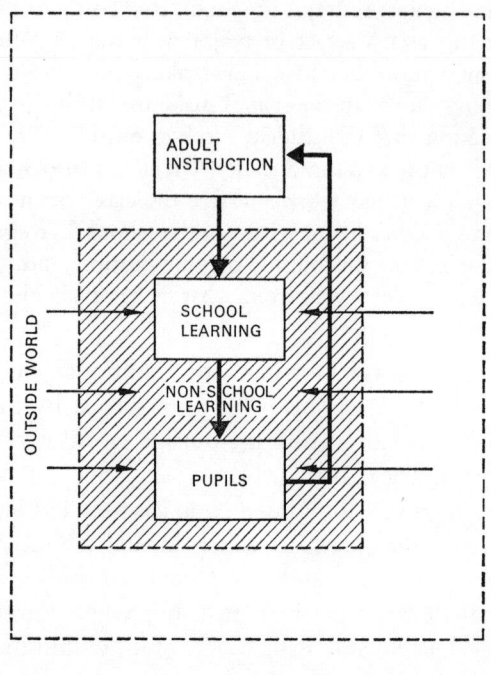

FIG 6

This is because messages transmitted in linguistic channels can only be decoded by the roof-brain, as Sir Arthur Sherrington called it. From the earliest times, the process of education has interpreted itself as a training of this part of the cerebral system, a kind of top-dressing which was intended to regulate the primitive nature of human behaviour. Intellectualism presupposes a well-developed roof-brain, and modern educational thought agrees with that of ancient Greece in insisting that this is *the* attribute by virtue of which man is man. This Platonic homage to the

'Christ, What a Way to Grow Up!': The Drop-out Generation

ideal of the severed head, which finds its clearest expression in the *Phaedo* – 'Thought is best when the mind is gathered into herself and none of these things trouble her, *neither sights nor sounds nor pain nor any pleasure, when she takes leave of the body and has as little as possible to do with it*' – it largely responsible for the emergence of that class of peculiar people who call themselves educated.

Uneasy lies the head that wears an intellectual crown, however. For beneath the newly evolved roof-brain lurks the ancestral cerebral core, seat of the passions and the old Adam. This core cannot decode messages couched in intellectual forms, but is acutely sensitive in terms of auditory, visual and sensori-motor perception. Normally, its activities are monitored and censored by the roof-brain. Circumstances may arise, however, in which disturbance in the central nervous system causes an uncontrollable spasm, almost as if a quiescent volcano had erupted.

> There is an ancient part of the brain, of no great size, which relatively modern parts have outgrown and overgrown. Unlike these latter with the development of cognizing and inferring it has not extended, or but little. Experiment and medical observation show that if it be damaged, still more if it be destroyed, the effective character and motor behaviour of its individual change. The individual's normal activity and affective sympathy are blunted and replaced by stolidity. The individual's motor initiative and emotive reactions are frozen. He has become emotionally unreactive. His facial expression registers no play of feeling. There is torpor and a drowsy state.
>
> When on the contrary electricity is applied to activate this part of the brain, the eyes dilate, the hair bristles, the breathing quickens. The animal bites and claws. In short there is presented a vivid picture of emotional excitement. Or again, when this part of the brain is freed from the control of the great overlying roof-brain by removal of the latter the animal becomes emotionally supersensitive. Irritable and excitable, it exhibits, without provocation, fits of rage.[10]

The first half of this passage might be taken as a vivisectionist caricature of educated, literate man as a gutless wonder; the second admirably illustrates the outburst of primitive mental energy and all the manic-depressive effects associated with the onset of an age of electronic communication. Hot jazz with its fevered drumming, the beat group and its dervish antics, zoom lenses that jolt the eyeballs, souped-up instruments and power-packed machines that make common assault on the nerves – none of these 'make sense' intellectually. Like the occupant of a top-floor flat, the roof-brain thoroughly disapproves of these wild goings-on down below; it reads a Beatles lyric and dismisses it as meaningless gibberish.

McLuhan, with his uncanny knack of putting his finger on an issue only to obscure it, has attributed this state of intense excitement to a distortion of sense ratios. This inspired guesswork, it should be said, finds a measure of support in one of the most reliable research studies yet reported in this doubtful field, Mialaret's *Psychology of the Use of Audio-Visual Aids in Primary Education*:

> In the audio-visual situation the attention aroused is a response to the commanding nature of the message source; the force of this command will be proportional to the difference between the stimulus intensity of the message and that of the rest of the room, and attention is likely to be correspondingly intense. Two consequences of this should be noted: certain authors have not hesitated to compare this situation, in which attention is strongly focused, to a pre-hypnotic situation such as that induced by psychiatrists at the end of the last century: this has been used to explain in part the effect of the cinema on spectators. The same problem appears from another angle to have a second consequence: certain authors have spoken of the subject's being asleep to all that was not part of the message he was listening to or watching. Differences of intensity, either visual or auditory, foster this state of indifference to all that does not constitute the main field of perception, and it is frequently observed that an attentive spectator at the cinema pays no attention to his immediate neighbours, whereas this indifference is less often observed at the theatre (for which there are also other reasons which we shall not enter into here).
>
> Here we again come upon the experimental results pointed out long ago by Pavlov and now being used in deep-sleep therapy. Pavlov had observed that when he eliminated experimentally all

sources of external stimulation from a dog the animal fell asleep. Similar situations are produced in the present-day techniques of sleep psycho-therapy, with the addition of weak period stimulus and the use of certain chemical substances. *A change in the balance of stimuli has another psychological effect which is important in the study of audio-visual situations. The reduction in the intensity of messages received within a given sensory area increases the meaningfulness of the messages received in other sensory fields.*[11]

As the bits and pieces of evidence begin to take shape they appear to point to a conclusion which is even more sensational than McLuhan's. Since the inception of mass education, school-learning has neglected whole areas of sensory awareness, notably those connected with touch, smell, movement and kinaesthetic activities, each of which has an indispensable part to play in awakening a spirit of *joie de vivre*. Addressing its messages to the roof-brain, it has concentrated on the manipulation of symbols (letters and numbers) and more or less sealed off the ancestral brain, whose energies have been held in abeyance. Learning to read was *par excellence* the basic skill which ensured that any inner turbulence was kept in check. Through reading, the child's experience was enormously enlarged conceptually and vicariously, but only by focusing his attention on the silent, word-by-word world of print. Letters were his anodyne. Kept busy with cognitive tasks, he was conditioned to a state of mind in which messages from other sources were so damped down as to be meaningless, or excluded as being too distracting. What went on down below, he was taught, was beneath his notice. Not nice. Not nice at all. Taboo.

Seeing that the intellectual gains from school-learning are as manifest as they are impressive, it may seem positively wrong-headed to assert that they have been accompanied, and offset, by what amounts to a starved emotional life. But all the time the old ancestral brain has been waiting its turn, biding its time. One by one, the new channels of communication flash their signals to it directly. Their messages find an instantaneous response and make the most telling impact because they do not have to be decoded by the roof-brain, acting as an intermediary. These messages are encoded not in static sequences of symbols but in dynamic patterns of light and sound; and they announce the advent of styles of learning so pregnant with power as to make the established styles of literacy and numeracy seem tame and slow.

In what context? The mass media would hardly exert the appeal that they have, had there not been an enormous vacuum in the life of the masses. It is no accident that their appeal is strongest among the semi-literate sections of adult society and among young people, and weakest of all in the ranks of literary intellectuals. For the former, the media have opened up and expanded ranges of experience which were previously inaccessible to them, including the kind of experience which had tended to atrophy during the heyday of literacy.

With what effect? Initially, with effects very similar to those described by Sherrington: excitability, hyper-sensitivity, frenzy, irritability, rage. The alternating moods of ecstatic, switched-on enthusiasm and sour apathy, so characteristic of the drop-out's behaviour, reflect the dissonance in the central nervous system. The 'old' brain is awake again and finds itself at odds with the 'new' brain which has held the driver's seat so long. Admittedly, this is a fuddled, figurative way of trying to explain what is happening. More precisely, if the brain is considered as a system, the indications are that it is currently in a state of meta-stable equilibrium. This could mean a turning point in its evolution, with social consequences which cannot be envisaged – another way of saying that anything can happen. Not since the second half of the sixteenth century has the spirit of the age been so compounded of uncertainty, yearning and near-madness as it is today. It is not a time for clinging to outworn dogmas, least of all those which identify rationalism with logic and language. It is a time for shrewdness and for humility – the kind of shrewdness which discerns in the hippy the man who has the future in his nerves, the kind of humility which is prepared to admit that what the drop-outs, in their inarticulate way, are trying to say is that we have been offering them a stone.

REFERENCES

1 Eric James, *An Essay on the Content of Education* (London, Harrap, 1949), p. 41.
2 Jacques Ellul, *The Technological Society*, translated by John Wilkinson (London, Cape, 1967), pp. 7–9.
3 cf. G. Patrick, 'A Glasgow gang observed', *Scottish Educational Studies*, No. 3 (1969).
4 Act III, Scene iii.
5 James Boswell, *The Life of Samuel Johnson*, Aetat 69.
6 W. C. Trow, 'The systems approach', in L. H. Clark (Ed.), *Strategies and Tactics in Secondary School Teaching* (London, Macmillan, 1968), p. 28.
7 Peter Abbs, *English for Diversity* (London, Heinemann, 1969), pp. 18–19.
8 Wilbur Schramm, 'Educators and communication research', in L. H. Clark, op. cit., p. 8.
9 ibid., pp. 10–11.
10 Sir Arthur Sherrington, *Man on his Nature* (Cambridge University Press, 1940), pp. 231–3.
11 G. Mialaret, *The Psychology of Audio-Visual Aids in Primary Education* (London, Harrap/UNESCO, 1966), p. 31.

CHAPTER TEN

Stuff and Nonsense in the Curriculum

The number of books about education, like the incidence of crimes of violence, has to be plotted as a steadily mounting curve. The fact that they cater for addicts does not make them any less a drug on the market, buoyant as it is. To the extent that this literature is preaching to the converted – for its readership rarely extends beyond the ranks of teachers, students, academics and administrators – it is curiously inbred. It has been remarked with justice that there have been few even moderately good books about education, and only one great one – and that it took the greatest philosopher of all time to write that one. Sooner rather than later, the learned papers, the bulky official reports, the meticulous monographs and the most painstaking empirical studies are quietly pigeon-holed, consigned to the same limbo that awaits all pulp literature.

The trouble is that, in writing them, educationists must observe so many punctilios that, inevitably, their style becomes flat-footed. For the sake of appearing to be objective they have to resort to arguments whose rationality is as impeccable as it is ascetic, and to evidence whose half-life is, at best, brief; to be 'thin on research' is, of all faults, the one they seek to avoid, to which end they eke out their chapters with statistical tables and bespatter their pages with jargon. Only very exceptionally, then, does one come across a book about education which speaks out loud and bold, or one which can be said to be truly heart-warming.

A good deal of contemporary writing on curriculum theory is very nearly unreadable, even by those who are well versed in educationese. A few samples, chosen at random, may be taken as typifying the high level of generality and abstraction which is all-too common:

> Because children react as total organisms, learning experiences must be selected for their influence on the learner's total development and their contribution to balanced and maximum growth.
>
> In the first instance, conceptual frameworks or structural frameworks are visualized as the principles or network of principles which integrate and explain man's observations about particular areas of his environment.
>
> The basic requirement of any organizational scheme or plan is that it should maximize the total effect of the selected learning sequences.

It is hard to see how the average teacher can be expected to get his teeth into sentences of this sort, harder still to believe that the layman will be able to make much sense out of them – and only too easy to agree that they are a blend of stuff and nonsense. What they have to say may be true enough: it is the way they say it which befogs their meaning.

THE LANGUAGE OF EDUCATION

In world-weary cultures words somehow lose their potency. Language itself shows signs of becoming a geriatric case. No amount of education can prevent this happening. Indeed, if the precedents set by the Ancient World are anything to go by, a fully developed education system only becomes possible when a civilization is already in decline. True, Greek and Latin survived the demise of Athens and Rome as centres of European culture and were more widely used in the centuries following their submergence as political powers than they had been during the days of Aeschylus or Virgil, but it is significant that neither proved to be the medium of a virile literature thereafter. By the same token, it is on the cards that English usage will remain a force in the world long after the British Empire has been forgotten, but short of believing that history repeats itself, it is not obvious that anything can be done to prevent people living in these islands from gradually relapsing into a has-been frame of mind. Of all the contextual variables which the curriculum-maker has to reckon with, none is more vitally important than the state of the nation: this, more than anything else, sets limits to what can be done. What he has to say, therefore, must be widely intelligible, not restricted to a select audience of intellectuals. But how? Like the poets, authors of books about education may well complain that, every attempt

> Is a wholly new start, and a different kind of failure
> Because one has only learnt to get the better of words
> For the thing one no longer has to say, or the way in which
> One is no longer disposed to say it. And so each venture
> Is a new beginning, a raid on the inarticulate
> With shabby equipment always deteriorating. . . .[1]

The language of educational discourse is a cross-breed of many terminologies, abstruse in its idioms, intricate in its conventions, and lacking in expressiveness when it comes to plain speaking. As graphic substance it is less than graphic, more a masquerade. No educationist, even in his cups, would dream of addressing his audience in such terms as, 'Get knotted' or 'Watch it, mate' – the equivalents of which in his language might be parodied as, 'It appears that the disagreement between us is so fundamental that there is no point in continuing the dialogue' and, 'Have a proper regard for the consequences of your behaviour'. The educationist is not to be blamed for observing the decorum of his profession, of course, any more than he is to be blamed for the frequent use of technical terms borrowed from psychology, sociology, economics, technology and other studies which make no pretence of appealing to the common touch. Since education has to do with bringing about changes in people, nevertheless, the educationist is under a moral obligation to say what he has to say in some kind of popular language. As things are, this obligation is easier to dodge than it is to fulfil. In the same way that the Augustans prided themselves on artifices of style and diction which had become progressively effete, so we are largely unaware of the extent to which our modes of thought and expression are embedded in an outworn grammar.

In this situation it is timely to ask whether the language of education is due for the kind of renewal which Wordsworth announced for verse in the Preface to *Lyrical Ballads*:

> The principal object, then, in these Poems was to choose incidents and situations of common life, and to relate or describe them, throughout, as far as possible in a selection of the language really used by men, and, at the same time, to throw over them a certain colouring of imagination, whereby ordinary things should be presented to the mind in an unusual aspect; and further, and above all, to make these incidents and situations interesting by tracing in them, truly though not ostentatiously, the primary laws of our nature: chiefly as far as regards *the manner in which we associate ideas in a state of excitement*.

Dealing as he does with an essentially practical activity, the educationist cannot give free play to his imagination, but why should he retreat so often behind a smoke-screen of pedantry? Is there no way in which he can report his findings more zestfully? At a time when the association of ideas is in a state of more than usual excitement, must he represent learning and teaching as being duller than they are? If he cannot take his cue from Wordsworth in looking for a plainer and more emphatic language in the conditions of 'humble and rustic life', might he not at least acknowledge that there is something to be said for 'the language really used by men' in an industrial society?

Thanks to the work of Basil Bernstein, most educationists are familiar with the functional and structural differences between 'elaborated' and 'restricted' codes of spoken English, and have not been slow in seizing on them in order to account for the inherent inequality of opportunity in British education. If the full implications of these differences have yet to dawn on us the reason is that we are still, for the most part, utterly convinced that the standards of rectitude laid down by literate-mindedness are the only acceptable ones.

The 'elaborated' code is complex, logical, articulate, couched in a verbally explicit phraseology which is carefully deliberated, orderly, rational, above all polite. By contrast, the 'restricted' code is simple, often incoherent, impatient of conveying its messages by words alone, limited by its context, disorderly, impulsive, gauche to the point of rudeness. The one uses the syntax of the roof-brain: the other is more of a *cri de cœur*, an ejaculation from the cortex core.

The distinctions between the two usages run parallel to the dual classification of people as middle class and working class, highbrow and lowbrow, well educated and partly educated which everyone recognizes. In each case it is taken for granted that the distinction is between superiors and inferiors; any querying, let alone rejection, of the right of the 'elaborated' code to be considered correct is practically unthinkable.

Why should it be? Those who prefer plain speaking – and in an age in which oral communication is staging a come-back their numbers are by no means confined to unskilled and semi-skilled workers – tend to look upon received standard English usage as merely mannered, stuffy, long-winded and, as often as not, dissembling. To their way of thinking, 'Get knotted' is not only plainer and more emphatic than the word-games which the *cognoscenti* delight in, it is also more honest. A 'restricted' code may be the language of the dumb ox, but it can be used with devastating effect in situations where a wink is more eloquent than the most elegant phrase, in the quick fire of unanswerable repartee, in the telephone kiosk and a host of other contexts.

Suppose, then, that we begin by asking why it is that the spoken word only looks good on paper if it is delivered in 'elaborated' code, and why transcriptions of it in 'restricted' code usually fail to 'make sense'. One reason is that in the first case the transmission is conceived in terms of print, or at any rate strongly influenced by habits of reading and writing; that is to say, its aspect of doubletalk is due to its being twice-removed from the message source. The very fact that its sentence formation is so studied and its punctuation so fastidious is a reminder that the thought processes going into it are conditioned by the rules of continuous prose. The speaker is literally watching his Ps and Qs. He is out to make an impression – the impression of a bookman.

This explanation is only partly plausible, however. How to account for the syntax of the *Iliad*, itself the product of a pre-literate culture, it may be asked? The question immediately prompts an alternative explanation, for the Homeric style of declamation, typified by Achilles as a 'speaker of words and a doer of deeds', has nothing in common with the 'elaborated' code's liking for the passive voice. The latter is symptomatic of the conceptual thinker, not the man of percept and the man of action. It is the kind of language which prefers to give sound reasons rather than to vent strong feelings. It is also the language of a bureaucracy.

Confronted by the new non-verbal languages which are entering common use, a bureaucracy's first reaction is one of outrage: as McLuhan says, it is inclined to ride off into the Middle Ages hoping it is the future. In an age of high-speed oral communications, however, all forms of sham are easily seen through even if they cannot easily be swept aside. For its part, the 'restricted' code can now be seen as having closer affinities with the sound-track of *I am a Camera*, the impromptu exclamations of the television commentator or the burblings of the disc jockey than with the bookman and the writer. For certain purposes – and the range and scope of these is widening all the time, just as their social prestige is increasing – this kind of language is more spontaneous, livelier and more punch-packing than the tame, villatic styles of literacy. Significantly, authors of genius have been the first to recognize this.

Let us watch the camera at work:

'In the flesh, Mrs Opal Emerson Mudge fell somewhat short of a prophetic aspect. She was pony-built and plump, with the face of a haughty Pekinese, a button of a nose, and arms so short that, despite her most indignant endeavours, she could not clasp her hands in front of her as she sat on the platform waiting.'

'Angus Duer came by, disdainful as a greyhound, and pushing on white gloves (which are the whitest and most superciliously white objects on earth). . . .'

'At the corner of the Greek Confectionery Parlour, while they [i.e. the local youths] ate dreadful messes of decayed bananas, acid cherries, whipped cream and gelatinous ice cream, they screamed to one another: "Hey, lemme 'lone", "Quit dog-gone you, looka what you went and done, you almost spilled my glass swater", "Like hell I did", "Hey, gol darn your hide, don't you go sticking your coffin nail in my i-scream".'

'She saw that his hands were not in keeping with a Hellenic face. They were thick, roughened with needle and hot iron and plough handle. Even in the shop he persisted in his finery. He wore a silk shirt, a topaz scarf, thin tan shoes.'

'The drain pipe was dripping, a dulcet and lively song: drippety-drip-drip-dribble; drippety-drip-drip-drip.'

The method throughout is the photographic. Click, and the picture's ours.[2]

That the novelist and the novel as a literary form, have been influenced by cinematic, televisual and other techniques which were still only in the offing in Sinclair Lewis's day is obvious enough. Decidedly less obvious are the ways in which modes of apprehension are being reslanted by new styles of communication. Film and television have been with us long enough for most people to get the hang of techniques of presentation – flashback, split screen, lapsed time, jumped sequence, montage, zoom shots, mixed image and all the other topsyturvy tricks of the trade – which are completely at odds with the orderly snail's pace of ordinary prose narrative. Accustomed to them as we are, all the same, it is easy to overlook the ways in which they remould outlooks and loosen the hold of old decorum. It is not simply that our ideas about what constitute the basic skills are undergoing a sea-change: much more subtle and fundamental is the shift from verbal conceptualization to figural perception in the learning process.

While it may be a disservice to Bernstein's theoretic models to represent the 'elaborated' code as exemplifying the values of a literate culture, the fact is that, in many respects, modern communication systems operate in a fashion which is much more akin to the one characterized by him as 'restricted'. The latter is economical, sparing in its uses of words because, intuitively, it realizes that invariably there is more to the message than can be conveyed by a literal statement. It knows that the look on a man's face means more than anything he says, no matter how eloquently he says it. A nod, a wink or a shrug of the shoulders may not be so explicit as a verbal proposition, but perceptually they share one quality of the electric media in being instantaneous. Among other things, this spells the end of the era of chalk and talk in the schools.

FALLING STANDARDS IN THE CLASSROOM

It was said earlier that only once in a long while does one come across a book about education which is genuinely heart-warming. One such book is John Blackie's *Good Enough for the Children?*, which deserves to rank alongside that earlier minor classic, Edmond Holmes's *What Is and What Might Be*. Both represent the considered verdict, based on long experience as Chief Inspectors of Schools, and in both cases that verdict amounts to a scathing indictment of the English system of education. It is not the intention here to recapitulate Blackie's strictures on the curriculum of primary schools, parts of which he designated as 'a lot of poor stuff – bad, crude illustrations, badly written and emotionally threadbare stories, nambypamby verses, books of reference marred by inaccuracies and too thin and childish in content, much that is vulgar and second-rate.'[3] Still less it is the intention to make capital out of such criticisms or to jibe at the lack of sensitivity and imagination in teachers; as he said, 'Before we condemn let us be quite certain that we do not make the same mistake.' In any case, the primary school's way of life can no longer rightly be accused of being either shallow or inhumane: of all the stages in the continuous process of education it is the only one which can claim to be largely free from disaffection – free because its approach is child-centred.

It is at the secondary stage that the charge of flat-footedness has to be laid. If this sounds unreasonable, let those who object to it remind themselves that while there is plenty of evidence to show that more and more pupils are voluntarily staying on beyond the legal school-leaving age, on the debit side there is also a good deal of evidence which indicates that the schools are failing to hold the interest of a fair proportion of the thirteen to fifteen age groups. In view of the powerful social and economic pressures ranged against the potential drop-outs, indeed, it may well be that beneath the surface calm there is a silent majority for whom going to school is a case of Hobson's choice, the next best thing to doing nothing at all. For some, evidently, the goods on offer are simply not good enough.

Why so? It is easy to point a finger of scorn at the flashy attractions and shoddy, makeshift satisfactions to which teenagers turn – the early leaver who worships his second-hand motor bike and sports a studded leather jacket, and his 'bird' who has eyes only for cosmetics advertisements and ears only for the Top Ten. The unscrupulous manipulation of modern youth by pop culture profiteers provides a never-failing excuse for indignation on the part of educational do-gooders. Without saying that this scandalized posture is typical of all teachers, as a class their attitude towards pupils' out-of-school activities too often tends to be at best condescending, at worst contemptuous. Either way, it is the attitude of the sophist, the Pharisee, the pedagogue. Because it is incapable of understanding what happens in the translation from one medium to another, it assumes that popularization – the film of the book, for example – is necessarily vulgarization, and doggedly refuses to countenance forms of learning which do not fit in with its own narrow-minded requirements.

Today the boot is on the other foot and it is the pupils' turn to be contemptuous. And for good reasons. As they see it, the sheer professionalism of the discotheque, the cinema or the television programme is streets ahead of the kind of performance put on by the most proficient teacher on the classroom floor. Today it is not canned music (as it used to be called) but chalk and talk which is open to the criticism of being cheap and nasty. It is not simply that the film show in the classroom cannot compete with wide-screen projection, that the record-player in the music appreciation lesson fails to reproduce the intensity of a beat group session, and that educational television rarely matches the excitement of programmes viewed at home. To say that such aids to learning lose some of the power and allure in a school setting which insists on drawing a hard and fast line between education and entertainment is too crude an explanation, though in this connection it is worth bearing in mind the Newsom boy's comment, 'It could be made of marble, Sir, but it would still be a bloody school.' Accustomed as they are to high-powered, slick productions, it is not surprising that teenagers find the daily round of lessons tame and monotonous. The even tenor of the instructor's voice lacks the varied modulations of their Radio One mentors at the breakfast table; textbooks have a lacklustre look to eyes that take the technical expertise displayed in colour supplements for granted; procedures, rituals and methods of keeping discipline more or less rule out any serious regard for those uninhibitable primal emotions which are constantly titillated in their daily lives and which find their rawest expression nowadays in the dance hall. Over-stimulated, choosy, difficult to please, they may be, inattentive, scatter-brained, opinionated, irresponsible and so on and on. Instead of blaming them for their faults, why not accept them as the creatures of their time and begin from there?

But this is precisely what the school cannot do so long as it adheres to norms of behaviour and rules of procedure which have been deemed necessary and proper hitherto. It is one thing to agree that the ultimate purpose of all teaching is to render itself unnecessary – that is, to enable the learner to go his own way under his own steam; it is quite another to agree that the days of the old-style teacher are numbered, that the young are different animals compared with their counterparts of thirty or forty years ago, much less dependent, much more aggressive in urging their demands. As yet, the manifestations of pupil power are no more than a rumour, and a ridiculous one at that, and the authorities can take refuge in the belief that it can't happen here. Different animals indeed! – the notion is too preposterous to be taken seriously. Not so in the U.S.A. evidently:

> New York, 28 February
>
> High school students here, their ages ranging from fourteen to eighteen, are insisting that in a number of the city's schools they shall have majority control over most policy decisions, including entrance requirements, discipline and the appointment of staff.
>
> Specifically, they demand that such decisions shall be reached by a majority vote of a twenty-member board of which ten members shall be students, five parents and only five staff, including the principal. Students want the decisions of these boards to be 'final, absolute, and binding on all teachers'.
>
> These and other, still more audacious demands reflect a new wave of student militancy which has begun to spread through the nation's high schools and is of the kind already disrupting scores of American colleges. As with so many trends, it has developed fastest in New York.
>
> Elected representatives of the city's 275,000 high school students are also demanding full freedom of expression, not only in the classroom, but everywhere in the school, with a guarantee that no student shall be penalized for any idea he expresses, no matter how inflammatory or far-out.
>
> They also want guarantees that the schools will not call in police if the students threaten to commit any crime. And they insist upon the right to receive through the schools whatever personal advice they need on abortion, contraception, drugs and military service without prejudice to their school records.
>
> In presenting these demands the students rejected concessions offered by the New York Board of Education aimed at damping down the high school revolt. The board was prepared to let the students have some say in policy decisions but certainly not the last word. When these board proposals were presented to a representative gathering of students the students became so disruptive that the meeting broke up. A second joint meeting this week also broke up in disorder, but the board is still prepared to make a third attempt. . . .
>
> 'These children are so much more mature than we were at their age', said one Board of Education official. 'They are also more politically aware. The system has to adjust to them a bit.'

Stuff and Nonsense in the Curriculum

There is also some realization of this on the national level. At a recent conference of high school principals, Mr Robert H. Finch, Secretary of Health, Education and Welfare, warned: 'We sense intuitively that the first thoroughly televised generation in the history of the world cannot simply be passed into and through the same institutional structures that its parents travelled.'[4]

Things have come to a pretty pass when pupils dictate terms to their teachers, it may be thought, and that such a state of affairs could ever arise in Britain seems as unlikely as it is undesirable. We find it convenient to forget that a similar state of affairs existed in the eras of the *grammaticus* and the *studium generale*, and that the first university at Bologna was controlled by students, with the *doctor* and *magister* on tap rather than on top. It would be more realistic to make up our minds here and now that what is happening in New York will sooner or later happen here too, since the educational services carry within themselves the prophecy of the eventual release of the young from a subordinate role. Far-fetched as it seems to ascribe the trend towards active participation, towards corporate living rather than individualism, towards co-operation rather than competition to exposure to television – and even more far-fetched to assert that this exposure has erased all sense of personal identity in young people – the trend is unmistakable. To ignore it, and to try to resist it is to ask for trouble.

The education system as we have come to know it functions as a bureaucracy, and a bureaucracy is never fully aware of what is going on in the world around it until it is faced with a *fait accompli*. Its institutions flourish so long as their members are content with a passive role which allows of their being kept subservient; they break down when there is no audience, only actors. Thus, the school as an institution with its egg-crate structure of classrooms has to be seen as a relic of nineteenth-century industrialism which is in many ways out of keeping with the conditions of an age of technology.

It is easy to imagine what would happen if compulsory school attendance were to be abolished overnight; the chances are that before long most secondary schools would be as empty as the churches. Sound as they are from an economic and political point of view, the arguments in favour of raising the school-leaving age gloss over the fact that for many teenagers schooling is no better than an enforced holding operation. However well-intended, and education is nothing if not well-intended, the school is a device for segregating the young from the rest of society and keeping them, as it were, out of circulation. When teachers go on strike newspaper editorials are the first to voice public concern for the children's well-being, as if their future prospects were being placed in jeopardy and held to ransom in pressing for better working conditions and more pay; but this profession of concern is to some extent disingenuous, for, as everyone knows, what hurts most is the inconvenience suffered by parents and employers.

Whether or not sociologists are correct in thinking that rules of procedure and the structure of institutions are the real cohesive elements in any society, there can be little doubt that they are the ones which alone prevent the educational system from falling apart at the seams. Threatened by external forces, of which the mass media are only one example, as well as by internal forces which are potentially no less disruptive, the danger is that the school will become much more concerned with its own organizational maintenance than with trying to come to terms with drastically changing circumstances. In that case, the policy of a holding operation will need to be implemented more sternly than it is at present, and the curriculum as an artificial contrivance – digging holes and filling them in for the sake of keeping the young occupied and out of harm's way – will become even more artificial.

The 'boundary maintenance' solution, that is, the attempt to safeguard the school's survival as a centralized institution by sealing it off as far as possible from influences which interfere with its work, is the one most likely to be tried. Nevertheless, it is a recipe for disaster. For one thing, the young will not stand for it. Gone for ever is the docility which kept them chained to their desks. Authority has been dislodged from its pedestal and cut down to size. Far from looming larger than life, as they once did, the powers-that-be look decidedly smaller on the television screen. Who's afraid of Big Brother or the big bad wolf? Not they. The espresso bar and the discotheque are greater levellers than the comprehensive school. Little folk are no longer resigned to thinking of themselves as nonentities: each is bent on 'doing his own thing', a poor thing, possibly (like roaring around the streets on a second-hand motor bike, say), but his own. Dumb insolence? Too big for their boots? Heading for a fall? Be that as it may, any sense of allegiance to established codes of behaviour has been so weakened as to make it extremely unlikely that such codes can be imposed from now on.

Black pamphleteers may rail against any move which looks like truckling to this uppity mood in the same way that, in the U.S.A., not so long ago, pro-war 'hawks' denounced anti-war 'doves' for being 'soft on communism'. Progressive methods, they argue, are responsible for falling standards of attainment and sloppy discipline in the schools. Were this not so preposterous a lie there would be no point in rebutting it. In the first place, as we have seen, progressive methods have made relatively little impression on secondary schools in Britain; the situation might have been a good deal healthier if they had. In the second, all the available evidence (for example, in the Newsom Report and in the Scottish Council for Research in Education's Report on Rising Standards in the Primary School) shows that formal scholastic attainments, at any rate in English and arithmetic, have steadily improved over the years. Granted, the improvement is not universal – the proportion of backward readers is twice the national average in the London metropolitan area, for instance – but to pretend that standards were higher at the turn of the century when the curriculum of the elementary school consisted of the Three Rs and little else is merely perverse.

There remains the criticism that school discipline has been allowed to become so lax as to leave the teacher in a position of impotence. Adolescents show scant respect for their elders, are too headstrong and self-assertive, have more money than is good for them, are too fond of living it up, too naked and unashamed in their sex life, tend to be work-shy – the list of complaints can be added to almost indefinitely. What is not obvious is how any of them can be connected with the use of progressive methods in the schools. When adult society is unsure of its values, the young are the first to see through any attempt to impose upon them. As regards the change in their attitude towards the world of work, Bryan Wilson offers his own explanation:

> In the early stages of industrialization we typically relied on the heightened socialization of individuals as the guarantee that men would perform their economic roles. A man's character was the guarantee of his attitude to work. A man who was 'conscientious, reliable, frugal, willing' and possessed the rest of the catalogue of Victorian virtues, was necessarily a good worker. But this was a blanket guarantee of his attributes necessary for the economic operation of society. Today in a more developed society work situations can be controlled much more effectively by equipment – the conveyor belt, electronics, data processing – and so there is no need to socialize the whole man so thoroughly. Increasingly, control is exerted at the point at which a man works, and not over his whole life activities: so long as he is there, he can be specifically controlled by equipment and need not be controlled through socializing processes in early life, and perhaps – as secondary socialization – job preparation.
>
> Because total moral dispositions of individuals are not now required for the work-order of society, the economic underpinning of morality has gone – and the changing moral standards of society and the changing patterns of socialization, from free expression in the schools to the permissive morality in the wider society, are associated with the changing character of social control in economic activities.[5]

As an explanation, this may not satisfy the puritans but at least it earns credit for locating the influences affecting the learning situation in society at large. Whether or not we agree that in advanced industrial economies there is less need for built-in moral codes and for personal dispositions such as trustworthiness, there is little doubt that the pressure on non-academic pupils to toe the line and work hard for success in school has eased. For those for whom leaving certificate requirements are not binding as incentives, the categorical imperative which decreed that it was a case of 'get on or get out' has lost some of its force, for although formal education may still be regarded as the royal road to a well-paid job and a satisfying career, it is no longer the only one open to the young.

At high speeds, patterns of change become plainly visible, so we are told. Today, at long last, the young are beginning to discern the deceptions in much of what they are taught. Time and again, the history of education shows that the stuff of learning in one age is nonsense to the next; but it is only when, as now, the pace of events is stepped up to racing pitch that the metamorphosis can actually be seen taking place. During the heyday of the Classics pupils saw nothing wrong with the kind of instruction which set them to resolve such nice problems as:

> Whether it is credible that a crow really perched on the head of Valerus in his duel with a Gaul, and flapped his wings in the latter's face.

or, seeing that there is no end to these fatuities,

> Suppose there is a law that a priestess must be chaste and pure and her parents chaste and pure. A virgin is captured by pirates and sold to a procurer who lets her out for prostitution. She asks her clients to pay her and yet respect her chastity. A soldier refuses to do this and tries to violate her. She kills him. She is accused of murder and is acquitted and returns home. She asks to become a priestess. Plead for and against.

Exquisite nonsense, we tell ourselves, as if there were no question of its being replicated in many an examination paper nowadays. Is it really so astonishing 'to realize that for almost a thousand years teachers and pupils struggled their way through countless exercises of this sort?'[6] If so, is it not even more astonishing that educationists should be so complacent as to think that such dreary pedantry cannot possibly be perpetrated at the present time without being shown up for what it is worth? It is true that we have come a long way from the crass regimen of rote learning, and that with the benefit of hindsight we can condemn the soulless methods of teaching exemplified in Mr Gradgrind's cross-examination of poor Sissy Jupe; we have no further use for the refined tortures of brain-teasing spelling tests which were in vogue a century or more ago for instance,

> While hewing yews Hugh lost his ewe
> And put it in the Hue and Cry,
> To name its face's dusky hues
> Was all the effort he could use.
> You brought the ewe back by and by
> And only begged the hewer's ewer
> Your hands to wash in water pure
> Lest nice-nosed ladies not a few
> Should cry, on coming near you, 'Ugh'.

Unthinkable that such pitiful balderdash could ever find a place in the modern classroom, we say. But is it so unthinkable that the content and methods of teaching which now strike us as being perfectly sound will come to be seen as just as rubbishy as those which passed muster for the Victorians?

Looking back, it is hard to decide dispassionately which was worse – the evils of child labour or the blessings of literacy as interpreted during the first half of the nineteenth century. 'Every town in the district has the same tale to tell', an inspector of schools reported sadly in 1855. 'At Coventry I am told that the children are employed in making ribbons; at Bromsgrove in making nails; at Redditch in pointing needles. In the colliery districts they open and shut doors in the pits. In the agricultural districts they drive teams, tend the cows, watch the birds. At Malvern they drive the donkeys; at Newport go to the forges.' Which was the harsher fate, one cannot help wondering, to be left to make ribbons and tend the cows, or to be herded into a school-room, there to chant the alphabet in unison and fall in with the rest of its rigmarole? And which was the more reprehensible, the blatant profit motive of captains of industry who saw children as a source of cheap manpower, or the piety of philanthropists and reformers who saw schools as the training grounds for cheerful subservience and stoical acceptance of a life of drudgery? It seems that accompanying the Three Rs all along have gone the Three Cs – Cant, Collusion and Conditioning; and in their train have come the Three As – Anxiety, Alienation and Absurdity.

Oliver Twist's daring to ask for more symbolizes the starting-point for the growth of less pliable frames of mind on the part of the masses. Timid at first, self-assertiveness has been fed by the educational services themselves, still more by the technologies which have helped to bring about an affluent society, and has now reached the point where it feels capable of forcing a show-down with the authorities. The latter may seek sanctuary inside their bureaucratic enclaves, but the hunt is up, and it begins to look as though the game may be up also.

> It is the students' role to cause the wave which has built up in society finally to break (thinks Richard Hoggart). They are more intelligent and emotionally articulate than most; they are at the moment free of continuing professional, financial and domestic responsibilities. More than anyone else they are able to stand, as it were, apart from society and ask what it's all in aid of. They are acting out a phase in what could be one of the most important secular changes of the last two or three hundred years. We could be seeing the beginning of the end of the Protestant Ethic in its two main forms of expression: in its attitudes to competitive work and to the sexual life. Both are coming under powerful challenge.[7]

The charge pressed by student activists boils down (or up) to saying that the universities have betrayed their trust by allowing themselves to be turned into service stations, at the beck and call of industrial and political agencies; and that so far as their teaching is concerned they have become increasingly preoccupied with advanced professional training and less concerned with the general welfare of students. Above all, it asserts that students are entitled to have more of a say in the way a university orders its affairs. Would this charge have produced the response that it has already produced if academics had been left to follow their own devices? But for the uproarious misbehaviour of the sit-ins, teach-ins, protest marches and violent invasion of Senate chambers would the dissidents have gained so much as a hearing? Universities are supposedly the power-houses for creative ideas, yet the record shows that they have been persistently withdrawn in their attitude to extramural affairs, slow and unwilling to reform themselves, and chronically uninterested in the methods they employ. During the Renaissance they remained wedded to outdated studies which they had inherited from the medieval schoolmen; in the eighteenth century they were so far sunk in torpor as to be hopelessly out of touch with the forward march of knowledge (which it was left to the Dissenting Academies to advance); in the nineteenth they remained obdurate in the face of the ascendant claims of the natural sciences and had to be forced out of their splendid isolation by governmental intervention. To this day, their entrance requirements remain one of the chief stumbling blocks to curriculum development in the schools.

According to Bryan Wilson, 'The shift to science and technology in universities, and the shift to scientific styles of procedure in the humanities, reflect the increased emphasis on instrumental procedures and the decline of concern with the humanistic affective aspects of discipline.'[8] Just how far the history of humankind can be seen, as he suggests, as a 'pushing back of the affective sphere of life into the activities of socialization' is debatable. If anything, the signs are that the 'affective sphere' is being forced more into the forefront of the modern consciousness. As was said earlier, what we have to reckon with is a massive release of nervous energy which finds its expression more often than not in non-intellectual forms, in the neo-romantic vogue of the man of feeling and percept.

Unrest in higher education makes headline news because a body of students – not to be identified with the student body – is vociferous enough and has an undeniable strength of conviction which is not to be placated or side-tracked by smooth talk. If that conviction does not carry all before it, at least it disturbs the equanimity of the authorities and causes them to think twice, and think hard, about the purposes and procedures of the institutions under their control. The same can hardly be said as yet for those in charge of the secondary schools in which protest, if it is heard at all, is necessarily muted. Yet the same forces which are causing upheavals on the university campus are silently at work in the classroom, and the fact that to date it has been easy to contain them is no excuse for shutting our eyes to their existence. It would be mischievous, of course, to suggest that the typical classroom is a battlefield in which the teacher has to contend with a concealed fifth column or a mutinous rabble; though this is what it sometimes feels like, the great majority of pupils comply with school regulations and see no reason to complain about the treatment they receive. A fairer analogy might be with the House of Commons where Ministers of the Crown have to face an organized Opposition. Teenagers are past-masters in the art of 'playing up' and getting together. Quite apart from all the other reasons for thinking that the desire for participation and belief in the need for shared decision-making and collective action will become more popular, young people cannot fail to be influenced by the multifarious forms of agitation going on around them – anti-Apartheid demonstrations, stop-the-war, ban-the-bomb, down-with-bloodsports, save-our-this-that-or-the-other marchers, dockers, dustmen, teachers, nurses, old age pensioners, even the blind carrying placards and shouting slogans. The publicity they receive makes them infectious and hot-blooded youth is quick to catch the infection. To be up in arms in some cause or other has become fashionable, though at times the pretexts for protest are so flimsy that it is hard to decide whether what we are witnessing is the moral equivalent of civil war or of morris dancing.

Even if the causes for grievance have nothing else in common, common to them all is a conviction based on strong feeling rather than rational argument that corporate action is essential if the stranglehold of bureaucratic authority is to be broken.

In the same way that anthropologists distinguish between the material and non-material aspects of a culture, sociologists distinguish between the 'instrumental' and 'expressive' components of a society. Broadly speaking, the 'instrumental' component refers to the knowledge, skills, institutions and procedures which make up the society, while the 'expressive' component reflects its values and norms of approved behaviour. As with the material culture, the former is visible and survives through its artefacts, whereas the 'expressive' component, which alone can explain what it feels like and 'means' to live in a given society at a given time, is always invisible. These two components, needless to say, are as intimately related as body and mind, substance and form. Normally, they are in harmony, in which case everyone is agreed on the need for accepting the established values, observing norms of behaviour and learning the skills and procedures expected of members of the society. But just as snakes start squirming before they slough off their dried-out, itchy skins, so a society begins to be uncomfortable when it senses a disharmony between its institutions and its way of life.

Which brings us to the hard luck story of British education. The burden of it has been harped on *ad nauseam* ever since the publication of the Crowther Report and is easily summarized:

> The transmission of the expressive component is concerned with preparing children for their adult roles in society, whereas the instrumental prepares them more specifically for their occupational roles. Moreover, a man's occupational role is consonant with his more general non-occupational adult roles. Together they constitute a part of his life style. The content of the expressive component is largely middle class and it is easily assimilated by children from middle-class homes. One of the major sources of conflict in the educational system is that many working-class children need to learn and accept middle-class values and standards of behaviour in order to succeed academically. This appears to be most difficult for the less able working-class children. . . . Clearly the educational system confirms the values of middle-class pupils. It may also confer new values on some working-class pupils, the successful ones. This is an aspect of the socializing function of education. In that it may begin the process of changing some working-class children into middle-class adults, education also acts as an agency of embourgeoisement.[9]

Leaving aside the fact that the concept of 'class' is now so hazy as to be less than helpful, there is no doubt that formal schooling tends to arouse feelings of inferiority, inadequacy and insecurity in the minds of many pupils. The Sissy Jupe syndrome remains uncured. A hundred years ago, when the lines of cleavage between upper, middle and lower classes were a good deal more pronounced than they are today, there was some excuse for singling out social class as the most important variable. As things are, any worthwhile analysis must take into account a whole set of variables. If only in rag-bag fashion, some of these can be listed as follows:

Tradition	Innovation
High culture	Mass culture
'Middle class'	'Working class'
General education	Special education
Establishment	Opposition
Elitism	Egalitarianism
Grammar school	Comprehensive or secondary modern school
Literate	Non-literate
Academic	Anti-academic
'Elaborated' code	'Restricted' code
Conceptual learning	Perceptual learning
Theoretic studies	Practical activities
Rational legitimation	Affective legitimation
De jure authority	*De facto* influence
Individual competition	Group participation and co-operation
Bureaucratic control	Personalized control

At first glance, such a list seems to make confusion worse confounded. This is because contemporary society is in a schizophrenic state in which the pros and cons of any issue are evenly and delicately balanced. In so far as the classroom is a microcosm of that society, it has to be recognized that the relationship between the teacher and his pupils is now one between equal partners, and that any pretence of maintaining a master–servant relationship has to be avoided.

As the pace of social change accelerates, pretence in any shape or form becomes easily detectable. Today, the young are well aware that what is taught has covert as well as overt intentions. They do not need a social scientist to tell them that, for example,

> The traditional school assembly may have certain religious functions but from the point of view of the school as an organization it is of more importance as a daily display of the authority relationships within the school. The holder of most authority, the head teacher, is on prominent display, perhaps wearing his gown as the regalia of his office. Teachers and pupils stand in his presence unless given permission to sit. Teachers are placed separate and distinct, as are prefects. The pupils with the lowest status, the first year, are placed at the front. Within age groups the lower stream pupils stand in front of their more esteemed age-mates of the upper stream. The whole assembly takes place in the school hall which is saved if possible, at great expense, for this daily ten minute ceremony. The routine of the ceremony emphasizes the continuity of the authority pattern on display from day to day. In the day school the assembly is a daily reminder to the child that he is now, once again, a pupil. It is significant that in maintained schools the assembly must usually begin the school day. It would be of little use to remind pupils of these essential authority relationships at the end of the day.[10]

Essential they may be. At the end of the day, nevertheless, pupils may be forgiven for thinking that there is an air of duplicity about many of the rules of procedure which they are expected to observe. More disposed to speak their mind than they used to do when books and letters cramped their style, they are not to be overawed by rituals which appear to them as the outward and visible sign of an inward and spiritual disgrace. For all its veneer of respectability, they are unimpressed by styles of teaching which smack of double-talk. Corporal punishment may be on the way out, but violence of the tongue is still not uncommon, hurtful even when it is quite unintentional – and they know it.

What it amounts to is that the age-old question, 'What should children learn?', is being answered by the children themselves. If there is one lesson which the curriculum theorist needs to take to heart it is this. The young are telling us that the kind of general education offered so far has not been to their taste, often substandard, largely pointless and a waste of time. If we care to listen, and most of us prefer not to, they are telling us that they no longer need the kind of teaching that has been thought necessary in the past. What they are asking for is not more efficient instruction but more sympathetic guidance – 'the process of helping a person to develop and accept an integrated and adequate picture of himself and of his role in the world of work, to test this concept against reality, and to convert it into a reality, with satisfaction to himself and benefit to society.'[11]

Theirs is no unreasonable demand. This, surely, was what Froebel had in mind in urging that the teacher's duty is to be passive, following the dictates of the learner, not his own – and what Mager means when he assures us that if we give each learner a clear statement of objectives we may not have to do much else.

REFERENCES

1 T. S. Eliot, 'East Coker', *Four Quartets* (London, Faber & Faber).
2 E. M. Forster, *Abinger Harvest* (London, Arnold, 1936), pp. 128–9.
3 John Blackie, *Good Enough for the Children?* (London, Faber & Faber, 1963), p. 16.
4 *The Observer* (1 March 1970).
5 Bryan Wilson, in W. R. Niblett (Ed.), *Higher Education: Demand and Response* (London, Tavistock Publications, 1969), p. 22.
6 Martin Ballard, *The Story of Teaching* (London, Longmans Young Books, 1969), p. 22.
7 Richard Hoggart, 'Higher education and personal life', in W. R. Niblett, op. cit., p. 217.
8 Bryan Wilson, loc. cit.
9 Ronald King, *Education* (London, Longmans, 1969), p. 21.
10 ibid., p. 39.
11 D. E. Super, *The Psychology of Careers* (New York, Harper & Row, 1967), p. 197.

Index

Abbs, Peter, 239
adolescent subcultures, 186, 232
Aeneas Sylvius, 22
aims, *see* objectives
algorithmic learning, 225–6
American high school, evolution of, 47 ff., 153, 170
Aristotle, 3, 4, 22, 200
Armytage, W. H. G., 21
Arnold, Matthew, 23, 216
Arnold, Thomas, 21
artes liberales, 22, 23
Association of Education Committees, 82
Auden, W. H., 113
Augustine, St, 23
authority, concept of, 114 ff., 262 ff.
Ayer, A. J., 215

baccalauréat examination, 105, 106
Bacon, 22
Banks, John, 141
basic skills, American view of, 46
redefinition of, 38–9
Basil, St, 23
Beeby, C. E., 67, 68, 221
behavioural technology, 183
Beloe Report, 77, 79, 87
Bernstein, Basil, 253, 257
Berthoin reforms in French education, 104
Biological Sciences Curriculum Study, 56–60
biology teaching, reasons for innovation in, 55–6
Bishop of Woolwich, 214

Blackie, John, 257
Bloom's taxonomy of educational objectives, 154
Bonhoeffer, 214
boundary maintenance in educational institutions, 122–5, 262
Briault, W. H. T., 171
Broudy, H., 199
Browning, Robert, 216
Bruner, J. S., 4, 6, 26, 155, 156, 158, 182, 194, 210, 221
Brynmor-Jones Report, 38

cahier de classe, 94
Cavendish Laboratory, 24
Certificate of Secondary Education (C.S.E.), 78, 79, 91, 222
Chaucer, 214
CHEMStudy, 60
Chemical Bond Approach, 60
child-centred curriculum, vindication of, 224 ff.
Circular 10/65 (D.E.S.), 140
Circular 600 (Scottish Education Department), 140
'Classes Nouvelles', 100
cognitive structures, 198–9
Comenius, 7, 63, 118, 152
Commissariat Général au Plan, 100
Compagnons de l'Université Nouvelle, 99
comprehensive school principle, 81
Conant, J. B., 49
Condillac, 98
'conditions of learning', 155
Condorcet, 98

conseil de classe, 94, 106, 108
Consultative Committee on the Curriculum (Scotland), 132
continuous assessment, 37, 94, 222
convergent thinking, 159
Copernicus, 113
cost-benefit analysis, 177
Council for Curriculum Reform (1945), 75, 76
creativity, 27
Crowther Report, 82, 270
culture générale, 102, 103, 105
curriculum, artificiality of, 162
  child-centred *v*. discipline-centred, 7–10, 26–7
  cyclical process of change in, 22–3
  definitions of, 4 ff.
  lumber in, 265 ff.
curriculum development, 11 ff.
  guidelines for, 33–40
  in England, 71 ff.
  in France, 97 ff.
  in Scotland, 127 ff.
  in U.S.A., 45 ff.
  national strategies for, 29–30, 34
Curriculum Study Group, 82

Darwin, Charles, 113
decimalization, 39
decision-making, computerized, 115, 116, 186
  levels of, 34
de Gaulle, General, 98
Dent, H. C., 77
Descartes, 98, 113
Dewey, John, 7, 10, 25, 45, 150, 163, 195
Dio Chrysostom, 206
discipline in schools, 166 ff., 259 ff.
disciplines of knowledge, 26, 76
  criticism of, 198–9
  definitions of, 196–7
  structure of, 181 ff., 199 ff.
discovery methods, 225 ff.
Dissenting Academies, 268
divergent thinking, 159
Divine Right of Kings, 114

dossier scolaire, 106, 108
drop-outs, 233 ff.

earlier physical maturity, 19
Ebbingham, H., 155
Eccles, David, 78, 82
educability, amplification of, 210–11
  concept of, 28
Education and the Working Class, 237
educational laboratories, 66
Educational Services Inc., 53
Eggleston, J. F., 222
Einstein, Albert, 113, 159
elaborated code, *see* language of education
elementary school tradition, 72–3
Eliot, T. S., 170
Ellul, Jacques, 230, 232
English tradition in education, 153
Erasmus, 23
Ethics and Education, 164
European Economic Community, 101
evaluation as a long-term process, 28
extra-curricular activities, 4

faculty psychology, 17
Farrar, Dean, 24
formal discipline, 17
Forster, E. M., 144
Fraser, Rev. James, 240
Froebel, Friedrich, 27, 273

Gagné, R. M., 155, 156, 157
Galileo, 113
General Certification of Education (G.C.E.), 77, 79, 81
general education, 18, 49, 174
General Education in a Free Society, 174
General Teaching Council (Scotland), 94, 137
generation gap, 170, 233 ff.
Goodlad, J., 34
grammar school tradition, 71, 72
Grandes Ecoles, 99, 108
'Great Tradition of English Literature' 217 ff.

Index

Hadow Report (*The Education of the Adolescent*), 73–4, 81, 163
Halls, W. D., 99
Handbook of Suggestions for the Consideration of Teachers, 137
Harvard Committee Report, 174, 196
Heisenberg, Werner, 220
Herbartian pedagogy, 182
Herriot, Edouard, 103
heuristic methods, 225 ff.
Hilgard, E. R., 155
Himmelweit, H., 212
Hirst, Paul, 10, 198
Hoggart, Richard, 267
Holmes, Edmond, 257
Humanities Curriculum Project, 89 ff.
Hungarian Education Act (1961), 97
Hutchins, R. M., 50
Huxley, Thomas, 23

IBM, 65
innovation in education, 15–20
in-service training of teachers (Scotland), 135
intelligence, *see* educability
interest, 162, 164, 167, 203
Isaacs, Susan, 134

Jackson, Brian, 237
Jacksonian democracy, 47
James, Eric, 229
James, Henry, 149
Jevons, F. R., 218
Johnson, Samuel, 189, 233
Johnson, L. B., 60
Journal of Curriculum Studies, 10

Keats, John, 179
Kennedy, John F., 64, 175, 176
Keppel, Francis, 48, 195
Kerr, J. F., 10, 222
Khruschev, 97, 163
Kneller, G. F., 162
Koehler, W., 155
Koffka, K., 155

Landa, A. N., 225, 226
Lane, Homer, 134

Langevin Plan, 101, 102, 109
language, *see* learning
language of education, 251 ff.
learning, algorithmic and heuristic, 225 ff.
  as 'knowledge of words', 216 ff.
  'cerebral' and 'sensational', 169
  content of, 218 ff.
  dimensions of, 200–1
  hierarchical, 157 ff.
  interaction of intelligence and feeling, 151 ff.
  interest in, 162 ff.
  language and, 202–3
  non-verbal, 255
  theories of, 155
learning objectives, *see* objectives
Leff, G., 26
Le Gorgeu Commission, 100, 101
Levis, F. R., 23, 217
Lewis, Brian, 181
Lewis, Sinclair, 256
life adjustment education, 45–6, 50, 163
Lily's Latin primer, 23
literacy, 18, 38
local education authorities, differences between England and Scotland, 138
Locke, John, 7, 153, 155
Lockwood, Sir John, 83, 85
Louis XIV, 98
Lowe, Robert, 239
lumber in the curriculum, 265 ff.
Luther, 113
lycée, 98, 99, 101, 105, 106, 200

McGill, Donald (H.M.I.), 131
McGill Journal of Education, 212
Mackenzie, R. F., 133
McLuhan, Marshall, 213, 246, 255
Mager, R. F., 177, 178, 191, 273
management of conflict, 33, 116
Manzer, Ronald, 95
Marsden, Denis, 237
Marshall, Sybil, 134
Marx, Karl, 113

Massachusetts Institute of Technology, 51
Master of Education degree, 129, 136
Mead, Margaret, 162
media and communications, 213 ff.
  effects of on young people, 243 ff.
Mee, A. J. (H.M.I.), 131
Mialaret, G., 246
Michelet, 99
Monnet, Jean, 100
Montaigne, 103
moral education, 215, 264, 267
Morris, Henry, 134
Musgrove, Frank, 10, 31, 32

Napoleon, 98
National Council for Educational Technology, 87
National Defense Education Act (U.S.A.), 53
National Institutes of Pedagogy (France), 104
National Science Foundation (U.S.A.), 53
National Union of Teachers (England and Wales), 76, 82
nature–nurture controversy, 209
Neill, A. S., 133
New Education, 78
new mathematics, arguments for, 53–4
New York Board of Education, 260
New York State Board of Regents, 50
Newman's 'Idea' of a university, 32
Newsom Report, 79, 263
Nicolson, Max, 161
Nuffield Foundation, 85, 86
Nuffield Science Project, 131
numeracy, 18, 38
Nunn, Sir Percy, 190

objectives, 36, 175 ff.
  affective and cognitive, 152 ff.
  Bloom's taxonomy of, 154
  conflict between in school, 167 ff.
  distinguishable from aims, 185
O'Connor, D. J., 208
O.E.C.D., 12, 13, 14

operational research, 177
'oracy', 38
organization theory, 122, 237
Oxford English School, 24
Owens, J. G., 119

Pask, 181
Pavlov, 155
payment by results, 27
Pestalozzi, 27, 195
Peters, R. S., 164, 185, 189, 203
Phenix, 26, 199
Physical Science Study Committee, 51 ff.
Piaget, Jean, 155, 158
'picturacy', 38
Plato, 3, 22, 159
Plowden Report, 225
Politics (Aristotle), 4
problem-solving, behaviourist view of, 157 ff.
  indeterminate, 177
  logical and mathematical, 156 ff.
programmed learning, 178
progressive education, 163
'Protestant Ethic', 267
pupil power, 259 ff.
pupil–teacher ratio, 171

Quintilian, 38

religious education, 215, 272
Resources for Learning Project, 87
restricted code, see language of education
Richardson, Marion, 182
Robbins Report, 117
role expectations, 123–4
role theory, 122
Rostow, W. W., 67
Rousseau, Jean-Jacques, 7, 27, 31, 188, 239
Rowntree, Derek, 180
Rugg, Harold, 6

Salerno, 123
Salon des Refusés, 152

Index

School Mathematics Study Group, 53–6, 69
Schools Council for the Curriculum and Examinations, 83–95, 121, 132, 141
Schramm, Wilbur, 213, 240
Schumann, Maurice, 100
science, teaching of, 217–18
Scottish Council for Research in Education, 143, 263
Scottish education system, 127 ff.
secondary modern school, curriculum of, 80 ff.
  evolution of, 74 ff.
Secondary Schools Examinations Council, 83
Seneca, 103
Sherrington, Sir Charles, 244, 248
Skinner, B. F., 155
social class influences in education, 270
Societé des Agrégés, 105
Socrates, 3, 22, 157, 195, 203, 206
Spears, Harold, 50
Spencer, Herbert, 23, 195, 206
Spender, Stephen, 217
Spens Report, 74
Sputnik I, 51
Stages of Economic Growth, 67
Stirling University, 129
structure of knowledge, 183 ff., 204
student protest, 216, 267–9
studium generale, 123, 261
subjects in the school curriculum, arguments against, 75–6
  origins of, 24–5
Swedish Board of Education, 85
systems analysis, 29, 117, 121–2, 125, 237
systems engineering, 177

Tanner, Robin, 182
Taylor, P. H., 10
Taylor, W., 80
teachers, professional competence of, 67–8, 221 ff.
  role of, 164–5, 171–2

technology, impact of on education, 230–1
Television and the Child, 212
Television in the Lives of Our Children, 213
The Technological Society, 230
Thorndike, E. L., 155
Time, 65
Tomlinson, George, 71
transfer of training, 17
Trenaman, Joseph, 212
Tucker, Nicholas, 214
Turing's theorem, 204
Tyler, Ralph, 177, 194

uncertainty principle in modern knowledge, 218 ff.
Understanding the Mass Media, 214
university entrance requirements, 268
University Institutes of Technology in France, 105–6

Vernon, P. E., 81

Wall, W. D., 170
Watson, J. B., 155
Weber, Max, 22
Wheeler, R. K., 201, 218
Whitehead, A. N., 61
Who Shall Be Educated?, 46, 62
Wiener, Norbert, 231
Wilson, Bryan, 264, 268
Winnetka Plan, 163
Wittgenstein, L., 150, 215
Woods Hole Conference (U.S.A.), 143
Working Paper No. 1 (Schools Council), 88
Working Paper No. 2 (Schools Council), 88
Working Paper No. 5 (Schools Council), 92
Working Paper No. 11 (Schools Council), 88, 89, 91

Xerox, 65

Zacharias, J. B., 51